First Strike

First Strike

Educational Enclosures in Black Los Angeles

Damien M. Sojoyner

University of Minnesota Press
Minneapolis • London

The University of Minnesota Press gratefully acknowledges financial support for the publication of this book from Scripps College.

"Fear Not of Man" words and music by Dante Smith. Copyright 2000 EMI Blackwood Music Inc., Empire International Music Inc., and Medina Sounds Music. All rights administered by Sony/ATV Music Publishing LLC, 424 Church Street, Suite 1200, Nashville, Tennessee 37219. International copyright secured. All rights reserved. Reprinted by permission of Hal Leonard Corporation.

Published by the University of Minnesota Press
111 Third Avenue South, Suite 290
Minneapolis, MN 55401-2520
http://www.upress.umn.edu

Printed in the United States of America on acid-free paper

The University of Minnesota is an equal-opportunity educator and employer.

22 21 20 19 18 17 16   10 9 8 7 6 5 4 3 2 1

Library of Congress Cataloging-in-Publication Data
Sojoyner, Damien M., author.
First strike : educational enclosures in Black Los Angeles / Damien M. Sojoyner.
Minneapolis : University of Minnesota Press, 2016. | Includes bibliographical references and index.
Identifiers: LCCN 2016019157 (print) | ISBN 978-0-8166-9753-3 (hc) | ISBN 978-0-8166-9755-7 (pb)
Subjects: LCSH: African Americans—Education—Social aspects—California—Los Angeles. |
    Educational sociology—California—Los Angeles. | Racism in education—California—
    Los Angeles. | Discrimination in criminal justice administration—California—Los Angeles. |
    School discipline—California—Los Angeles.
Classification: LCC LC2803.L6 (print) | DDC 371.829/96079494—dc23
LC record available at https://lccn.loc.gov/2016019157

To Elaine and Godfrey, whose love has always been unconditional.

*To Shana, whose love has enabled me to reach levels
I never thought possible.*

To Naima and Nesanet, whose love gives my life true meaning.

Contents

The Problematic History between Schools and Prisons

I sat on the hard, black rubberized seat feeling the tight coil of the en-meshed springs wanting to release years of pent-up tension upon my legs. The bus driver, towing a group of rambunctious teenagers who were all-too-excited to get out of the confines of school, took very gently to the precarious conditions of our route. The circuitous road curved and twisted along a path that led us to an area known as Rancho Palos Verdes. Although a mere ten miles from my hometown of Carson, California, I had never ventured along these streets and was slowly taking in my new surroundings. We were on a field trip to study the various life forms that inhabited the Pacific Ocean, and I for one was excited; though I had lived relatively close to water all of my life, it was a rare occurrence to go to the coastline other than to play along the beach. As the bus driver nimbly took the mass of yellow steel along an avenue that cut through a valley of small hills, I was awestruck by the size of huge houses that sat along the hillside. With massive windows that provided panoramic views of the ocean, the homes rested in a fashion that gave the appearance that they had been built in isolation. From my vantage point there was no access road that led to their location, and there definitely were not any street markers that provided directions to these monstrosities on the tiny mountain.

As the bus slowly pulled up to a stop sign for what felt like forever, I was stuck in a momentary feeling of confusion. Outside of the thick pane window I saw what I thought to be a large park. It had all of the signifi-ers of what a park in a neighborhood of such wealth should be—a series of very well-kept buildings outlined by a large, painstakingly manicured landscape. Flanked by children play areas on the property, I looked to the sign posted along the street to find out the name of the park, only to be shocked to read that it was not a park. It was a school. My first and most long-standing memory of the event since then was one of befuddlement: there were no gates, no fences, no large imposed barriers. These had been the signifiers of a school in my childhood and early teenage years. Every school that I had attended since kindergarten had an increasing level of steel and barbed-wired tapestry that surrounded the outside and was intimately interwoven within the fabric of the school. These barriers not only were fundamental to schools, but they were often praised as a means of educational progress under the guise of public safety.[1]

That moment however, sitting atop of a large hill in Ranchos Palos Verdes, brought a small sense of clarity. My guess is that the residents of Ranchos Palos Verdes, mostly white, and mostly possessing relatively large sums of money and real estate, had never given thought to what I learned on that morning.[2] There was something profoundly unnatural about the barriers that very often were presented as a means of safety to communities such as those in Carson, Compton, Long Beach, and South Central Los Angeles. Ranging from large, black, steel, arrow-tipped gates to metal detectors, the physical manifestation of these barriers continues to serve as the literal and metaphorical device for the multiple forms of enclosure that Black youth face both inside and out of school. It is here, between the imposition of enclosures on one hand and the lived experience and knowledge formation of Black people in Southern California on the other, that this book, *First Strike,* takes form.

While researching and writing this book, I found that the title phrase *first strike* was a metaphor that extended in three different directions. The first and perhaps most apparent is the 1994 passage of Proposition 184 in the state of California, better known as the Three Strikes Law. The law increased the time of incarceration with each felony conviction, or strike, and the legislation mandated that by the third conviction the convicted individual be sentenced to a term of twenty-five years to life in prison (Brown and Jolivette 2005). With the expansion of felony charges to encompass many nonviolent crimes and the explicit targeting of Black people, the law had a devastating impact upon Black communities throughout California (Mauer and Huling 1995; Urizar 2009). The passage of the law occurred during a period of intensification of formal policing mechanisms within predominately Black public schools in California. Proposition 184, in conjunction with the presence of Los Angeles County Sheriff and Los Angeles Police Department officers and substations on campuses, meant that students could and would garner their first strikes while in school.

The second meaning of *first strike* is in reference to W. E. B. Du Bois's discussion of the general strike of Black southern laborers that effectively ended the Civil War (Du Bois 1935/1998). In *Black Reconstruction in*

America, 1860–1880, Du Bois argues that rather than rely on the benevolence of white abolitionists or presidential decree by Abraham Lincoln, Black workers in the U.S. South developed a strategy to stop working for the southern planter bloc, and in droves joined the ranks of Union forces. This effectively ended the war because the Confederacy lost both its labor supply and any potential numeric advantage. The Reconstruction period that followed brought about many changes, but of great importance was the demand by southern Blacks for the establishment of a public education system. Prior to this call, formal education had been the purview of wealthy white men and/or an agent of colonization (Franklin 1974; Lomawaima 2009; Woodson 1919). However, in a two-pronged strategy, the demand for public education was meant to wrestle economic power away from the plantation base (through a tax system) while also providing a means to educate the masses of poor Black and white populations. It is within this context of Black freedom movements that education has been the centerpiece of liberation struggles and figured prominently as a tool of both intellectual development and organizing.

The direct contestation to Black education brings us to the third meaning of the title. *First strike* in this sense is the first point of attack by efforts to undermine a truly democratic social vision. From the derailment of public education by northern capitalists following Reconstruction to the codification of permanent racial inequalities within education policy from the civil rights era to the present, the formal education of Black people as articulated by the U.S. nation-state has been about the suppression of Black freedom (Anderson 1988; Ladson-Billings and Tate 1995; Watkins 2001). Rather than looking at the official doctrine of the nation-state (that is, education policy) as a totalizing top-down force, it is key to understand it as a reactionary agent against the mobilization of Black people, with education being the linchpin. The framing of *first strike* in this manner highlights two important points: first, rather than focus only on the effects of policy and legislation, it is even more important to study the people, communities, and movements that these policies are in reaction to.

Second, we have to resituate our understanding of schools away from a model that funnels students into some other structure and look at the ways in which schools themselves are the locus of contestation. It is within this vein that current analytic devices and campaign slogans such as the "School-to-Prison Pipeline," while well intentioned, do not address the historical and contemporary root causes of planned malaise within

Black education and as a consequence are not adequate in either analyzing critical issues or providing viable solutions.[3] Within a burgeoning field of schools and prisons, *First Strike* builds upon the insights of Erica Meiners and Kathleen Nolan, who argue for the need to reconceptualize the framework of School-to-Prison Pipeline. Meiners persuasively argues:

> Linkages between schools and prisons are less a pipeline, more a persistent nexus or a web of intertwined, punitive threads. The nexus metaphor, while perhaps less "sexy" or compelling than the schoolhouse to jailhouse track, is more accurate as it captures the historic, systemic, and multifaceted nature of the intersections of education and incarceration. (Meiners 2007, 31–32)

Furthering Meiners's critique of the School-to-Prison Pipeline in her study of Urban Public High School (UPHS), Nolan states, "The lived experience of many students at UPHS can be better understood through a nuanced description of daily life rather than the pipeline metaphor." She further argues, "To gain sufficient understanding of the everyday life experience of students at the school, it is useful to highlight a more mundane but pervasive phenomenon: how the lives of impoverished urban students are managed by a complex interpenetration of systems" (Nolan 2011, 72).

It is within this current social milieu that I argue that the most comprehensive manner in which to understand the relationships between schools and prisons is through the lens of enclosures. As a tool of analysis, enclosures are powerful because they provide a means to understand both the importance of Black communal traditions and the reactive tendencies of the U.S. nation-state.

Enclosure

Although it cannot be easily placed within a catchy slogan or tagline (I have tried on multiple occasions), the term *enclosure* encapsulates the multifaceted processes that have brought us to this current moment of mass incarceration, intense racialized policing, and a full-on assault upon public education. Enclosure most readily signifies a physical barrier such as a wall, a fence, or anything that is meant to limit the freedom of movement. Yet, enclosure also refers to the unseen forces that are just as powerful as the physical manifestations. In this sense, enclosure is representative of social mechanisms that construct notions of race, gender, class, and sexuality; and just as important as the imposition of the physical and unseen, enclosure embodies the removal/withdrawal/denial of services and programs that are key to the stability and long-term well-being of communities.

Enclosure is also very useful because it is not a static term. Rather, enclosure refers to historical contestations over power, resources, and ways of life that have ushered us to the present. This utilization of enclosures in this manner is perhaps best seen in the work of Clyde Woods. In his masterful text, *Development Arrested: The Blues and Plantation Power in the Mississippi Delta,* Woods carefully documents the long-standing struggle between the southern plantation bloc and Black working-class communities (Woods 1998). Woods uses enclosure as a method of analysis to understand "the historical origins and current manifestations of planter bloc hegemony, the appeasement of it, resistance to it, and the roads still open to regional development based on economic democracy, social justice, and cultural sanctity" (Woods 1998, 24). Within this process, he develops his conceptualization of the Blues Epistemology. According to Woods:

> The blues epistemology is a longstanding African American tradition of explaining reality and change. This form of explanation finds its origins in the processes of African American cultural construction within, and resistance to, the antebellum plantation regime. It crystallized during Reconstruction and its subsequent violent overthrow. After two hundred years of censorship and ten short years of open communication, the resurrected plantation bloc thoroughly demonized all autonomous forms of thought and action for another century. The blues became the channel through which the Reconstruction generation grasped reality in the midst of disbelief critiqued the plantation regime, and organized against it. The Mississippi Delta is the home of the blues tradition in music, popular culture, and explanation. It is therefore fitting that this popular consciousness is used to interpret both the continuous crisis in the Delta and African American attempts to create a new regional reality based on cultural freedom and economic and social justice. (Woods 1998, 25)

Through the course of his text, Woods describes in painstaking detail how the plantation bloc, over the long range of history, utilized various forms of enclosure to dampen the power of the Blues Epistemology. From forced removal of Black laborers from the land to elimination of key social policy that provided the bare modicum of communal stability to the utilization of crises (that is, natural disasters) as a means to advance particular economic and political interests, enclosures figure prominently as a means to understand the extent to which the plantation bloc tried to control southern Black communities.

It is within Woods's treatment of enclosures that I argue that we frame our analysis of schools and prisons in a historic conversation that reveals the nuanced details that have given life to the complex relationship between schools and prisons that exists today. It is only then that we can understand that, rather than a funneling or pipeline system that transfers students from schools to prisons, particular forms of enclosures have been developed with particular aims. Some of these forms were developed long ago, without consideration for schools or prisons, but have become key facets in both. Some were developed explicitly with the intent to prevent the education of Black people and have had tremendous influence upon the development of prisons. Others were designed solely for the management of the massive prison apparatus and have bled throughout society, including into the realm of education. It is from the vantage point of these historic and contemporary realities that no sleight of hand or one-size-fits-all solution is going to "fix" schools or remedy the problematic framing of an "achievement gap" between Black students and white students. The utilization of enclosures as a method of analysis allows us to perform the serious level of engagement that is needed to address the uncomfortable truths and harsh realities that have been instrumental in the development and maintenance of the structured dysfunctionality that marks our education system and the ubiquitous nature of the U.S. prison system.

Yet, just as it is important to address the particular forces that have been instrumental in the development of enclosures, it is even more important to detail the Black communal epistemologies that have forced the enactment of such enclosures. Documenting the various forms of resistance and cultural traditions is vital to both debunk racist, class-based, gendered, and sexed myths of Black people while asserting the legitimacy of Black forms of knowledge and realities. From this stance we can then develop a comprehensive perspective of the relationship between schools and prisons and build models that are in tune with the legacy of Woods's Blues Epistemology.

Policy and Enclosures

Throughout the course of the book I address manifestations of state power in two primary capacities: formal and informal. *Formal* refers to what we commonly consider to be the main organs of government such as elected officials and legislative bodies. *Informal* is signification of entities such as philanthropic organizations and nongovernment agencies that have the power to shape key structures (that is, education, health care). A main argument that carries through the text is that both formal and informal actors of the state develop and/or reproduce enclosure processes through policy. Although policy is usually discussed in distinct forms, such as economic policy or education policy, I demonstrate that during the past forty years there has been coordination among economic, political, criminal justice, and education policy mandates to disrupt and/or neutralize Black social visions of freedom. Modeled upon policy enclosure formations that date back centuries, the collaboration of these policy initiatives into a cohesive approach represents a contemporary wrinkle in policy development. I argue that this recent shift has been central to the buildup and legitimization of prisons in the United States.

The state has also built upon previous policy models that co-opted Black freedom movements via incorporation into the state bureaucratic apparatus. Indebted to the theoretical framework established by Beth Richie, I argue that such co-optation methods have been very detrimental to Black communities. In Richie's work on the connection between violence against Black women and the buildup of what she calls the "prison nation," Richie asserts that the strategic incorporation of antiviolence movements into the state proved detrimental to the initial objectives of the movements. Rather than develop models that addressed state complicity in structural forms of oppression against women, Richie states that those who chose to work in conjunction with the state soon became "apologists for the system" (Richie 2012, 75).[4] Similarly, the incorporation of radical social movements and actions pertaining to communal, educational, and gendered marginalization that were willingly or forcefully subsumed into the state process lost their radical potential and also functioned to reproduce violence upon Black communities.

It is from this position that the book questions that effectiveness of common sense renderings of the relationship between schools and prisons such as the School-to-Prison Pipeline (STPP). Although community activists developed the STPP as an organizing model during the 1990s, the model has been wholly subsumed into the state via policy initiatives, positivist research agendas, and official government mandates. Manipulated in this manner, the framing of the STPP is no longer a viable option to understand the complex relationship of the enclosure processes that have brought us to the current moment. Devoid of historical and cultural analysis and situated in a top-down configuration of power with respect to Black communities, the STPP framework reproduces the same tropes of ideological and pragmatic dogma that have been central to Black oppression. An intervention in such scholarship, the book pushes away from such thinking and, through detailed analysis of enclosure models, posits for the development of analytical frameworks immersed in Black social visions of libratory practice.

Structure of the Book

The scope of *First Strike* is intentionally broad in order to account for the multiplicity of issues that have given rise to the relationship between schools and prisons in California. The book is not solely situated within a particular time and place, which is very common to ethnography as a mode of inquiry, nor is located within a specific historical moment. Rather, the text takes the reader along the contours of interconnected issues and brings the focus upon central interstices that provide meaning to the complexities of schools and prisons in California. To this end, *First Strike* is an ambitious project that covers fairly large swaths of history, several methodological traditions, and fundamental issues of race, class, gender, and sexuality.

Emanating from the tertiary trajectories that *First Strike* provides as a metaphorical device and built upon the centrality of enclosures, it is best to read the chapters in the book as both discursive projects that provide narrative to particular reads of *first strike* and models of enclosures that have given rise to the relationship between schools and prisons. The foundation of the book is invested within multidisciplinary traditions that are central to the field of Black studies and the legacy of continued interventions made by Black scholars within anthropology and the social sciences broadly speaking. Each chapter provides both a historic overview that is desperately needed to present context to particular contested struggles and an ethnographic description of the lived experience of students, care-givers, teachers, staff, and administrators. The following provides an over-view of the chapters in the book and a general discussion of the major themes that develop throughout the text.

The first chapter, "The Problem of Black Genius: Black Cultural En-closures," is a twofold chapter that traces the genealogical development of cultural enclosures within education. Focused upon the metaphorical tra-jectories of first strike that understand Black culture as key to struggles for Black liberation on one hand and the attempt to counter such movements on the other, the chapter situates the dialectal tension in its historical con-text and brings the conversation to the present through the experiences and insight of Black students at County High School (CHS). With respect to the latter, the chapter maps out the manner in which Black manifesta-tions of cultural autonomy ranging from music to visual art have been systematically eliminated from public education. This discussion is book-ended by a discussion of the central force that fomented Black cultural enclosures: Western Christianity. Heavily indebted to the work of Cedric Robinson, my argument is that the planned imposition of a Christian doc-trine negated the cultural manifestations that have been key to Black re-sistance and cultural maintenance (Robinson 2000). Signaling the signifi-cance of Western Christianity upon Black life, Robinson states:

> Ethnocentrism, legitimated by the authorities of church and igno-rance, the two fountains of medieval knowledge, became the basis for world knowledge. Ultimately, with the evolution of Christian ideology into a worldview, it was enough to know that mankind was divisible into two collectivities: the army of Light and the army of Darkness. . . . Europe was God's world, the focus of divine atten-tion; the rest of mankind belonged for the moment to Satan. For perhaps a thousand years or more, western European world his-torical consciousness was transformed into theosophy, demonol-ogy, and mythology. And, indeed, in a most profound sense Euro-pean notions of history, both theological and pseudo-theological, negated the possibility of the true existence of earlier civilizations. The perfectibility of mankind, the eschatological vision, precluded the possibility of pre-Christian civilization having achieved any

remarkable development in moral law, social organization, or natural history (science). (Robinson 2000, 86)

Springing from the bowels of a wretched metaphysical manipulation, the cultural enclosures that manifested within CHS were born through the demonization of Black cultural practices—the same cultural practices that have been instrumental in revolt, organizing, and community building in Southern California and throughout the African Diaspora.

The development and maintenance of particular forms of ideology is the most important job of education within the United States. From mythical creations and continual iterations of a colorblind society to an overemphasis upon the incessant need for "law and order," schools are vital to the production of the social dogma that defines the nation-state process.[5] Key to ideology is the manner in which it becomes commonsense. That is, to question the existence of prisons or to speak the specific conditions of Black oppression, the most readied response is stern objection and charges of race baiting or racism. William Watkins's historical mapping of the racial underpinnings that were key to the formation of Black education, as detailed in the chapter, provide a blueprint to understanding the power of ideology to counter Black demands for education (Watkins 2001).

Following Watkins's path, I explore in chapter 2, "In the Belly of the Beast: Ideological Expansion," how ideology is made normal. Framed within the genealogical strain that looks at first strike as the imposition of a social order based upon a set of exorbitant rules of engagement, I argue that the conceptualization of the prison regime, as articulated by Dylan Rodríguez (2006), has become the central mode of ideological framing of the U.S. nation-state. As a result, the belief in the incessant need of prisons has become an enclosure with profound implications. Ranging from prisons understood as a social good to the military apparatus associated with notions of freedom, the enculturation of the prison regime has served as a powerful tool to counter the facts of history.

Chapter 3, "Land of Smoke and Mirrors: The Meaning of Punishment and Control," analyzes the mechanisms that have fueled the rise of draconian discipline policies and normalized violent excess within public education. Most closely related to the Three Strikes Law that ties in with the metaphorical device of first strike, the chapter traces the contemporary history that gave rise to punitive policy formation in Southern California and questions the intent of such legislation. Building upon the growing body of research that documents the ill effects of formal policing within education, the ethnographic detail in the chapter brings to bear the adverse effect that discipline policies have upon the processes of learning and safety within schools (Na and Gottfredson 2011; New York Civil Liberties Union 2007). A major goal of the chapter is to intervene within the ubiquitous utilization and invocation of Michel Foucault's analysis of docile bodies and biopower (Foucault 1990). Given that Foucault has remained the "go-to" theorist on discipline, his misreading of race and emphasis on a hierarchal formulation of the power relationships renders his analysis insufficient with respect to the current moment of attacks upon education and massive Black incarceration. Rather, I argue that what is needed is a comprehensive understanding of racial capitalism and how the tentacles of perceived power are merely illusions of power that have proven not to have long-term staying power in the face of Black communal organizing.

The fourth chapter, "Troubled Man: Limitations of the Masculinity Solution," was the most difficult chapter to construct. Much of the difficulty was attributed to the manner in which problematic constructions of Black masculinity have been framed as the quintessential first strike in developing simple answers to deeply rooted, complex problems. Given the multiplicity of issues facing Black men in the United States, there have been a broad range of purported solutions, and yet I continued to find that many of the solutions were invested within a heteronormative, patriarchal formulation of masculinity. Long after the academic dismantling of the Moynihan Report by Black feminists, the saliency on Black family degeneracy and the focus on Black women's immoral proclivity as contributing to the failure of the development of Black men has remained potent. In particular, Black communal investment within such renderings of Black masculinity and, by extension, the Black family have further enclosed Black communities. Set against this backdrop, chapter 4 presents the harsh realities that young Black men face in the gendered social hierarchy that presents a very limited set of problematic solutions as models. Situated within a liminal space that advances violent expressions of masculine behavior, the stories of Black male youth explore the consequences when Black males reject these notions of masculinity. Bridging the issue to manifestations outside of the formal school site, I argue that the historical rendering of a bourgeois respectable political construction of Black masculinity has assisted in the silencing of Black radical movements on college campuses and has been central in the criminalization of poor Black people. The dire consequences of abiding by such a construction of masculine performance are further discussed through violence inflicted upon Black women. That is, the steadfast belief in a sacrosanct model of patriarchal heteronormativity has resulted in the literal and metaphorical silencing of multiple forms of violence against Black women.

The fifth chapter of the book, "By All Means Possible: The Historical Struggle over Black Education," provides a historical foundation on which to understand the development of first strike as a metaphorical device. The chapter elucidates a needed connection between the competing visions of the education of Black people and current iterations of the educative process. The construction of this chapter in this manner is of great importance because a major flaw in the School-to-Prison Pipeline analytic framework is a historical representation of the issues that are central to schools and prisons. Additionally, much focus of the School-to-Prison Pipeline and recent urban education literature focuses exclusively on the "heavy hand" of school discipline policies (that is, policing, metal detectors); and problematically, there has been very little attention given to the "soft" side effects (that is, education policy, curriculum) upon processes of enclosure.[6] Specifically, the historical development of policy formation and decisions pertaining to curriculum guidelines have been essential to the removal of Black cultural traditions from education. Discussing the centrality of education to the Black radical tradition and communal formation in the United States, I argue that education, as a tool of organizing, political and social development, and intellectual empowerment was understood as a threat to the progression of the U.S. nation-state process. Resultantly, the formal education of Blacks was under continual attack by the southern planter class, northern industrial elites, and formal U.S. state policy. This brief historical description leads into an ethnographic rendering of the current moment in public education that has been dominated by a perverse logic of accountability. This section of chapter 5 is to provide the inner workings of a public education system intentionally stripped bare. In its place, a structural apparatus of testing and policy-driven standards has been implemented that has severely restricted critical inquiry. Following in the tradition of the southern planter bloc and proponents of industrial education, the current manifestation of education has sought to limit the power and effectiveness of Black education through a vile imposition of asinine, meaningless tasks.

The construction of this book has taken me on a long, fruitful journey. A question that I have been asked many times during the process is what I hope that the book will do. First, on a fundamental level, my goal is that the text will challenge what has become commonsense about the education of Black youth in the United States. It has become quite apparent with school closings and mass consolidation of resources away from Black communities that the education of Black people is deemed expendable. Specifically, the book reframes the narrative of Black educational failure away from rhetorical invocations of Black cultural failure and teacher incompetence to a historical and structural analysis that exposes the root causes of formal Black educational calamity. Second, I want to link the enclosure models that have developed within schools and prisons. With this in mind, the basis of any option for addressing issues of education must have a philosophy of abolition at its core. It is only then that we can begin the work to abolish enclosures that dominate both prisons and public education. Last, I hope to have accurately portrayed the lives of the people who are central to this book. Having spent countless hours with students and their families, I have learned more from them than one text can hold. Their stories and the stories of their genealogical antecedents are the basis of this book and are key to developing solutions that are immersed in a radically democratic vision of the future.

The Problem of Black Genius

Black Cultural Enclosures

Toward the middle of the school year in February, and after several conversations and personal interactions with Black students at County High School (CHS), I questioned whether the school was a site of daily struggle based on racialized and gendered oppression. Where were the spaces of Black autonomy that have historically been sites of resistance (that is, music, art, spiritual)?[1] If the school was effective in enclosing these spaces, then what were the policy and informal, nonstated mechanisms that allowed for the circumvention of Black resistance? Further, how, if at all, did the school define and control the parameters of Black cultural production?

Rather than a monolithic engagement, Black students had a variety of responses to the school's effect within their lives. Some aligned themselves with the school project and adopted conservative stances toward Black culture (that is, that it was not refined or dysfunctional). There were a large number who chose to remain silent and become as invisible as possible as a means to complete school. Others decided to reclaim spaces of autonomy through cultural manifestations that articulated both resistance and continuity of a Blackness whose philosophical underpinnings were located within the Black freedom struggle. In particular, one Black male student, Sidney, with whom I had the privilege to work at CHS, chose the latter approach. In the face of modern race-making practices that are lodged within individualized notions of being, he tapped into communal-based, cultural strategies that protected him from racist onslaughts of the school and simultaneously constructed an alternative masculinity that countered the school's interpellation of Black males (Awkward 1995).

Cultural Enclosures

In an attempt to answer the aforementioned questions, this chapter details the primacy of Black cultural forms within processes of enclosure. My use of *culture* here is influenced by the work of Stuart Hall, who argued that culture is "*something*—not a mere trick of the imagination. It has histories and histories have their real, material, and symbolic effects. . . . It is always constructed through memory, fantasy, narrative and myth" (Hall 1990, 226). Black culture as an agent of social transformation has always been a first strike against violent modalities of white supremacy. Ranging from the confluence between music and spirituality to initiate the Haitian Revolution to the duality of Black spirituals as vehicles of cultural expression but also cautionary warnings and markers of direction to fugitive Blacks during slavery, culture has been central to Black liberation (James 1989; Levine 2007). The response to these Black cultural manifestations was the development of enclosures to limit Black freedom. Exemplified by the passage of laws during the eighteenth and nineteenth centuries in the mainland colonies and the Caribbean that were aimed at preventing Blacks from playing music or congregating together, and a strict surveillance of Black spiritual practices, the enclosure of Black cultural forms has had a long historical past.

The key to looking back at the historical past is to study the ways in which these enclosures inform contemporary processes of cultural enclosure. In the case of Black Los Angeles, the genealogical impact is quite profound. Infamous incidents of Horace Tapscott's jazz orchestra surveilled by the Los Angeles Police Department (LAPD) in the 1960s and the hip-hop group Niggaz With Attitude surveilled by Federal Bureau of Investigation (FBI) during the 1990s indicate the contemporary manifestations of the contestation between white forms of domination and Black lives (Lipsitz 2011; Rose 1994). With respect to education, the relationship between Black cultural manifestations and Black freedom has played a central role in both social movements and everyday forms of resistance. The Black Arts movement in Southern California, for example, was heavily indebted to the cultural work that was done at secondary schools throughout Los Angeles. Perhaps there is no better coalescence of this occurrence than poet and activist Jayne Cortez. Cortez, whose passion for music and poetry was developed while a student at Manual Arts High School in South Central Los Angeles, became an iconic force of the West Coast wing of the Black Arts movement (Widener 2010).

It is with respect to the work that was done by Cortez and the many teachers, students, and community members throughout Los Angeles that Black culture became central to the organizing of Black people throughout Southern California. Realizing the role that schools played in the nurturing of Black cultural forms, public education became a key site to develop and initiate the process of Black culture enclosure. In the legislative tradition that prohibited expression of Black cultural forms, the elimination of music, performing, and fine art programs within Black schools was initiated in two primary ways. The first, covered in more detail later in the book, was under the guise of education policies that systematically removed the aforementioned programs under the rationale of budget cuts and/or replacement with enrichment classes that were geared to assist students pass standardized tests. The second, the basis of this chapter, was through forced cultural manipulation and assimilation via process of intentional misrepresentations and omission of Blackness—and as a result the assertion of whiteness as a ubiquitous demarcation of "refined" culture.

As a means to understand the process of cultural enclosure, the chapter is divided into two sections. The first is an ethnographic section that provides insight into daily manifestations and the lived results of Black cultural enclosure and the multilayered effects that it has upon teachers and students alike. A historic rendering of its genealogical antecedent, the Western Christian Church, follows the ethnography. The roots of Black cultural enclosure emanate from the establishment of Christianity in the "New World" and has provided the basis of enclosure models that have been continually refined and further developed. Although rarely discussed, the legacy of Western Christianity has had a profound impact upon cultural enclosures within Black education. As explained in the chapter, such a discussion is of particular importance given the glaring absence of culture in discussions within the School-to-Prison Pipeline (STPP) discourse. Without analysis of the linkage between Black culture and enclosures, all solution sets that derive will fail to provide the needed comprehensive detail with respect to prisons and schools.

Designed to Be Liminal

The biggest open secret on campus was that CHS did not give strong support for the musical arts. Ms. Briggs, the beginning band teacher, provided detailed information regarding the multiple issues that she faced as a music instructor at CHS. She explained that, counter to her personal experience attending schools in an adjacent school district that was heavily vested in music, the vast differences between the schools were a result of the investment that the districts placed in the students.

> Well, this is nothing like Vista Playa. I meet with the elementary and middle school students once a week for orchestra during zero period on Friday. I am not sure if you know, but zero period starts at 6:45 in the morning. I love the students because they all come so energized and they love music, but there is not really a lot that can get done if we only meet once a week. Then during the course of the school year, students drop out and I can understand. The majority of these parents work the graveyard shift on their jobs, so getting their children either to campus or to a bus stop is very difficult at such an early time. By the end of the year the group gets smaller and smaller. . . . Now this is so much different than in Vista Playa. In middle school we had rehearsals everyday and even in the evening sometimes. There were the opportunities for the all-district orchestras, there were the festivals at other schools. This was all in middle school. Then at the high school level, students were already trained in the basics, so the teacher could really work on the nuances. All of the orchestras and bands in the high school were pretty big. We had rehearsals in the evening every week and traveled all around playing. Many of the students were very good and started their own bands. Even the students in the beginning orchestra had played before, but here, many of these students here, it is their first time ever picking up an instrument. They are all so sweet, but they just don't have the training and they are already in the tenth grade. I have to start with the very basic foundations even with the advanced orchestra, it is very difficult and I want to play new things, but I just can't because we have to work on tuning and listening.

I had the opportunity to observe Ms. Briggs's class on several occasions and understood her frustration. Preparing for a holiday concert, the students were rehearsing a medley of traditional Christmas songs; however, they could not make it through one complete take of any song. The thirty-piece string orchestra consisted of violins, violas, cellos, and bass. Although the different instruments were separated into first- and second-part groupings, many of the second-part violins could not distinguish their complementary harmonizing from the main melody played by the violins. Consequently, they attempted to play their part in the same rhythmic pattern of the first violins, which created a chain reaction of events that led to what is referred to as a "crash and burn," whereby melodies are no longer recognizable and different instrumentation groupings are playing different rhythms. Though this pattern is common with younger musicians upon sight reading a piece for the first time, the advanced orchestra had been rehearsing this song for more than three months. Additionally, many of the students had yet to grasp the ability to play the music while simultaneously following the conductor cues or listening to other instruments around them. Upon several occasions during the rehearsal, when Ms. Briggs had stopped the piece, many of the students kept on playing because their attention was intently focused on the notes on the page.

The majority of the students used school instruments. It was very difficult for students to take instruments home to practice because many of the instruments had to be shared by multiple students in different groups. Even if the students did not share, many of the instruments were in such bad condition that the students simply could not practice. The deplorable state of the band room also prevented students from utilizing the space in an effective manner for rehearsal.

As we sat in the cramped quarters within the band room office, Ms. Briggs's frustration had resigned to defeat. With a small ten-inch black-and-white television adorned with bunny ears sitting atop a microwave that sat on top of a white mini-refrigerator, she barely had enough space to place her textbooks, sheet music, and music instrument parts that lined the floor of the office that she shared with her colleague. "We need practice rooms and students need space to rehearse. Look out there, there is not any space to do anything. Students can't practice. There is the room in the back, but it is cluttered with so many instruments that no one can practice back there."

Her insight into the physical space of the room was indicative of the school's treatment of the fine arts. The band room was located in the old shop facility that once was home to wood and metal classes before they were removed from the school curriculum.[2] Constructed as a series of three imposing rooms called the 700 Building, each room facilitated radically different capacities. Two were utilized as social studies classrooms (one of them was Mr. Davies's room) and the third, the band room. The original intent of the room was evident; although it was poor for acoustics (optimal for a band room), it was a perfect space for large tools needed to cut wood and metal. It was within this landscape of disinvestment from music that Sidney attempted to make a new path.

Sidney's Story

Sidney had the demeanor of a confident, modern-day, humble poet who was trapped inside of a world full of car salesmen. That is, Sidney fully understood the limitations that CHS presented to him. An artist of impeccable wit, Sidney confided to me that he resented having been kicked out of the charter school that he attended prior to enrolling at CHS. He explained that back when he was "on the quest for green," he became more entrenched in his job than in his books and, as a result, his academic pursuits became secondary.[3] After faring poorly in academics, he was expelled from his previous school and was forced to attend his home school, CHS. He explained to me that the academic material at CHS was a joke in comparison to his former school. Although he had taken and passed geometry in the ninth grade, he was forced to retake the subject upon entering CHS. He mentioned that he became disinterested in learning the subject over again and had to retake the class yet another time in the eleventh grade.

His third time taking the class, Sidney was understandably frustrated with his current situation. He explained that because he had to continually take and retake geometry, he couldn't participate in elective classes that were of interest to him. Very effectively, the school was enclosing life possibilities for Sidney. Having a limited math background and minimal elective classes, his chances of gaining admission into a four-year college or university were virtually nonexistent.

However, in spite of the school's attempts to encroach upon his aspirations and dreams, his passion for the arts kept him afloat, giving him the inspiration to move forward in spite of his current situation. His expressive mannerism was most readily conveyed through his drawings, paintings, and love of music. Talking during lunch one day, Sidney told me about his brothers and sisters. As he pulled the slivers of meat from the broiled chicken breast that he was holding, he spoke fondly of his family. Just as he completed his master creation of chicken, cheese, and lettuce in a soft-shelled flour tortilla, he talked about wanting to be a good example for his younger siblings.

After taking a bite from his taco, he expressed a great deal of remorse for failing out of his previous school and believed that his failure had a negative impact upon his younger brother and sister. He had a great deal of pride in his family and conveyed that as an older brother it was his duty to be a positive role model. While he took another bite, my eyes glanced down toward the metal picnic bench that we sat on and noticed a colorful picture on the cover of Sidney's notebook. A pencil sketch filled in with brilliant color of the popular children's show, *Sesame Street*, was spread across his folder. I immediately questioned whether he had any more drawings.

With a mouth full of food, he pointed to a section in his binder that housed his mini-portfolio. As I looked through page after page of wonderful illustrations, it was evident that Sidney had a true gift. Whether it was Charles Darwin's theory of evolution or cell mutation, Sidney displayed his understanding of multifaceted scientific theories through artistic expression. The depth of Sidney's genius was clear as he simplified complex phenomena through the medium of a children's puppet television program. He used the characters of Bert and Ernie as a means to convey processes of meiosis and mitosis. In one setting, Bert and Ernie were dressed as scientists, adorned in white lab coats and explaining through captions how the splitting of cells occurred. In another picture he drew the character of Big Bird in the center of an array of various species of birds. Atop of Big Bird's head was the word "Evolution?" I was shocked, yet taken aback by his nonchalant behavior toward his artistic ability. The stark contrast between two dissimilar objects could have been conveyed only by a person who had a firm grasp of both subjects.

Sidney and Music

Although his drawings were phenomenal, Sidney's true passion rested in his musical interests. The same creativity that he had displayed in his drawings was employed in his music. Further, his ability to turn mundane phrases into his unique creation was a trait that he used in both media. He carried a tenor sax that was as about wide as his thin frame and blew with it all of his will and might into the belly of the brass-colored horn. He loved music, desired to master all of the woodwind instruments, and described himself as an aspiring music producer. In a tight-knit space, he and four other members of the jazz combo slowly went through "Jammin' with Charlie," a slow and demonstrative beginning jazz standard that emphasized the connection between resting and playing.

A novice to the saxophone, Sidney was technically far behind his counterparts in knowledge of their respective instruments. Yet, his passion for becoming a solid musician was inherent in his passion for music. He drank up all of the subtle cues that were played by his quartet mates. During the sessions, Sidney was intent on mastering the fingering and stylistic flow of his sax. In this space, he was free to be expressive, ask about the unknown, and demand respect. This brief hour of time was a solace from the racially charged epithets that were hurled by teachers and staff members.

As the session continued, I noticed a surprising aspect of the students' instruments in relation to their dedication to their craft. Although Sidney and his fellow sax mate Lester spent a lot of time trying to make their instruments sound great, the limitations of the instruments was self-evident. Sidney's overcompressed tone was compounded by the fact that just about all of the pads at one time or another were stuck to the holes. Thus, as mightily as he tried, missed notes were a frequent occurrence. Lester's problems ran much deeper. As probably the most gifted of the musicians, his alto saxophone was in shambles. The cork that surrounded the neck of the instrument was falling apart. Lester brought up this fact to the director of the music program, Mr. Albert, who told Lester that he did not understand the concept of tone and was out of key because of his playing. Lester's analysis, however, was more than keen; he had to the hold the mouthpiece on the neck of the saxophone to keep it from resting directly on the body of the tattered instrument.

Yet, in spite of all this, Lester was not deterred from playing his horn as loud and punctually as possible. A young male of a slightly brown hue, built in the mold of a gentle giant, Lester was solid at the core, yet torn asunder at the edges by a structure that had long since labeled him troubled. He firmly understood that his teachers, in fact, hated him. Similar to the experience of Sidney, Lester was quick to explain that his teachers were racist. Upon pressing him as to how he came to this conclusion, he provided example after example of the teachers' treatment of non-Black students in a favorable manner compared to the Black students.

I was warned before ever stepping foot in the class that Lester was a troublemaker. I was provided explicit instructions not to allow him to go to the restroom because he would never return to the class. Furthermore, it was made known that Lester would easily disturb the class, thus gaining control of practice sessions would be impossible. It was evident that Mr. Albert would spend more time attending to a shot dog than on the future prospects of Lester. Within the hostile nature of this environment, it was firmly established that it was never intended for Lester to learn through the fundamental process that was prescribed by district administrators. Rather, Lester is a child of post-Reconstruction education. The basis of his existence had long since been determined by a structure that negated his right to exist.

As the quartet played "Jammin' with Charlie," it was clear that although they enjoyed making music, there was a gap between their desire to play and the styles they were being taught. The passion that was characteristic of Black music had been stripped away piece by piece. Though the notes were being played, there was a clear distinction between the playing that they wanted to achieve and the manner in which the music was produced. Given that they were playing a jazz standard, I stopped the band and asked them to name their favorite jazz artist. Silence filled the immense room and the students looked at me blankly. I ran off some names of popular musicians such as Miles Davis and Charlie Parker, and though the students had heard of them, they were not familiar with any of their songs.

Shocked and amazed, I grabbed my iPod out of my teaching sack and plugged it into an audio amplifier that I had brought for another class. Immediately, the scurrying sounds of Dizzy Gillespie's trumpet engulfed the room. In a roundlike cadence, Charlie Parker's unmistakable saxophone took hold of the listening space. "Hot House" blared through the walls and the band sat in awe, drinking from be-bop's glass and wanting more.

As the song continued to play, my eyes searched around the room for any pictures of Dizzy Gillispie, Charlie Parker, or John Coltrane. Suddenly, it was obvious that the band director had removed any notions of Blackness from jazz. Just above the rusted, cream-shaded lockers were posted pictorial representations of "jazz" that would give the viewer no indication that the musical form had any connection to Black people. Rather there were posters of white musicians, posing in various stances, signifying their mastery of the trumpet, saxophone, and a variety of other instruments.

Immediately, a conversation that I had with Sidney sprang to mind. Talking outside of the band room, on a clear and beautiful day, we were updating each other on a previous conversation about music.

"So, what are your plans for next year?," I questioned. "Are you going to keep on playing music?"

"Yeah," he replied, "I am going to play in the marching band next year, but I really want to play in the funk band."

I asked him why he was not going to play funk, given his mastery of the saxophone in such a short amount of time.

"I keep asking," he told me, "but nobody will give me information. I just hope the date for the tryouts had not passed."

It hit me with a weight that I could not bear. From my conversations with the assistant band director, I knew that the audition time period had indeed passed. Furthermore, given that there were only two weeks remaining in the academic calendar, the roster for the subsequent year's band had been set and rehearsal dates during the summer were being solidified.

It was shockingly clear: Sidney was intentionally being prevented from joining the funk band. Although it was almost normal protocol for Black students to be denied admission to the band after trying out, the band director did not even attempt to mask his blatant, racist practice. It was obvious that he had intentionally not informed Sidney about the funk band tryouts, and it further appeared that he instructed other members of the band not to disclose information about the tryouts. Given that there was only one Black member in the funk band and he seemed to be ambivalent about the state of his Blackness, the school had effectively removed a potential site of cultural autonomy and resistance from the Black student population.

Although Sidney had the opportunity to participate in the marching band, it coalesced within the framework of a hierarchal, militaristic organization that was aligned with Western cultural norms of performance. Counter to the possibility of the funk band, the marching band operated within the traditional "white" stylistic marching method that was based upon the U.S. Army Marching Band. The marching band participants marched in strict, stiff, military style to popular Broadway show tunes. Accompanied by flag bearers and baton twirlers, the band allowed very limited room for personal expression and creativity.[4]

Important to Sidney's desire to play music was the source of his passion. Located within a cultural tradition of music expression, Sidney had grown up in a family of musicians. During the year-end band concert, I had the pleasure of meeting and talking to Sidney's father about Sidney's talent for music. The concert was held at CHS West, the high school campus that housed only ninth-grade students. The white walls of the auditorium enclosed rows of nylon covered, metal-hinged chairs. Reminiscent of a 1930s single-room theater, the open space was labeled as multiuse, but it was not conducive for listening because of the poor acoustics. While a group of elementary school students cleared the elevated stage, Sidney's father spoke glowingly of Sidney's progress in music.

> Yeah, I was really surprised when he told me that he wanted to play music. I grew up playing music. I played the piano and sang. I had a band and we would practice in the garage. I never pressured him [Sidney] into playing music. I wanted him to find his own path and not seem like it was something that he had to do. He had been into painting and art and I thought that was real cool. So then, I was surprised, but happy when he told me that he wanted to learn music. So I still tried to keep my distance and let him do his own thing and that is when he told me that he wanted to play clarinet. Now I wanted him to learn piano if he was going to play music, because you know if you can play the piano then you can play anything. But I did not say anything and just allowed him to follow his own path. So he is around the house playing the clarinet and trying to get the notes and figure everything out. . . . Then one day he asked me if he could listen to some of my old records and he starts listening to my old funk records, you know of James Brown and all of them. I guess it was listening to all of those records that changed his mind, because he switched over to tenor sax right after that and boy did he pick it up really fast.

We concluded our conversation as the beginning band took the stage and the lights dimmed down signifying that the band was about to play. Although the band originally had five members, only three of the participants were on the stage. In order to supplement the sound of the band, the beginning band director, Ms. Briggs, joined the band. Playing trumpet, she accompanied Sidney on tenor sax, Frank on drums, and Freddy, who played the second trumpet part. Soon after the band engaged in the first song, I realized that Sidney was playing both the tenor and alto saxophone parts. His combo mate, Lester, was not at the performance and Sidney took it upon himself to play both parts. Playing solo phrases over Frank's syncopated rhythms, Sidney's confidence in his instrument had taken form.

I glanced to my right side, toward Sidney's father, whose joyous disposition was marked by a beaming smile and nodding of his head to the rhythmic pattern of the song. The band played another song and concluded their set with a mixed combination of elementary school students, ninth-grade students from the adjacent campus, and high school students from the senior campus. While the stage crew arranged the chairs for the elementary school students, Sidney's father turned to me and with a look of absolute joy said, "Man, did you hear him? He was playing in between the breaks and everything. He has gotten a lot better."

The lights dimmed once again, and the enlarged band consisted of the high school introductory band, an elementary drum ensemble, and ninth-grade band members from the CHS secondary campus. Ms. Briggs approached the microphone and introduced the members of the band. She also thanked the parents and the students for the time and energy that they put into the music given the limited amount of time that they were afforded to practice together as a unit. She sat down in the front row of the band and counted off from her seat. The wide-ranging level of experience in the band was masked by the dominating sound of the bass guitar that filled the room. At the conclusion of the song, the audience jumped up and gave the band a standing ovation. Ms. Briggs stepped to the front of the stage and thanked everyone for coming to the performance and looked forward to making more music next year.

Sidney, Manuel, and Frank walked off the stage with a bold and confident swagger. In contrast to the daily school environment, within this space their passion and love for music was validated. Sidney walked down the path of the linoleum floor and searched out his father. Upon seeing him, they embraced and Sidney thanked his father for coming to the performance. "What did you think, Daddy?," he asked his father.

Looking especially proud his father responded, "It was great son, just great. Did you have a chance to eat already? I would like to take you out, but I have to get back to work."

Sidney responded that he had not had dinner, but was planning to pick up something on the way home. His father pulled out his wallet and gave him $20. He hugged him again, shook my hand and then departed.

I had never seen Sidney look so happy. I told him how great the band sounded and that I was impressed by his performance and his ability to play both the tenor and alto saxophone parts. His enthusiasm became muted when I asked about his band mate, Lester. "Yeah, I don't know. He told Ms. Briggs that he was going to be here tonight, but then he didn't show up. He is going to fail the class now."

"Had he been coming to class?," I asked Sidney.

"Yeah, he had been coming to class, but he had gotten into some trouble, some sort of fight or something about his girlfriend."

During my conversations with both Sidney and Lester, I was humbled and excited by their ambition and resilience in the face of overt racism. It had been my experience at CHS that, rather than give up, students searched for specific activities in the school that they could join that would provide a sense of belonging and attachment to the school. However, for the majority of Black males on campus the spaces that had been associated with Blackness were being enclosed. Although Sidney had been denied access to the funk band and Lester was being pushed out of band all together, these were not isolated phenomena, nor were they strictly an issue at CHS; rather, the enclosure of Sidney and Lester and the withdrawal of resources as experienced by Ms. Briggs was an all too common occurrence that took place throughout Southern California and across the nation (Schnyder 2010).

Culture, Enclosures, and STPP

The ethnography described represents a gulf in the literature that permeates throughout the STPP analysis. Although there have been many solutions presented that connect suspensions, expulsions, detentions, and zero-tolerance policies to a pipeline created between schools and prisons, we have to move to a position that is absent of a singular "smoking gun" that will point to "the solution." For example, the framing of the STPP leaves us without the language to write about, discuss, and even consider the thousands of Black students like Lester and Sidney—students who may have not been arrested and who also do not fit neatly within the binary of either going to prison or on their way to "productively contributing" to society. The introduction of culture into the discussion begins to change the lens of how we understand the relationship between schools and prisons. In many ways the removal of Black culture from the grasp of Sidney and Lester was much more damning than any truancy ticket or suspension. It tore at the core fabric that provided a connection among home, community, and school. The effects were quite profound in the case of Lester, who increasingly saw CHS as a hostile environment in which he was not represented. Thus, as Erica Meiners and Ann Arnett Ferguson note, it is not surprising when Black students do not see failing a class as a major issue, because performance in school has very little bearing on how they understand their own intellect and abilities (Ferguson 2001; Meiners 2007). Extending that conversation further, it would be logical to understand that the self-removal of Black students from the formal educative setting is in order to protect their sanity. Hence, Lester's absence from the concert should not be understood as surprising. Not for the common-sense reasons such as misplaced priorities or lack of discipline and focus; he was merely reciprocating the level of respect that the school had extended him. It is within this context that the STPP discursive project becomes problematic. How do we talk about Black youth whose life opportunities have become limited by circumstances that we normally do not associate with prisons (that is, arrests, suspensions)? The issues of school failure and prison expansion are multifaceted and require multifaceted analysis. My main argument in this chapter is that Black culture is a major facet within the demise and rise of these state structures. However, just as the discussion of culture is completely omitted within the STPP analysis, it would be a severe mistake to locate the current manifestation of cultural enclosures within the temporal moment of educative politics. Instead, it is incumbent upon us to search for the root source(s) of the development of these particular enclosure models: Western Christianity.

Black Cultural Enclosures

The position of Black culture within Western expansion has been one of appropriation and enclosure. As a means to extract both labor and resources, a primary intent of European expansion and colonization throughout the African Diaspora was to eliminate sites of Black cultural autonomy. Yet, key to any study of Black cultural enclosure is an understanding of the relationship between the suppression of Black spiritual and cultural practices and the complex role that the many strands of Christianity played in the development of the United States. Specifically, it is important to tease out the distinctions between the containment practices of the English, whose Protestant-driven practices differed greatly from the Catholic-based religious tenets employed by the French, Spanish, and Portuguese colonizers and slave authorities. Central to both forms was the basis that Black spiritual suppression had everything to do with the revolutionary potential central to Black cultural practices. In turn, the proliferation of

Black cultural practices terrified white planters and colonial authorities alike. For their part, planters' fears emanated from two sources. Although loss of wealth was an evident motivation, more apparent was the realization that Black retribution would be swift and strike a dissident, far-reaching chord among the psyches of enslaved Blacks and white landed gentry. At the same time, colonial authorities worried that loss of revenue would diminish their ability to wield social and political power and that slave agency might counter the racist myth that propped white superiority atop the invented racial hierarchy. Thus, as a result of this very real threat, planters and colonial regimes utilized a plethora of strategies to limit black culture.

Protestant, British, and Ruthless

From the inception of colonial law to the imposition of martial rule, Black culture was under continual supervision by planters and Protestant clergy. However, it wasn't until the forging of alliances with missionary societies and religious leaders and slave owners during the nineteenth century that the most insidious method to limit the potential of Black freedom was realized. Still, prior to this period, Christianity proved to be a hard sell to slaves and planters alike. This was due in large part to the edict of the Anglican Church that once baptized, an individual was deemed free.[5] Given this framework, Protestant ministers had a difficult time convincing planters that conversion was in their best interest. Writing on this matter, Albert Raboteau commented, "Repeatedly, would-be missionaries to the slaves complained that slaveholders refused them permission to catechize their slaves because baptism made it necessary to free them" (Raboteau 1980, 99). A direct conflict existed in which "the Christian commission to preach the gospel to all nations ran directly counter to the economic interest of the Christian slave owner" (Raboteau 1980, 99). In an effort to assuage the technical problem of freedom and baptism, colonies passed legislation that made the conversion process financially feasible for planters. In 1644, a request was placed to the upper house in Maryland "to draw up an Act obliging negroes to serve *durante vita* . . . for the prevencion of the damage Masters of such Slaves must susteyne by such Slaves pretending to be Christ[e]ned [;] And soe pleade the lawe of England" (Raboteau 1980, 99). South Carolina followed suit with passage of the Act of 1701 that "declared [it] lawful for any slave or slaves to receive the Christian faith & be thereunto baptized." Though L. H. Roper makes known that the colony "retained the prohibition of conversion as a means to manumission or to alter the "estate & condition he was before" (Roper 2007, Section 19).

Thus, the seeds were planted for Christianity to become a socializing agent whereby the roots of a Black past could be remapped, and in some instances cut, in order to "transition" Blacks into docile workers. However, infusion with a foreign culture form into Black life was a problematic endeavor because very often Blacks understood or interpreted Christian rhetoric and verse as a text of liberation. In addition, as hard as it was tried, it was impossible to remove African spiritual and cultural practices from Western Christian norms. Yet, rather than the imposition of an artificial religious practice, key to the historical process is to question why. Why did plantation owners, after years of skepticism, seek to work with Western religious organizations? Why were plantation owners so intent on suppressing Black culture? Why did religious leaders seek out relationships with planters? The why provides insight into a complex web that belies the relationship between capital expansion and race. The question of why allows us to move beyond the mere fact or presence of imposed policy and invented cultural practices and analyze the ideological milieu that provided the foundation of such policy and cultural practices to become socially palatable and form social conventions.

Rather than a civilizing mission or matter of benevolence, the actions undertaken by planters, missionaries, and colonial officials must be understood within a historical and contemporary trajectory of Black subjugation to the economic and political demands that undergird the wealth of white supremacist projects. Throughout the modern African Diaspora, there existed a continual dialectical relationship between the vicious demands of plantation owners and the liberation desires on the part of Blacks. Key to revolutionary Black struggles was the organizational logic of African spirituality and religiosity that countered brutal regimes that sought to maintain the Trans-Atlantic enterprise.[6] Despite the attempts of a largely conservative missionary class to pacify the Black "subject" into docility, such maneuvers were outflanked by Black leaders and radical white organizers who incorporated Christian doctrine into already existing African spiritual practices.

It was at this point in Black liberation that the involvement of the planter class into the process of religious conversion took a drastic turn once the organizing and ideological power of Black spiritual practices was made real to the white planter bloc. Tolerant at best and largely disdainful of the missionary process, the planned insurrection of Denmark Vesey in 1822 and Nat Turner's revolt in 1831 quickly changed the ambivalent orientation to the conversion process. Turner, an enslaved Black laborer in Virginia, began a rebellion against the landed class that quickly spread through the vast network of plantations in southern Virginia. Although planters were shocked that their fears of violent revolt were realized, they were more astounded by the ideological construction that informed Turner's passion for revolt: Christianity. Upon being captured, Turner recounted to Virginia officials:

> I heard a loud noise in the heavens, and the Spirit instantly appeared to me and said the Serpent was loosened, and Christ had laid down the yoke he had borne for the sins of men, and that I should take it on and fight against the Serpent, for the time was fast approaching when the first should be last and the last should be first. . . . And by signs in the heavens that it would make known to me when I should commence the great work, and until the first sign appeared I should conceal it from the knowledge of men; and on the appearance of the sign . . . I should arise and prepare myself and slay my enemies with their own weapons. (Rose 1999, 126)

The message to the planter class was evident. In conjunction with Denmark Vessey's revolt in South Carolina, which similar to Turner's was informed by Christian theology, Black resistance provoked fear in the hearts of the southern aristocracy. If they did not gain control of interpretation of the Christian gospel, danger abounded. Black folks were not merely utilizing the Bible for apolitical metaphysical guidance. Rather it was clearly a tool whereby revolutionary prophets such as Vessey and Turner exercised the Bible as a means to organize and revolt against white terror. Yet the planter bloc had more than revolutionary slaves to deal with; its members had also fallen behind radical white abolitionists who had become quite adept at using the Christian doctrine as a means to alter the political landscape of the condition of Blacks during slavery.

Theodore Parker, a minister from the Unitarian tradition, was emblematic of this fountain of the Christian faith and also the power that religious movements could have on the destruction of slavery. Even within a considerably liberal framework as that of the Unitarians, Parker felt too confined to the limits that were established by the long-standing ministers. In an effort to break out of this space, during the 1840s Parker took to the road and held revival-like speaking engagements that drew thousands of people. His primary message focused on the destructive desires of capitalism that were on full display in the new burgeoning industrial system and the slow death of the "inner goodness" within people (Cruz 2001, 140).

As Parker's tour grew in popularity, so too did the scope of his analysis of social structures. No longer solely focusing on the intentions of northern industrialists' activities in the North, he concentrated his efforts on the perverse logic of southern planters. The passion and conviction that Parker spoke with had a great impact upon those who attended his rousing sermons. A member of Parker's traveling congregation was the journalist and abolitionist William Lloyd Garrison, who did much work to change the tenor of abolition in the United States. Another member of the congregation was Franklin Sanborn, who later became the first president of the American Social Science Association (Cruz 2001, 140). In conjunction with Parker, Sanborn and four others formed the Secret Six (Cruz 2001, 140). Similar to the ideological framework established by Nat Turner and Denmark Vesey, the aim of the Secret Six was to put theology into action. Perhaps their most notable effort was the financing of John Brown's raid of Harpers Ferry in 1859 in an attempted revolt against slavery in Virginia (Cruz 2001, 140). Parker also did a great deal to shift the tide against the further expansion of slavery into the North. With the passage of the 1850 Fugitive Slave Act, Parker formed the Boston Vigilance Group (BVG), an organization of ministers and abolitionists that sought to free Blacks from the clutches of southern intervention in northern politics (Cruz 2001, 145).

It is within the context of a radical theological praxis applied by the likes of Turner, Vesey, and Parker that we can understand why and how, in an abrupt manner, southern planters became intimately close to religious leaders and made it their business to gain control of the spread and management of the Christian doctrine.[7] Counter to the radical influences that were seeping into the Christian message, the tenor of southern Christianity took on a very conservative and anti-Black tone. While the practice of religious instruction changed, so too did the philosophical orientation of the instruction. In order to mask the gross exploitation that was at the heart of the Black labor project, the reformed gospel became infused with the benevolent nature of slavery and the moral strivings of hard work. Rather than adhere to a humane position, southern religious organizations aligned themselves with the obtuse desires of planters. White preachers began to teach gospels of subservience and remove the emancipatory logic that was central to the Black interpretation of biblical verses. In a not-so-sleight of hand, God became conflated with white plantation owners and freedom became synonymous with obedience.[8]

Complementing the work of individual preachers, sectarian factions of the Christian faith boldly claimed their allegiance to the repression of Black freedom. Proclamations such as the edict released by the Generally Assembly of the Presbyterian Church in 1861 stated that slavery instituted "real effective discipline" and was in fact the Black people's "normal condition" (Genovese 1976, 187). Similarly, the Alabama Baptist Association at its annual meeting in 1850 issued the claim:

> Intelligent masters with the light of experience before them will regard the communication of sound religious instruction as the truest economy and the most efficient police and as tending to the greatest utility, with regard to every interest involved. (Genovese 1976, 189)

At this moment that link of direct complicity of religious leaders and their organization is made known. In a broad stroke of pen to policy, these leaders within the prominent denominations of the Protestant church willingly joined the ranks of a terroristic project to enclose Black existence beyond of the realm of laborer.

Plantation owners, however, did not merely stop at enlisting the services of religious leaders; en masse they began to build Christian chapels on plantation grounds and would force Black laborers to attend church services with them (Genovese 1976; Raboteau 1980). Although the façade put forth was that planters were concerned with the spiritual strivings of Black people, the reality was that these actions were nothing more than a form of social control. The real concern was that Black folks were gaining spiritual instruction from radical sources (that is, Turner and Vessey) outside of the purview of the white gaze. To this extent, laws were put in place that even limited the time and location of Black funerals and their ability to be held in public spaces (Genovese 1976).[9]

Given that the fear on the part of white southerners was substantiated by plots of Black revolt, it is understandable that planters would want to prohibit Black organizing. However, the question arises: How, even in broad daylight and in public spaces, often in front of white overseers, did Blacks organize? This question of how allows us to comprehend the savvy and intellect of Black cultural practices. Additionally, it provides a platform by which to understand why planters, government officials, and religious clerics alike sought to contain Black culture at all cost.

Similar to the Haitian Revolution, Nat Turner utilized Black cultural practices as a means to communicate with his fellow compatriots in the struggle for Black freedom. In a very coy manner, Black liberators such as Turner would employ common Christian hymns as signifiers of meeting times and location. In an effort to coordinate the rebellion against the Virginia plantation bloc, Turner used the spiritual "Steal Away to Jesus" as a means to establish meetings (Cruz 2001, 109). Similarly, Harriet Tubman used the same tactic, invoking the song "Wade in the Water" as a way to communicate to fellow Blacks how to attain freedom.[10] Although on the surface the song describes the process by which Moses leads the Israelites out of Egypt (which by itself bears parallels to Tubman's important role in the Underground Railroad), it bore specific instructions of how to evade the tracking ability of bloodhound dogs—to literally wade in the water in order to disrupt the scent pattern (Cruz 2001, 109).

The ability of Black liberators on southern plantations to utilize cultural practices informed by the Christian faith to achieve freedom forced the hand of planters to develop new methods to corral such libratory practices. By and large, plantation owners employed two means to counter Black resistance. The first was by means of outright violence in response to the singing of Christian hymns. After several revolts, the landed class had figured out that a primary means for Black organizing was through the coding of Christian hymns and songs (Cruz 2001, 109). Building upon the impulses of slavery, planters passed draconian measures and brutal regulations that aimed to prevent Blacks from organizing via means of song. In 1849, St. John's parish in Louisiana prohibited Blacks "from beating the drum or dancing after sundown" (Epstein 1977, 60). Charity Bower, a former enslaved Black laborer, noted that following the Nat Turner revolt, Blacks on southern plantations endured beatings for singing "There's a Better Day Coming" (Cruz 2001, 109).

Although outward physical violence was a common occurrence of slavery, plantation owners were also aware that brutal force brought about intense resistance. Thus, plantation owners implemented coercive policies in an attempt to prevent slaves from invoking specific gospel melodies. Planters were particularly sensitive to slave songs that implied that their living and working conditions were deplorable and would soon be remedied by the coming of the Lord (which was very worrisome given that the Lord had instructed Nat Turner to rebel against his masters). Rather, they demanded that if slaves did sing, they were only to sing songs that connoted a cheerful and positive orientation to life. Francis Kemble, an English actress who was the wife of a plantation owner, commented that it was commonplace to prohibit "melancholy tunes or words" and sing only songs that were "nothing but cheerful music and senseless words" (Cruz 2001, 113). She made the particular note that Black laborers who sang downtrodden songs had a much more adverse disposition to work and could not be easily managed (Cruz 2001, 113).

Although many sects within the Protestant faith had developed clever methods, such as censoring songs, to enclose the parameters of Black cultural expression and physical movement, the Catholic Church was slightly ahead of their Christian brethren. Due in large part to its tiered structural orientation, Catholic authorities had implemented a model that proved highly effective in marginalizing Black culture and consequently limiting potential threats to its power base. With respect to the historical relationship between Black people and the Catholic Church, it is important to situate Catholicism both as a religious institution and also as a colonial agent within the nation- and empire-building process.

Catholic and Complex

Counter to the loosely based conglomeration of dominations that make up the Protestant faith, the Catholic Church has maintained a strict top-down hierarchal relationship between the pope and its tightly regulated global network of churches, seminaries, and convents. The basis of this chain of command is the belief that the pope is the vessel of God and in turn provides instruction and guidance to priests around the world. In between the priests and the pope are a host of bishops who control specific geographic regions and ensure that priests implement the pope's mandates. Importantly, priests who reign over the lay community of their particular parishes are the "mediator(s) between God and humanity" and hold the "keys to the kingdom of heaven" (Ochs 1990, 10). An emblematic example of the tiered relationship between the lay congregation and the religious clergy is the requirement that all participants of the Catholic faith have to perform confession to priests, who in turn provide forgiveness once repentance has been articulated. In order to assist the work of the priest at given parishes, nuns, in addition to their assigned tasks at the church, perform duties (that is, nurse, teach) that are specific to their religious orders.

As can be imagined within a relatively inflexible chain of leadership, the lines of the Catholic hierarchy are drawn specifically along constructions of gender and sexuality. All of the members of the clergy (that is, priest, bishop, pope) are presumed to be men, heterosexual, and celibate; all of the nuns are presumed to be women, heterosexual, and celibate. Thus, within the implicit governance, the Catholic Church is a heteronormative patriarchal institution whereby men (pope) give orders to other men (bishops) who in turn give orders to other men (priests) who finally give orders to women (nuns). The terms of these orders are to be final and not questioned or deviated by the underlings who have been assigned the task of carrying out the work of the church. Although this is a very simple description of a complex institution, it provides a framing for understanding how and why the Catholic Church has historically been slow to respond to issues of social justice.

Important to the foundation of the Catholic Church is the education of both the clergy and the lay congregation. Protestantism is home to a multiplicity of authorities (this variety is formed by the multitude of faiths that make up the religious practice) who may or may not have been formally trained. All Catholic priests, in contrast, are mandated to be ordained and trained within seminaries that operate under the tight control of the Papal Council. Although there are slight deviations for cultural differences of particular locales, all doctrinal interpretations and governance patterns are established within the confines of the seminaries. Similarly, the pope and the Catholic hierarchy in Rome tightly regulate the teaching of the lay community in the form of Catholic schools that range from the elementary level to doctorate-granting institutions.

The governing parameters of the Catholic Church provide an outline for understanding how the organizational structure of the church systemically dictated the relationship between the African people and the church from the fifteenth century on. This concentration of power allowed the church to gain wealth at the expense of Black bodies and was able to wield an immense amount of influence on the U.S. nation-building process. Key to this process, the church played a central role in the development of white supremacy within the United States. The irony of this process is that the Catholic movement, which was heavily based within non-English speaking countries (that is, Spain, Portugal, and Ireland [Gaelic]), was considered to be outside of the realm of proper whiteness.

In order to understand the mechanisms of the Catholic Church's enclosure process upon Black people in the United States, it is key to expound upon the white supremacist ideology that informed the governing structure of the Catholic hierarchy. First, the church's hard-and-fast stance against the ordination of Black priests in the United States. It was not until 1866 in Boston, Massachusetts, when the first group of Black priests, three brothers named James, Alexander, and Patrick Healy, that the U.S. church made headway with Black clergy (Ochs 1990, 10). However, it must be noted that in addition to passing for white, historical records show that these very light-skinned brothers did very little to advocate for Black priests or congressional causes and actively sought to stay clear of such issues (Davis 1998, 32). As a matter of practice, Catholic bishops actively prevented aspiring Black priests from being ordained in the United States. In the rare instances when Black students were sent to Europe or Canada to undertake training, it was the bishops who ensured that their request to return and preside over U.S. Black congregations was denied.

The rationale for this exclusionary access to clergy is best understood within the philosophical framing of the Catholic Church with respect to slavery. During the middle of the sixteenth century, the Catholic Church posited that based upon the work of Aristotle, slavery was a natural fit within the order of social relations (Davis 1990, 23).[11] The church utilized this argument as a rationale for enslaving Black peoples throughout the European colonization project. However, unlike their Protestant brethren, the Catholic Church made it a point to baptize slaves, who were deemed to be heathenish pagans. Further, the underlining premise of such a forced conversion was very troubling: Black culture as a whole was worthless and needed to be eliminated. Gomes Eannes de Azurara, a chronicler of Portugal's involvement in the slave trade, commented unfavorably upon the condition and treatment of Black Africans during the Middle Passage. However, such brutality was justified by the caveat that at least they can be rid of their degenerate culture and way of life. Writing in the middle of the fifteenth century, he stated:

> And so their lot was not quite the contrary of what it had been; since before they had lived in perdition of soul and body of their souls, in that they were yet pagans, without the clearness and the light of the holy faith; and of their bodies, in that they lived like beasts, without any custom of reasonable beings—for they had no knowledge of bread or wine, and they were without the covering of clothes, or the lodgement of houses; and worse than all, they had no understanding of good, but only knew how to live in bestial sloth. (Raboteau 1980, 97)

The power of Azurara's logic was its ability to establish broad-based common sense that would last throughout the colonial epoch. Raboteau argues, "Azurara's rationalization . . . was to be repeated for over four generations by successive generations of Christian apologist for slavery" (Raboteau 1980, 97). This process had exceptional limits, of course, because matters of colonization were never simple. The most notable occurred when Spain, beginning in 1700, offered freedom to Black laborers who fled their plantations in Georgia and the Carolinas, converted to Catholicism, and fought on the Spanish side in Florida against the British (Davis 1990, 30). The caveat was that Blacks had to convert to Catholicism in order to make this process complete.[12]

Yet the dominant narrative of Catholic involvement with slavery in the United States was its participation in the thriving enterprise. In 1636, the Jesuits received more than 12,000 acres of land in southern Maryland from Cecil Calvert. Irish indentured servants initially worked the land; however, by 1700 the Jesuits had introduced slavery to the region and soon thereafter had amassed a sizable plantation. Roughly 130 years later, because of internal strife over the mission of the Jesuit community, it was decided that the Jesuit Order would shift its focus away from slavery. In order to maintain the moral standards of the church, it was decided that rather than free the enslaved laborers the best way to achieve this goal was to sell the slaves to Catholic landowners and that all slave families would be kept together. However, because capital and morality are often in conflict, families were torn apart as financial gain overrode ethical concerns and the Jesuits sold all of their slaves to planters throughout Louisiana (Davis 1990, 37).

Rather than an exception, the Jesuit model set the tone for the relationship between the Catholic Church and Black laborers in the United States.

The practice of slavery was ingrained within the foundation of orders of nuns throughout the country, beginning with the Ursuline in 1721. In addition to the Ursuline of New Orleans, the Carmelite of Port Maryland, Daughters of the Cross of Missouri and Louisiana, Visitation of Washington, D.C., and Dominican of Kentucky were all slaveholders. Many orders such as the Loreto of Kentucky were started as a direct result of selling enslaved Black workers who in turn enabled Mother Ann Rhodes to purchase the land for a convent (Davis 1990, 39). What is particularly striking about nuns was the integration of slavery within the ordination; many of the women brought slaves with them to the religious orders as a part of their dowries (Davis 1990, 39). Catholic historian Cyprian Davis argues that as members of the landed gentry, the members of the orders of convents in fact were beholden to the "sentiments of the slaveholding class" (Davis 1990, 39).

As stakeholders within slavery, it did not come as a surprise that many of the clergy sided with a pro-slavery style of capital accumulation during the Civil War. Building upon an intertwining of Aristotelian thought and religious conversion, the enslavement and forced labor of Black people was rationalized as necessary. Many Catholic bishops, priests, and nuns benefited from the legitimization of profiting from slavery with an understanding that Black laborers left to their own devices would never rise out of their inferior state of being. This point of view was well articulated by Bishop Augustus Marie Martin, originally from France and in 1829 ordained in the Vincennes parish of Indiana. Writing upon the subject of slavery in 1861, he stated:

> The manifest will of God is that in exchange for a freedom of which they were incapable and for a labor of the whole life, we should give these unfortunate ones, not only the bread and the clothing necessary for material life, but also and especially their legitimate portion of the truth and the goods of grace, which consoles them in their present miseries through the hope of rest in the bosom of the Father, to Whom they are called under the same title as us. (Davis 1990, 52–53)

The indebtedness of the Catholic clergy to the sustenance of slavery positioned them in direct opposition to the religious leaders and political figures who supported an abolitionist stance. The radical Republican,

Thaddeus Stevens, commented that the Catholic clergy "support[ed] the pro-slavery party [the Democrats] and cry 'Down With the Nigger'" (Ochs 1990, 37). Proving Stevens's claim, Catholic Archbishop John Hughes of New York took particular exception to the likes of radical minister Theodore Parker and urged President Abraham Lincoln during the war to refrain from advocating for the freeing of Black laborers. He wrote to then–Secretary of War Simon Cameron that if Catholics "are to fight for the abolition of slavery, then, they will turn away in disgust from . . . patriotic duty" (Ochs 1990, 32).

Yet the Catholic position on abolition was complicated by the nativist position that had gained afoot within the Republican Party. In response to the migration of Irish immigrants into the United States, the Know-Nothing movement was based upon a platform of anti-immigration and anti-Catholic in particular. Similar to the claims that many within the Catholic clergy interpellated upon Black people, the advocates of the Know-Nothing movement argued that ills of U.S. society were to be blamed on the inferiority and uncivilized nature of Irish immigrants who made their way across the Atlantic Ocean. However, rather than take a position of alliance with abolitionist and/or radical religious members whose analysis was centered on matters of capital accumulation and gross exploitation, the hierarchy within the U.S. Catholic clergy sought to protect their financial interests located within slavery. As a marked strategy, several prominent clergy claimed that abolitionists were at the core of the problems that were tearing the nation asunder. Specifically, they linked the abolitionists to the Republican Party and thus as members of the Know-Nothing movement. Archbishop Augustin Verot argued that the radical abolitionist preachers were against the Catholic Church. He stated, "There has been, in the northern part of the country, an actual conspiracy against justice and truth. . . . This conspiracy is headed by fanatical preachers . . . who desecrate and pollute the Divine word" (Davis 1990, 54). In driving the connection further between unrest and the attack upon the Catholic Church, he charged, "Now, beloved brethren, they are the same who heretofore assailed, calumniated, vilified our church, and have resorted to the vilest and most iniquitous devices . . . to destroy our holy religion" (Davis 1990, 54).

It was very true that the abolitionists were trying to destroy the core of the American Catholic Church; at the center of the expansion and maintenance of the U.S. Catholic Church was a firm investment in both slavery and white supremacy. On the account of slavery, the Catholic Church's place within the United States was directly linked to its financial stock within the plantation system of the southern United States. As previously discussed, many orders of clergy and nuns were established directly as a result of slavery. Rather than benign participation in matters of the southern economy, high-ranking clergy recognized the need to maintain dominion over Black people. Just prior to the Civil War, Archbishop Francis P. Kenrick of Baltimore argued that as long as slave owners respected the basic rights of food, shelter, and a place to practice their religion, slavery was neither deplorable nor did it go against the tenets of Catholic spirituality (Ochs 1990, 18). In line with an Aristotelian perspective of slavery, the Catholic Church was able to exploit the tenet that slavery was merely part of the natural pattern that governed social rules.

However, the exploitation of Black labor was not merely an economic endeavor; key to the process was the promotion of a white supremacist agenda that while denigrating Black people simultaneously created false allusions of whiteness. Perhaps the most arduous defense was presented by Catholic convert and writer Orestes Augustus Brownson. On the eve of the end of the Civil War he penned an article entitled "Abolition and Negro Equality." In it he wrote, "We may talk as we will, spin any fine theories we like, praise the negro as we please, and sneer at the boasting Caucasian to our heart's content, but we cannot alter the fact of negro inferiority, or make it not a fact that the negro is the most denigrate branch of our race." Just in case his readership was not clear on his position of his definition of inferiority, he furthered his point:

> The inferior races, the yellow, the red, or the black nearly all savage, barbarous, or semi-barbarous, are not . . . types of the primitive man, or so many stages in man's progressive march from the tadpole, chimpanzee, or gorilla up to Bacon, Newton, Napoleon Bonaparte, George B. McClellan. . . . They mark rather so many stages or degrees in human degeneracy. The African negro is not the primitive man, the man not yet developed, the incipient Caucasian, but the degenerate man, who through causes which neither you nor I can explain, has fallen below the normal human type. . . . He has ceased to be progressive, and when a race has ceased to be progressive, nothing remains for it but to die. (Davis 1990, 61)

Although his position regarding Black people is evident, what is more important in Brownson's commentary is the creation of a mythology about the superior notion of white people. Brownson's marking of European achievement as the pinnacle of human development simultaneously forged a new type of whiteness that up to that point was not fully formed. It was no secret that until roughly the middle of the twentieth century, German, Irish, and later Slav and Italian immigrants were not considered in the same racial category as Anglo-Saxons. The early formation of the United States was marked by a series of nativist movements that sought to assert a particular type of whiteness at the direct expense of other racial groups. The irony of Brownson's statement is that it came on the heels of the aforementioned Know-Nothing movement that positioned Catholicism and the surge of Irish and German immigrants as outside of the boundaries of whiteness. Brownson, fully aware of these tensions, articulated the Catholic Church's stance on such political formations. Although the Catholic Church actively sought to defeat the Know-Nothings, they desperately wanted in on the business of being white.

Thus, the first matter at hand for the church was to fully distance themselves from Black people. Once this had been established by the Catholic hierarchy through their stance on slavery and the ideological orientation of the supremacy of whiteness, the second matter was the creation of a white subject. The difficult task was to shift the tide against the notion that the Irish immigrants were in fact not white but some sublevel race below proper Anglo-Saxons. This was achieved through the drastic reduction in the number of priests and resources for Blacks in the South and the articulation that the newly arrived Irish immigrants were white—this message was driven home by Archbishop James Whitfield of Baltimore. Although he wished he could service the Black population, he claimed that there were not enough resources to service what he considered "white" immigrants in the North, whom he deemed to be the successors of the religion (Ochs 1990, 15).

In order to affirm the place of the Irish as white was the disavowal of Black people as members of the clergy. This was no more evident than during the 1866 Catholic Council when there appeared to be a slight headway on the part of the Roman Propaganda to push the American Catholic Church to ordinate Black priests. The resistance against such an action from the U.S. clergy was swift and strong. Archbishop Peter Kenrick of St. Louis (brother to Archbishop Frances Kenrick) stated that the role of the bishop was to preside over his diocese, not abide by the rules of the Propaganda, and further, if Rome issued such a decree, he would resign (Ochs 1990, 41). Archbishop Jean-Marie Odin from New Orleans was adamant that Blacks in Louisiana did not need Black priests and such intervention would disrupt the activities of the church base. This sentiment was echoed by Archbishop John McCloskey of New York, who argued that because there were very few Blacks in the North, the plight of Black people did not weigh on the conscience of northern bishops (Ochs 1990, 41).

The resistance against Black priests in the United States allowed the Catholic Church to achieve two vital goals. With respect to the whitening process, to be a priest was synonymous with being white (to the extent that being a priest meant that one was not Black and hence moved that much closer to whiteness). This project was especially important for both the expansive lay population of Catholic Irish immigrants and also to the range of Irish clergy who either recently immigrated or scrounged for whiteness under the scrutiny of nativist movements in the United States. The second and powerful objective that the Church sought to fulfill was the prevention of the development of a radical Black clergy. Already buttressed by the hierarchal nature and strict guidelines of the ordination and education of the Catholic Church, the U.S. clergy fortified their boundaries with an all-white clause. This represented a sharp contrast to Protestant sects that were not governed by one homogenous body. Thus, it is of no surprise that the first U.S. Black preachers came out of Protestant denominations.

However, counter to the Protestant church, the structural concentration of power in the Catholic Church provided it with the ability to make bold decisions that had sweeping consequences. Yet when given the opportunity to make drastic social change, even in the face of blatant attacks upon the Catholic Church, it chose to align with its capitalist interests. During the same time period as race-based attacks against Irish immigrants and their religious affiliation with Catholicism, the church supported pro-slavery positions. For example, Archbishop John Hughes, born in Ireland, was wholeheartedly in support of the Fugitive Slave Act of 1850. His basic argument was that, given that abolition did not have any provisions for compensation of planters for their loss of property, the concept itself promoted larceny (Sharrow 1972).[13] This sentiment was buttressed by Brownson, who argued for the Act and stated, "If the master has a title to the bodily services of his slave which is good in morals, as he certainly may have, he has the right in justice to recover his slave, the same as would have in the case of any other species of property" (Davis 1990, 60).[14] Brownson's and Hughes's assertions have to be placed within the context that the U.S. Catholic Church attained vast amounts of property, land, and wealth as a key player in slavery. Further, much of the Catholic hierarchy thoroughly understood the threat that abolitionists posed to their financial wealth and power. Additionally, the last thing that the church wanted was a priest in the mold of Nat Turner or Denmark Vessey preaching radical theology to a congregation of Black laborers in the South.

It is from the perspective of Turner, Vessey, and their fellow revolutionary apostles that we can understand why the Catholic Church in the United States was adamant about keeping Blacks from the pulpit. The integral role that Black-centered religious practice played in the overthrow of the Catholic-dominated French plantation system in Haiti, along with the threat of Turner, struck fear in the hearts of the wealthy Catholic hierarchy (Raboteau 1980).[15] It is out of this fear that the U.S. Catholic Church imposed harsh policies against both the ordination of Black priests and upon potential Black clergy. In contrast to the Protestant religions that allowed for the freedom of cultural expression, the Catholic Church also placed severe boundaries upon Black clergy.[16] The church instituted the forbiddance of dance, drumming, and vocal expression. Elizabeth Ross Rite, a Black enslaved laborer who worked for a Catholic plantation owner, stated, "We was all supposed to be Catholics on that place, but lots didn't like that religion. We used to hide behind some bricks and hold church ourselves. You see, the Catholic preachers from France wouldn't let us shout, and the Law done said you gotta shout if you want to be saved. That's in the Bible" (Raboteau 1995, 119).

The drastic measures that the Catholic Church undertook in the repression of Black cultural practices were the church's attempt to remove the essence of what gave Black people pride, dignity, and the means to revolt against a brutal system. Not by chance, the Catholic Church and Catholic plantation owners set up a dual-tiered system of preventing the freedom of Black cultural expression. The doctrine dictated that all slaves within the jurisdiction of the Catholic Church (that is, those countries that were financially and religiously tied to the church) be baptized as Catholic. This thereby ensured that as workers the only type of religious ministry they received would be at the hands of the Catholic Church.[17] Once inside the clutches of the Catholic regime, if they were fortunate enough to attend mass, they were forced into a situation that attempted to strip away the possibility of resistance. For the vast majority of Black laborers who toiled under the weight of the church or Catholic plantation owners, there was no opportunity for service. The landed gentry often did not build churches on their land and prevented Blacks from leaving the plantation for fear that they might escape (Ochs 1990, 20). Given the church's guidelines that service could only be presided over by a priest and that the church did not provide enough priests to minister to Black laborers, very little in the way of "church" was provided and plantation owners took full advantage to work the enslaved to levels that could only be describe as absurd (Raboteau, 1980).[18]

It is here at the intersection between the political economy of northern industry and the plantation bloc on one hand, and the religious decrees of Western Christian theology on the other, that the formation of cultural enclosures become a necessity. In order to continue the expansion of a most vile racial capitalist system, Black cultural traditions were understood as a grave threat to the legitimacy and proliferation of Western expansion. The sophistication of Black organizing strategies that utilized Black cultural media proved too a mighty of a force to counter with mere rhetorical strategies. In order to enclose the impact of Black liberation efforts, the U.S. state apparatus, in conjunction with Western religion, developed legal and moral protocols that attempted to dismantle Black cultural traditions. The result was the formation of an enclosure model that sought to stop dissent through rearticulating Black culture as both dangerous and against the will of God.

Rather than a fleeting example of the flexing of power, the enclosure of Black cultural traditions became a staple of the Western tradition. Understood most readily in the well-documented attempts to silence both the formation of blues and later hip-hop, I argue that more profound are the mundane daily manifestations of the Black cultural enclosure model such as at CHS (Rose 1994; Woods 1998). Similar to the enclosure of Black cultural traditions, the struggle over ideology has been highly contested and violent. The next chapter details that role of ideology in sustaining the enclosure model marked by Dylan Rodríguez's (2006) conceptualization of the U.S. prison regime. First, it provides insight into the decisions that students are faced to make in light of issues beyond their immediate control yet are framed as their own volition. Second, it addresses the direct connections among ideology, Blackness and education within the U.S. nation-building process.

2

In the Belly of the Beast

Ideological Expansion

> *The obscuring of the Black radical tradition is seated in the West's*
> *suppression of Europe's previous knowledge of the African (and its own)*
> *past. . . . It was also a process that was to transport the image of Africa*
> *across separate planes of dehumanization latticed by the emerging*
> *modalities of Western Culture.*
>
> —Cedric Robinson, *Black Marxism*

The key component of public education is its ability to transmit state-sanctioned ideology to its subjects, the students. According to Antonio Gramsci, schools are responsible for socializing students to the "intractable laws to which man [*sic*] must adapt himself if he is to master. . . . These laws of the state and of society create human order which historically best enables men to dominate the laws of nature, that is to say which most facilitates their work" (Gramsci and Hobsbawm 1988/2000, 311–12). Central to Gramsci's claim is the need of the state to make work seem as if it were a natural function of daily life.[1] Through this process, rather than a space of enlightened attainment, school is a space where students both "learn to labour," become indoctrinated in ideological laws that appear natural and "are sites for popular culture practices that stage or reproduce social inequality" (Foley 1990, xv; Willis 1977).

What happens, however, in a political and economic environment where jobs are scarce and wage labor has more resonance as a theoretical principle than a social fact? What is the state-sanctioned ideology in that space, and how do schools disseminate it to students? Ruth Wilson Gilmore argues that within such an economic paradigm, the climate is ripe for radical social transformation (Gilmore 2007).[2] Although the transformation could result in the complete overhaul of the production of social relations to eliminate social hierarchies, capitalist states have never chosen that option. When national, state, and local policy makers were presented with such a situation during the 1970s, they chose to intensify regimes of racialized terror and unleashed a "civilization maddened by its own perverse assumptions and contradictions" (Robinson 2000, 318).[3] The result was a massive disinvestment from social services and the expansion of a prison enterprise like none other in the world. As described by Dylan Rodríguez, all models of social organization are bonded to a new logic—the prison regime (Rodríguez 2006). He describes this new regime as a

> dimension of processes, structure, and vernaculars that compose the state's modalities of self-articulation and "rule" across . . . macro and micro scales. It is within this meso range of dynamic, fluctuating articulations of power that the prison is inscribed as both a localization and a constitutive logic of the state's production of juridicial, spatial, and militarized dominion. (Rodríguez 2006, 41)

The naturalization of ideology is vital to the success of the new prison regime given its overt use of violence and terror. Gilmore posits that "while already-existing material inequality shapes political landscapes, the contested grounds are also ideological, because how we understand and make sense of the world and ourselves in it shapes how we do what we do. In a society, those who dominate produce normative primary definitions of human worth . . ." (Gilmore 2002, 265).

Enclosure, Ideology, Prisons, and Schools

A key intervention that Rodríguez and Gilmore make in their respective works is to resituate how we conceptualize the mental and physical geography of prisons. Their call to move beyond the physical site of prisons is very powerful because it necessities that not only do we shift our economic and political analysis beyond the physical walls of prisons but also our rendering of the ideological fortress that buttresses the very need for prison. They provide grounding for us to understand that the logic of prison—the normalization of its existence in all of its grotesque sensibilities—is the ideological enclosure within the current moment.

Through an analysis of the prison regime as an ideological construct, startling truths come to the fore: there is nothing normal about a prison; there is nothing normal about the destruction of Black communities via means of surveillance, warehousing, and killing of Black people; there is nothing normal about massive government expenditures that are granted to ensure Black oppression. There is serious work that has to be done to make these processes seem normal. Just as in previous epochs, there was nothing normal about slavery, nor sharecropping or Black people crammed into small urban dwellings, yet these forms of enclosure were made normal along ideological terrain. Whether it was through the commonsense understanding that Africa contained no culture or civilization or moral claims about the dysfunction of Black families, the ideological remapping of Black communities has been in an effort to make Black oppression appear normal. Within the current moment, the ideological enclosure as described by Rodríguez has been a crude yet sophisticated attempt to justify the existence of the prison regime via the imminent threat of Blackness to the destruction of "American" life.[4]

Building upon Rodríguez's claim of the prison regime, my argument within this chapter is that public education has been at the forefront of ushering in the prison regime as a mechanism of ideological enclosure. It is my contention that in order to understand the vast impact of the enclosure of the prison regime, we have to resituate the position of education within current discourse pertaining to prisons and education. Counter to the pathway established by the School-to-Prison Pipeline (STPP) trajectory of schools funneling students into prison, schools laid the foundation for the expansion of the prison regime in the United States. Further, and important, the STPP discourse does not reckon with the undergirding ideology of the prison regime. The advocacy logic of the STPP model posits that changes to policies within a racialized discipline code will serve as an equalizer within respect to education. However, the ideological basis of education within the United States has mandated that the education of Blacks serve a particular objective. Dating back to Reconstruction, the historic record indicates that schools were crucial in order to prevent Black dissent and key to this process was the ideological enclosure of the educative process of Black youth (Anderson 1988; Watkins 2001). Within the current moment, the buildup of the prison regime was laid bare by the wrestling of the ideological notions of "freedom" and "protest." In response to protest, anger, and a planned school strike, city and school board officials and the LAPD (Los Angeles Police Department) developed a "Police in Government" course taught by LAPD officers to Black youth during the later part of the 1960s through the '70s (Sojoyner 2013). The emphasis of this course was to teach Black youth the "true" meaning of their rights and how they should and should not act within a very narrow scope of a legal apparatus that already severely limited Black freedom. In addition, the utilization of "lockdowns" and the normalization of the "need" to have continual police surveillance on Black youth were made real by 1969. All of this work that was done through the coordination of police, city, and school officials predates the massive buildup of the physical prison system that took place in California. Central to making this happen was the use of schools as a model to implement a new ideological enclosure that constructed Black communities and youth in particular as dangerous. Although there had been iterations of such ideological stances in the past, such as the construction of the Black male rapist as justification for legal and extralegal lynching, there was a marked intensification of this process that called for the permanent surveillance and control over the movement of a newly configured dangerous Black youth. Although some of this can be attributed to the racialized fears presented by integration, the rationale for the enclosure was the highly effective means of organizing by Black communities against racial terror in Los Angeles (Sojoyner 2013). Once again, it is key to reiterate that this was not normal. Police were not teaching classes to white youth in Los Angeles; there was no such thing as a lockdown on predominately white secondary campuses. This had to be made normal, and though getting white Angelinos to buy into this new system was of concern, the major focus was instituting this new ideological enclosure upon Black communities—and here is where the schools became a central agent.

From the late 1960s to the present, in concert with the buildup of the U.S. warfare economy both home and abroad, there was a continuous amplification of the ideological enclosure of Black education. In the form of curriculum and discipline policies, by the time that physical prisons had firmly entrenched themselves in the drought-stricken, barren fields of central California, Black schools were in the depths of enclosure. Police academic magnets had been established in predominately Black schools, and Black schools had become eviscerated of cultural ties. Left in its place was a cold pedagogical apparatus that justified Western imperial projects and validated the need to enclose Black people. Yet over the decades, as the racial demography of Southern California changed and the backing of a U.S.-supported coup in El Salvador brought forth a mass migration of displaced El Salvadorians into the state, Blackness soon became easily used as a proxy to reinforce racial hierarchies and further entrench the ideological enclosure (Coutin 2007; Vargas 2006). Thus, the model that was established in the later part of the twentieth century was easily transferred to the twenty-first century, even though the racial dynamics had radically shifted. Blackness as dangerous and counter to the U.S. nation-state had already been thoroughly incorporated within the curriculum as a means to both justify Black oppression and to legitimate the expansion of war both domestically and abroad, which Black social movements and communities had been connected to and fought against. Thus, by the time that I entered the classroom at County High School (CHS), the ideological enclosure model that reified the prison regime was in full bloom.

It was in the context of CHS that my awareness of the functionality of public education to socialize racialized subjects to the ideological framework of the prison regime was made hypervisible—the violent technologies of discipline and control have been naturalized to the existence of an orderly civil society. I was highly intrigued as to why the students at CHS had a varied response to this process. Although some "bought into" the lure of the ideology, others resisted based upon their daily encounters with state-sanctioned racialized terror. Through the course of this chapter, I analyze the acceptance of the prison ideology by the very people whom the structure seeks to subjugate. Further, through an ethnographic analysis of the students and curriculum as CHS, I flush out how this ideology is maintained and describe how students utilize the educational tools at their disposal to counter dominant ideology of normalized behavior.

What Makes Dollars Don't Make Sense: Twelfth-Grade Decisions

Toward the end of the school year the student workload slowly dissipated. Teachers spent the majority of their time preparing final exams, and students began to think about summer work plans or their futures once their tenures at CHS were completed. Students in Ms. Allegro's twelfth-grade Language Arts class often engaged in these conversations, and, as the summer neared, many of them approached me with questions about job opportunities. At the crux of their inquiries was a desire to earn the most amount of money possible without a college degree. I sat in the front of the class when three Latino males, sitting adjacent to my four-legged stool, asked for my opinion on jobs. In return, I asked them what they wanted to do and whether they possessed any skills that could be used to earn money. Martin, a senior who had recently become a father, contemplated the possibility of owning a barbershop.

> Yeah, it's something that I want to do, because you know that barbers who have their own shop can make from one to two thousand dollars a week. But I don't know if I want to have all the responsibility of owning a place, finding a location and then getting barbers in there [the shop]. So I might just stay a barber in the shop that I work in right now and keep cutting hair. It makes enough money for me and my girl and the baby, but I could make more money, I guess.

Martin talked about his future plans, and the two other students, Daniel and Miguel, looked on and occasionally nodded their heads. Martin's indecisiveness was in stark contrast to Miguel's confident rationale of Martin's issue. "You need to own your own shop. There is way more money that you can make in being a barber if you own your own place." Martin, however, was not convinced of Miguel's explanation and just sat looking at his desk with a slightly worried expression. Miguel immediately seized the moment of silence as an opportunity to ask questions regarding his future. "Hey Mr. Sojoyner, do you know anything about being a parole officer or a corrections officer? I hear that they make good money," he said.

In an effort to dissuade him away from pursuing a violent career path within the criminal justice system that would reproduce racialized, gendered, and sexual oppression I told him, "I am not sure about a parole officer, but I know that you do not want to be a corrections officer. But are you good with your hands?" He responded with an affirmative head nod.

"You know that down at the Cerritos Auto Square, the mechanics get paid more than the salespeople. Now all you have to do is enroll in the auto mechanics program in Cerritos College and you can have an 'in' into the Auto Square," I informed him, hoping to push him away from the punishment and control professions.

"Yeah, that is cool," he responded, "but I talked to this guy who works down at the juvenile hall and he told me that he can help me get in. He is a Black guy that has been working there for a long time and told me that I don't need to have a college degree and can start making good money as soon as I go through the process."

It hit me like a ton of bricks. As much as I wanted to believe that out of their experience in dealing with the police and various forms of the state (that is, Immigration and Naturalization Services) the students would take a stance against the state, the cruel paradox was that the enclosure apparatus of the prison regime presented itself as the only solution. It was within this context that Miguel's logic made perfect sense. A young Latino male who stood about five foot, eight inches, and walked with the humble confidence of a proven heavyweight fighter, he was forced to deal with the reality of his situation. He did not have the grades or test scores to immediately attend a four-year college or university. He needed money to assist his household and attending college was going to cost him money. He did not want to turn to the informal economy because he had lost his older brother to violence and wore a dog-tag chain around his neck in memory of his slain sibling.

The choice was obvious; he could earn a little over $36,000 working as a corrections officer while enrolled in the Basic Correctional Juvenile Academy sponsored by the California Department of Corrections and Rehabilitation. Once he completed the training program, Miguel could earn in excess of $72,000 a year. If he continued progressing in the system, his salary would amount to $96,000 a year. The job also included a tremendous benefits and retirement package laden with incentives ranging from bonus pay for his bilingual expertise to the possibility of earning close to his highest-grossed salary for the rest of his life upon retirement. This would be in addition to his 401(k) package (California Department of Corrections 2008).

I was stuck without any viable argument to counter the economic logic of becoming a corrections officer. The minimum wage in California at the time was $8.00 an hour, which meant that even to earn the bottom-level salary with the Department of Corrections, including benefits, he would have to work more than a hundred hours a week, for fifty-two weeks a year.[5] After speaking with Miguel, the reality of the situation became strikingly concrete: there were truly no other opportunities for the vast majority of the students at CHS. The record of these activities is best viewed in the rapid expansion in the employment of law enforcement and prison guard officials during a time of economic instability and budget cuts. Since 1984, California has built more than forty-three penal institutions, and the budget for the Department of Corrections in the state has grown by nearly $7 billion between 1998 and 2009 (*California Progressive*

Message [CPM], 2011).[6] Importantly, of the current $11 billion Department of Corrections budget, 70 percent funds the salary, overtime, and benefits of prison guards and staff (CPM, 2011). However, just when I thought I reached the summit of hearing the unthinkable, I was struck by the shrewdest bit of irony.

Be All That You Can Be: Saved by the Army

I posed the same question, "What are you going to do after high school?" to Mr. Washington's U.S. Government class. However, on this occasion, the students threw a wrinkle in the response. Although some said they wanted to attend college, quite a few said that they wanted to join the armed services. After hearing this response, I asked how many in the class were considering joining the armed services. By my quick arithmetic, fifteen out of the thirty-two students said that the military was a serious option for their post–high school plans. Though I was not shocked by the response because the military is now a main employment venue of many former Black and Brown high school students, it was the rationale behind joining the armed services that completely took me by surprise.

"So why do you want to join the military? You know that if you join, many of you will be sent over to fight in Iraq or Afghanistan," I stated to the class. "Yeah," responded Julio, "and what is wrong with that?" Julio a tall and strongly built Latino male, was on the football and wrestling teams at CHS. Full of confidence and quick with a retort, I responded back to him, "What is right about that?"

He fired back with the common "armed forces phrase" that the military is protecting the freedoms of the U.S. citizens and the safety of the country. I then questioned him about the connection to the U.S. military's expansion into countries and the U.S. response once those same people enter into the U.S. borders. "So when the U.S. went into El Salvador and upset the stability of the country causing El Salvadorians to flee the country for their safety, it is ok then to call them illegal aliens and tell them to go back home?" I did not anticipate his next response:

"Well, if they did not come here legally then they need to go back home," he responded. "This country has too many problems to deal with to allow all of the people who want to come in to come in," he responded. By this time, some of the other students were dying to join into the debate.

I called on Julissa, a young Filipina whose quick wit and verbal confidence was quite spectacular. "That is okay, you keep on thinking that. When Hilary gets in office, you won't have to worry about any illegal immigrants, they all will be legal."

"No woman is ever going to lead this country. I will move away from here before I live in a country with a woman president," Julio immediately responded. I was taken aback. Although I had heard this line of reasoning before from the mouths of conservative commentators of color, I was shocked that a young Latino male growing up in the oppressive community that contained explicit police and school repression and racism would take such a conservative hardline stance. Yet the more I thought about Julio's and Miguel's situation, I realized that their plights, though articulated in very different manners and tones, were undergirded by the same rationale: the organizational logic of the prison regime.[7] Further, as I began to think about my experience of teaching at CHS, it became clear that there was an effort afoot to dampen any resistance to the ideological enclosure that governed the school. Much more savvy than outright attacking students who offered counter viewpoints, the school merely presented perverse forms of history, literature, economics, and politics that denigrated Blackness in order to legitimate the superiority and normalcy of Western ideology. The result was that when students such as Julissa spoke out about issues of gender, race, and nationality, they did so to a student body who by the very nature of their educative process, were equipped with rhetorical devices (no matter how absurd) to quickly counter a libratory analysis of power.

Yet, I also found that the converse held true. That is, when students were exposed to material that had been removed from their purview they were very adept at applying the newfound knowledge to their lives. The following two ethnographic sections of the chapter detail how students, when given just the smallest amount of information, were very fast to make connections that were detrimental to the ideological enclosure of the prison regime. Implicit within the process was the danger that the non-Western ideological tropes proved to the sustainability of the prison regime as an enclosure. Thus, counter to what any standardized test score might indicate about the students at CHS, when given information that coalesced with the knowledge formation that existed within their communities, their appetite for learning was insatiable.

No Music, No Problems: Remove All Threats

Sitting in the cramped office space that was swallowed by sheet music, instruments, cases and general clutter, I began to look through the music appreciation textbook. Although the office appeared to be built for one teacher, both Ms. Briggs and Mr. Albert held their posts in the small space. Trying to come up with a new method to teach the class, I was surprised to find that the book was nearly twenty years old.

Mr. Albert sat at a desk that was roughly a foot adjacent to where I sat. The desk was marked by the presence of everything on it. From clarinet tubing to violin rosin, it seemed that his desk was a resting depot for instrument pieces. On the floor next to him were boxes filled with sheet music and more instrument pieces. Very serious about music, he often spent time in between classes and during his conference periods scouring the Internet looking for performance competitions to enroll his students in or searching for music components. A very big man, his presence loomed over the desk as he typed on his small gray and black laptop. Looking over to Mr. Albert, I questioned why the text was so old. "Man, don't even get me started on that," he replied.

> It is so stupid. Now does this make any sense? We have the new audio version on CD [compact disc] that accompanies the updated version of the text that I have, but the students have the old books. So when you want to play an accompaniment piece that is supposed to go with the text that I have, you can't. These books are completely pointless. And as you can see way outdated. I mean they have countries in that book that don't even exist anymore.

"Can you buy the new textbooks for the class?" I responded.

"I wish. The school will never buy the books especially now that we are in this budget cut. We will be lucky to survive this. I mean, we need new instruments, so the last thing the school is going to buy is new textbooks for a music class."

The insight that I gained from working with the students in the Music Appreciation class coalesced with Mr. Albert's plea for new books. The students detested reading from the textbooks and indicated that they were completely alienated from this material. This was due in large part because, though the students enjoyed music, the books effectively removed the soul from music. In addition to being grossly outdated and as a consequence having inaccurate information, the text wrote of music in very a technical manner that overemphasized mundane details and did not provide insight into how and why the music was developed. There was no discussion as to how the social, political, economic, racial, gender, and cultural impact infused the music with the very soul that the textbooks very effectively stripped away. This burnt a bridge that would have allowed the students to link their lived experiences with those of someone in another continent. Reviewing the information in the text, it became readily apparent that the students couldn't care less about the material they were supposed to "learn." One day we went over various styles of music that were the key terms at the conclusion of each chapter.

"Alright, who can tell me about Baroque music?," I questioned aloud to the class. Once again, no one in class exhibited the least bit of interest. I continued to press the issue. "Okay, who can tell me about the Romantic Period?" Very respectfully, the collective eyes of the student body gazed in various directions throughout the classroom, and once again, no one spoke up. A little frustrated, in a stern voice that surprised even me when it rang out of my throat, "Okay, let's try something a little different. Everybody put away their books and take out a sheet of paper." Once again sighs rang through the roughly twenty-foot walls of the chorus room.

Although the students gathered their papers and removed the books from their plastic-chair, metal-framed, wooden-flanked desk, I set up my iPod docking station that was equipped with dual front speakers. Setting the music device to the Fela Kuti playlist, I moved to the small whiteboard that was hidden behind a large white projection screen. In a green marker I wrote the words *Nigeria, colonialism,* and *Afrobeat* on the board. Once the majority of the class had their paper out, I stood in the center of the class. "Okay, who can tell me who Fela Kuti was?" No one raised their hand or spoke up.

"Have you heard of colonialism or racism?" The class all nodded their heads in agreement. "Getting back to Fela, why do you think I brought all of this information up?" Expecting the silent response that I received, I asked the class the location of Nigeria. Although some guessed it was in the Caribbean "by Jamaica," the majority correctly said it was in Africa.

"So what happened along the West Coast of Africa that is important to your history?"

While the usual hush fell upon the class, Sam Smith, the only white student in the class, spoke out. "Is it something to do with slavery?," he asked.

"Alright, now, we are getting somewhere. So since we are talking about slavery, what is the significance or importance of British colonialism?," I asked.

Once again Sam spoke up. "They enslaved the Africans."

"Good, good we are getting somewhere." I stated in response to Sam's answers. Sensing that I was getting excited about the response, the class became less withdrawn and a little more interested in the conversation.

"Now what do you think the Africans did in response to their enslavement?," I challenged the class. The inquisitive looks and silence was not surprising given the lack of teaching of any type of history that did not depict "the West" as the bastion of civilization and enlightened culture. "Do you think that the Africans just let the Europeans come in and take their land without resisting? How many of you guys just let people talk to you disrespectfully and not say anything back to them?" Once again no one raised their hand. "Alright, so do you think the Africans just let people come in and take without fighting back?" I answered my own question: "No. Now I am going to play a song by Fela Kuti that is a demonstration of this type of resistance to violence enacted by the West onto Black people. The title of the song is 'Africa—Center of the World.'"

The tiny speakers of the iPod docking station began to blare out the rhythmic harmonies of vibraphones, congas, timbales, and an organ. Suddenly, a chorus of voices sang out in a beautiful repetitive cadence: "Africa, center of the world . . . Africa, center of the world." The bright sounds of the vibraphones picked up the pace and energy of the song as Fela entered with a resounding cue that signaled to the entire band. An eclectic mix of saxophones, drums, singers, and trumpets bounced around the faded mixture of carpet and concrete that enclosed the room. The students' faces exuded a combination of confusion and intrigue as their heads bobbed up and down to the consistent bass beat that anchored the various melodies flowing throughout the song.

Just as the song began to pick up speed, I ran over to the docking station and stopped the song. "Alright, so what exactly is being said in the song?"

Looking at me in unison they said, "Africa, center of the world."

I realized that I had gotten one step ahead of myself. "Alright, let me back up, why do you think they are saying that over and over again? What is the point of singing the lyrics in that type of manner?"

Continuing to look at me with blank expressions, I moved from the docking station and took a few paces over to the whiteboard. Pointing to the words on the board I asked, "Who in here has ever heard of Pan-Africanism?" No one answered. "What does it sound like?," I asked in response to their silence.

Sam spoke up: "Something to do with Africa."

"That is right," I stated. "Now since slavery, where do you think the emphasis has been placed with regards to the history and literature that you read?"

Once again Sam spoke up, "Well, we always read old English stuff and material that is boring with o's and thou's."

"Sam, you are correct," I stated. "Now based on what Sam is saying, you probably would agree that you don't read much about Mexico, El Salvador, Nigeria, or Ghana. Nothing outside of Europe. This is what Fela is saying. There needs to be a recentering of the focus onto Africa and off of Europe. Now back to Fela, let's take a listen to another song. Write this down: 'Fear Not for Man'" (Kuti 2001/2006). Once again, the rumblings vibrated through the room. "Now as we listen to this next song, I want you to tell me what instruments you hear and what he is saying. Listen very closely to the beat and what is being said."

Pushing the play button function on the iPod, the syncopated rhythm of bass drum and crisp clack of the snare drum began to pulsate throughout the room. A heavy bass guitar brought in the underlining melody and was soon accompanied by the wonderful light sharp tones of the organ playing over the solid percussive background. As the track played, on the students looked attentively at the iPod. The song continued to play and I yelled, "Alright, what do you hear?"

"A guitar . . . some drums . . . some kind of piano," were yelled back at me from the class. Then in a firm and steady tone, Fela rang out with a powerful yell. Quieting down, in a strong vice he spoke over the colorful collage of music:

Doctor Kwame Nkrumah
The Father of Pan-Africanism
Says to all black people
All over the world
The secret of life is to have no fear
Now we all have to understand that.

Stopping the track after Fela spoke, I asked the class, "Now who in here has ever heard of Kwame Nkrumah?" A firm silence grasped the class.

"Kwame Nkrumah was the first prime minister of Ghana once they achieved their independence from England. He had a belief that all nations that had Black people should band together to achieve their freedom from the ills of slavery and colonialism. Now why do you think he said that you should not be afraid and have no fear?"

Sam answered aloud, "Well if you have nothing and you are living in slavery then you really have nothing to lose."

"This is absolutely correct," I responded to Sam's comments. "Similarly, if the police constantly are stopping you and shooting at you, what is there to fear? You have nothing to lose. Now this is the attitude that Mos Def had when he made his song, 'Fear No Man.'"

I quickly paced over to the docking station and scrolled through the various playlists until I reached Mos Def's album, *Black on Both Sides* (Smith 2002). Before I played "Fear No Man," I asked the class to listen very carefully to the song and see whether they heard any similarities between Mos Def's song and Fela's song. I pushed Play on the iPod and the drum set started, followed by the melodic playing of a Hammond organ. As the song continued and Mos Def began talking, I asked the class what they heard. Immediately they said that it sounded just like the Fela's song "Fear Not for Man." Stopping the track, I said that I wanted them to listen very closely to the song.

I turned the player back on and the song continued. Mos Def talked over the track in a style reminiscent to a parent talking to a child:

> . . . They wanna create satellites and cameras everywhere
> and make you think they got the all-seeing eye
> Eh . . . I guess The Last Poets wasn't, too far off
> when they said that certain people got a God Complex
> I believe it's true
> I don't get phased out by none of that, none of that
> helicopters, the TV screens, the newscasters, the . . .
> satellite dishes . . . they just, wishin'
> They can't really never do that
> When they tell me to fear they law
> When they tell me to try to

have some fear in my heart behind the things that they do
This is what I think in my mind
And this is what I say to them
And this is what I'm saying, to you check it

All over the world hearts pound with the rhythm
Fear not of men because men must die
Mind over matter and soul before flesh
Angels for the pain keep a record in time
which is passin' and runnin' like a caravan freighter
The world is overrun with the wealthy and the wicked
But God is sufficient in disposing of affairs
Gunmen and stockholders try to merit my fear
But God is sufficient over plans they prepared
Mos Def in the flesh, where you at, right here
on this place called Earth, holding down my square
Bout to do it for y'all, and y'all at the fair
So just bounce, come on bounce.

Stopping the song, I asked them for their opinion on the lyrics.

Manuel raised his hand and said, "Well, it's talking about not being afraid of what is out there, don't be afraid of all of these things that are always around us."

Sam chimed in, "Yeah, especially with cameras everywhere, it's like we have to watch everything that we are doing and how we do it. It can be very scary and stop you from just being yourself."

After Sam finished talking I interjected the following question into the conversation: "How does the song relate to Fela and what we just talked about, speaking about racism and colonialism?"

The class fell silent for a few moments and then Sam answered, "Well, since we were talking about racism, it seems like all of this stuff is still going on and just like Fela, Mos Def is saying that people don't need to have fear and just fight back."

As Sam finished speaking, I looked over to the clock and noticed that the bell was about to ring. The students also saw this and they gathered their backpacks and books to leave for the next class. The bell rang shortly thereafter and the students began to file out of the classroom.

Walking down the elevated steps, Sam approached me and in an inquisitive voice said, "No one has ever taught us stuff like this, why don't you teach here all the time?"

Although his questioning statement can be taken to be a compliment, in fact what it speaks to is the desire on the part of the students to critically engage with material that resonates with their lives and more important challenges them to think beyond what they have been taught.

Leave It to McKay: Countering Dominant Narratives

I substitute taught for Mr. Frank's Language Arts III class (the eleventh-grade English class), and to my great fortune the students were discussing the Harlem Renaissance. Not having a lesson plan provided me with the freedom to lead them through the writings of Countee Cullen, Langston Hughes, and Claude McKay (the text was noticeably absent of Black woman artists and writers of the time period). The class was full of Black and Brown faces that looked surprisingly alert for an early Tuesday morning. I recognized many of the students from having substitute taught for other teachers and for Mr. Frank in the past. Malik, a very energetic and involved student, walked through the door. "Mr. S, man I am glad that you are here. This is going to be a cool day. What we talking about today?"

"What is going on Malik?," I responded giving him the traditional hand dap that ended with a snapping of the fingers. "Today, we are going to read from the Harlem Renaissance and discuss some of the authors that you guys have been reading about." As the majority of the class filed in, I took roll and then asked them to open their books to Claude McKay's poem "If We Must Die." A relatively short yet insightful poem, we proceeded to analyze sections of the text. I began reading the poem in a purposeful and loud voice:

> If we must die, let it not be like hogs
> Hunted and penned in an inglorious spot,
> While round us bark the mad and hungry dogs,
> Making their mock at our accursed lot.

After finishing this line I prefaced my subsequent question by contextualizing that McKay wrote this poem while white supremacist groups across the United States attacked Black people who were moving from the South into major urban cities of the North. "Alright, what is going on in the poem? Why is Claude McKay writing about this?"

Malik immediately raised his hand and responded, "He is saying that Black people shouldn't take having white people just beat them up and hurt them without fighting back."

"That is great Malik," I responded and, before I could get another word out, Malik said, "See y'all I know what I am talking about."

As the class laughed at Malik's commentary, I read the last section of the poem, pacing up and down the aisle formed by the columns of desks throughout the classroom:

> So that our precious blood may not be shed
> In vain; then even the monsters we defy
> Shall be constrained to honor us though dead!
> O kinsmen we must meet the common foe!
> Though far outnumbered let us show us brave,
> And for their thousand blows deal one deathblow!
> What though before us lies the open grave?
> Like men we'll face the murderous, cowardly pack,
> Pressed to the wall, dying, but fighting back!

I finished the last sentence with a resounding tone emphasizing the exclamation that was noted at the end of the poem. "Alright, so what does this mean?," I asked the class.

Humberto, a tall and wide-framed young Mexican man who sat in the front of the class explained in very poignant terms. "You just can't stand there and let somebody continue to beat on you."

Malik then chimed in, "Yeah, that is right, like when someone tries to beat you down, you can't just sit there and take it."

Following up on the points that Malik and Humberto had just made, I asked the class how the poem could relate to their lives. Specifically, "Do you guys feel any pressure or force that is keeping you from doing anything that you want to do?"

Immediately four voices shouted out, "THE POLICE."

Humberto elaborated:

> Yeah, the police just stop you and harass you for no reason, just
> 'cause they can. I was walking with my girl and the police, they

just stopped the two of us on the street. They then asked us to pull up our sleeves, you know. That is the test they use to see if you are illegal, you know that scar that people from Mexico have on their arm [referring to the scar left by an immunization shot]. So he said, "Pull up your sleeve," and I said, "No, I ain't going to pull up my sleeve, for what?" He said it again, and I said "no" right back to him. He then looked me in the face and said, "I know that you're illegal and I am going to get you."

Malik immediately jumped into the conversation, "Yeah, they just stop you for no reason. Like you can be in the car with your homies and then the police just stop you and ask you all of these dumb questions."

Humberto, feeling the energy in the room, responded to Malik's comment:

Yeah, like I was driving down the street one day, I ain't got a license, but I've been driving for a long time and the police just pulled me over. Now I asked him why he pulled me over and he didn't have any reason, he just said give me your license. So when I told him that I didn't have one, I couldn't drive back and had to wait for my brother to come pick me up because the cop wouldn't let me drive.

Following up on Humberto's point, I commented to him, "Now Humberto, you know that you can't drive without a license, so you gotta watch out." He responded, "Yeah, I know, but I gotta get places. My brother works all of the time and my mom needs stuff from the store and for me to take her places, so what I am going to do." Brilliantly, Humberto placed my own normalization of the law square in my face. He quickly brought to the fore that, unlike the choices of answers on a standardized test, there is never a simple right or wrong answer.

Acknowledging his point and, important, my incorrect assumption that the law was always correct, I asked if anybody in the room had heard of the recent police shootings in the Boyle Heights projects that had taken the lives of two sixteen-year-old boys in the past two months, the most recent being a week ago. They said that they had not. But after I explained the circumstances of the Los Angeles Police Department chasing a young boy who was riding his bike, then by foot after he fled from his bike, and then shot him in the back and killed him, nobody in the class was surprised or shocked.

Humberto commented, "Yeah, I used to live over in the Florentine projects over there near Compton and that stuff happened all of the time. The cops just came in there and do what they want. My mom used to always say 'Don't go outside because it's too dangerous.' There were always shootings over there, it was not cool."

Dismantling Ideology

The twelfth-grade students at CHS were faced with tough decisions that had strong implications for their life outcomes. The majority of the students such as Miguel and Julio had skills and talents they would not be able to utilize in their projected endeavors once they left CHS. Although their decisions were strongly influenced by monetary compensation, both of their career choices were informed by the same hegemonic ideology that governs all state processes: the white supremacist organizational logic of the prison regime. In an effort to explain the basis of this logic, I borrow from the insight of Dylan Rodríguez, who analyzes the organizing effect of the prison regime beyond the physical site of the prison:

> The prison, precisely such a capillary site for the production and movement of power, exerts a dominion that reaches significantly beyond its localized setting. This is to argue that the post-1970s emergence of a reformed and reconceived prison regime has become central to constituting the political logic as well as the material reproduction of the U.S. social formation. (Rodríguez 2006, 46)[8]

Initially I was perplexed by the rationale of Miguel and Julio to engage in state systems that are antithetical to their very existence. Rodríguez's analysis, however, provides the necessary lens to capture the meaning behind their anticipated decisions. It is within the context of the current prison regime that state subjects are rewarded (socially, economically, politically) for adherence to state ideologies and technologies of power. The process of rewarding subjects is key to the legitimatization of the prison regime as the dominant logic within society. Michael Hardt and Antonio Negri posit that within the current era of material and social relations that simultaneously disperses and internalizes power, the legitimatization of power is key in the formation of imperial projects (Hardt and Negri 2001).[9] Rather than by force, they argue that legitimization is gained by an attraction to the potential power that is promised in return for an allegiance to constructed social norms (that is, heteronormativity, racially based, patriarchal) that are employed to govern society.[10] As a result, these processes become normalized as the correct course of action for the advancement of civil society. It is within this moment that becoming a corrections officer or joining the military is not only the best financial decision, it is constructed as that which will best help society.

On the interpersonal level, the process of joining the military or some facet of the prison system becomes associated with the politics of respectability. Borrowing from Edmund T. Gordon's theorization of respectability in regards to Black masculinity, men who abide by patriarchal norms of family and engage in proper civic behavior (that is, involvement in church and/or social clubs) are deemed to be the moral standards of society (Gordon 1997).[11] Gordon's analysis has particular salience as the politics of respectability are juxtaposed against that of "Reputation."[12] Within this framework, reputation is characterized by rebellious acts against social norms, "especially White authority" and performing a particular type of heterosexual identity that is associated with "real" masculinity. Gordon describes that "'Respectability' and 'Reputation' are constructed in dialectal relationship" and, given the moral authority ascribed to performances of respectable masculinity, the respectable man is charged with the duty to uplift his lower reputational brethren (Gordon 1997, 43). Gordon attributes the moral validation of respectable performance to white supremacist constructions of cultural and social production. As a result, the two forms of performance are easily categorized within the social structure as "good" (Respectability) and "bad" (Reputation) in comparison to their white normative constructions of proper behavior.[13]

Although these constructions limit the range of performance, the mechanisms that control their logic are framed within a heterosexual state of being. There is no space to exist outside of these boundaries, and through social acceptance of such sexual performance, the state is granted further legitimacy to maintain order. M. Jacqui Alexander explains that the state's connection to heterosexuality has been key to its ability to construct power hierarchies. Alexander comments:

> The state has always conceived of the nation as heterosexual in that it places reproduction at the heart of its impulse. The citizenship machinery is also located here, for the prerequisites of good citizenship and loyalty to the nation state are simultaneously housed within the state apparatus. They are sexualized and ranked into a class of good, loyal, reproducing, heterosexual citizens, and a subordinated, marginalized class of non-citizens who, by virtue of choice and perversion, choose not to do so. (Alexander 2005, 46)

Miguel's and Julio's adoption of respectable, heterosexual forms of being are attempts to gain some sense of power within a social context that otherwise negates their existence. I argue that within the prison regime, the most respectable action to take is to become civically involved in assisting the most "deviant" with specific racialized communities. Similarly, Douglas Foley argues that within schools, "the lifestyle and value of middle class youth are held up to rebellious working class youth as the cultural ideal. The socially prominent youth learn a new communicative style and ethic and become adept at managing their images and manipulating adult authorities. These new communicative competences in the art of deceit prepare them to be future civil and political leaders." He cautions, however, "As these youth gain materially, perhaps they lose a little of their humanity" (Foley 1990, xv). Given that social relations are governed by technologies of violent discipline and control, it is not only logical, but imperative to be a part of structures of normalized violence that will "reform" these wayward souls and protect society from threats against order. If we read Gordon's intervention in conjunction with Rodríguez's analysis of structural forms of white supremacy, a lens is provided to understand why students such as Miguel and Julio strive to join systems of racialized terror. Rodríguez states:

> White-supremacist regimes organic (if not unique) to the United States—from racial chattel slavery and frontier genocide to recent and current modes of land displacement and (domestic/undeclared) warfare—are sociologically entangled with the state's

changing paradigms, strategies, and technologies of human incarceration and punishment. . . . White supremacy may be understood as a logic of social organization that produces regimented,
institutionalized, and militarized conceptions of hierarchized
"human" difference. (Rodríguez 2006, 11)

The hegemonic discourse that Julio invoked was full of altruistic intentions (that is protect the freedoms of the United States, protect the establishment of law and order) that on the surface appear benevolent.
Yet, as Rodríguez describes, the basis of these claims is to protect a white
supremacist organization of social relations and enclose Black spaces of
humanity. The beauty/cruelty of such a structure is the absence of whiteness; rather, notions of individual responsibility that are key to current
manifestations of white supremacy are reinforced and further normalized
within social relations (Kelley 1997).[14] As a result, the upholders of the respectable identity appear to be making individual choices to protect their
community and better society, when in fact they are reinforcing an ideological construct (white supremacy) that dehumanizes Blackness through
the subjugation of women and non-heteronormative sexual performances
(Alexander 2005).[15]

The limits of abiding by the cultural norms as established by the prison
regime are constituted by the fact of whiteness. Following the logical conclusion of Gordon's argument, though Julio and Miguel may strive to
reach success through respectable forms, they will never be able to reap
the benefits of being a white patriarchal male. The thrust of the white supremacist ideology is to situate subjects as individuals in order to mask the
structural effects of racism. By *racism*, I mean "the state-sanctioned and/
or extra-legal production and exploitation of group differentiated vulner-
abilities to premature death, in distinct yet densely interconnected political geographies" (Gilmore 2002, 261). Thus, if Julio does join the military
or work for the border patrol rather than make his community safe, his
actions will contribute to the warfare state and increase the violent acts
of terror upon the very people he supposedly aims to protect. Angela Y.
Davis insightfully argues that the expansion of American imperialism via
the Immigration and Naturalization Service (INS) is directly linked to the
development of the prison system (Gordon 1999).[16] Further, both Gilmore
and Rodríguez theorize that the expansion of the prison regime is directly
linked to military expansion within the United States. Gilmore argues:

In the current period of globalization, we see the demise of military Keynesianism, and its successor militarist state rising on a firm foundation of prisons, peopled by the 2,000,000 and more who represent both the demise of golden-age capitalism and the defeat of alternative societies militantly pursued, throughout the golden age, by those who sought to make impossible the future we live today. (Gilmore 1999, 186)

Building upon Gilmore's argument, Rodríguez states:

The prison regime has become an indispensable element of American statecraft, simultaneously a cornerstones of its militarized (local and global) ascendancy and spectacle of its extracted (or coerced) authority over targeted publics. The specificity of the prison regime as a production of state power is its rigorous and extravagant marshaling of technologies of violence, domination, and subjection otherwise reserved for deployment in sites of declared (extradomestic) war or martial law. (Rodríguez 2006, 44)

Both Gilmore and Rodríguez elucidate the flaws within Julio's attachment to the prison regime ideology. His strident desire to join the ranks of the immediate prison regime infrastructure make him complicit in the destruction of the alternative possibilities that have provided for his existence. Contrary to the rhetoric of the prison regime ideology, the U.S. Army and/or U.S. Border Patrol did not provide for his freedom; rather, through the "technologies of violence" both entities have historically sought to limit and deny the freedom of nonwhite subjects. Instead, as Gilmore argues, it was the collective struggle of racialized beings against the U.S. imperialist project that have provided subjugated groups with the small fissures of freedom. Thus, Rodríguez's pontification of the U.S. imperialist project provides breadth to Gordon's claim of the racialized and gender limits of respectable politics—the militaristic expansion within the United States, as part of the prison regime, has functioned to preserve the integrity of a white supremacist agenda that privileges white male heteronormativity to the detriment of otherized subjects.

Gilmore, Rodríguez, and Hardt and Negri point to the shift of modes of production during the later part of the twentieth century as a key moment that blurs the lines between the military and the police. Given the expansive reach of capital beyond national boundaries, the state became a much more expansive concept including not just official structures, but also encompassing a vast network of private actors, including corporations and nongovernmental agencies (Hardt and Negri 2001). The question became, "Within an environment, what force could govern such a large body?" Traditional methods of military engagement became moot because the very idea of a traditional enemy was no longer viable, for often the enemy were citizens of the state (Hardt and Negri 2005). Hardt and Negri posit that in order to maintain control of the multilayered, multinational state, the police adopted the same role of enforcers of power that were also designated to the military:

> In the new state of war is that international relations and domestic politics become increasingly similar and intermingled. In the context of this cross between military and police activity aimed at security there is ever less difference between inside and outside the nation-state: low-intensity warfare meets high-intensity police actions. The "enemy," which has traditionally been conceived outside, and the "dangerous classes," which have been traditionally been inside, are thus increasingly indistinguishable from one another and serve together as the object of the war effort. (Hardt and Negri 2005, 14–15)

Hardt and Negri's analysis of the police and the military directly corresponds to the critique of the American project by the Black Panther Party during the Vietnam War. Central to the Panther's theorization of the state was a correlation of fascist activities enacted by the police within Black communities and the actions of the military in Vietnam (Seale 2002).[17] In response to the terror enacted upon Black people by the United States, Bobby Seale wrote:

> You can't just fight imperialism, the acts of imperialism abroad, without understanding and recognizing community imperialism abroad, without recognizing community imperialism here of Black people, Brown people, Red people and even to the point of protesting students and radicals and progressive peoples here, in America. Domestic imperialism at home is in fact fascism. But what in essence is it? I think Black people if we go over the concrete

experiences that we've had in America and what's going on now against us we can understand exactly what it is—to be corralled in wretched ghettoes in America and look up one day and see numerous policemen occupying our community, and brutalizing us. . . . (Seale 2002, 94)

Seale's critique of imperialism foregrounds current theoretical interventions that link the impetus of the military to that of internal forces (that is, police and prison).[18] Both structures are governed by the need to control and subjugate in an effort to contain and remove racialized threats to "order."

Similar to Seale's argument with respect to the function of the police in the lives of Black people, the intent of dominant ideological constructions of behavior is to enclose the possibilities of existence. As argued by Elaine Bell Kaplan, it is a double-edged sword that subjugates racialized populations for both abiding and/or not abiding by "moral" social conventions (Kaplan 1997).[19] In the face of such options, the choices appear limited; however, Frantz Fanon's analysis of the structural limitations of the racialized state renders that the only option is to assert an identity formation that both threatens the establishment and provides alternative possibilities of human existence (Fanon 1967).[20] These contestations to normative ideology are often articulated through cultural manifestations. As argued in chapter 1, whether through music, poetry, or daily acts of life, culture has played a pivotal role in the deconstruction and reconstitution of a new life that breaks the binds of forced violence and terror. Based upon Hall's description of culture, we can understand the linkage of struggles for material resources to innovative and "fantasy" aspects of the collective imagination. It is this linkage that undergirds the threat to dominant ideology— alternative cultural manifestations are based upon historical struggles that provide both critiques and counter-narratives to dominant ideology. Understanding the possibility of cultural threats to power, Western society has proven that it will do anything to prevent the dissemination of alternative forms of culture.

Among the various tactics utilized by the state, there are two key methods that are trademarks of cultural enclosure within the prison regime. The first is to prevent the proliferation of alternative cultural forms. The school, as a primary site of socialization, is at the crux of this process. Gramsci argues that a function of the school is to displace local and communal cultural knowledge with state sanctioned laws of reasoning and order (Gramsci and Hobsbawm 1988/2000, 311).[21] This is important because it removes the threat to the production of racialized forms of social production.

Within CHS, this process was exemplified by the systematic dismantling of the school's performing arts infrastructure. The music program was severely underfunded. The textbooks had not been updated in more than twenty years, and the teachers were forced to come up with clever tactics to teach current material. Within the climate, students often became bored or frustrated by the material that they knew was incorrect (that is, the students were learning material from a text that still discussed cultural forms indigenous to the USSR, a nation-state that had not existed in the students' lifetimes).

The curriculum was based upon a multicultural format immersed in what Hall calls "imaginative" forms of culture. Rather than based in any historic and material reality, it was as if particular groups from around the world were born with innate cultural practices that distinguished them from other communal groups. The result was the removal of political counter-narratives that were central to the development of cultural practices. The power of these counter-narratives was brought to light when the music appreciation class discussed the historical background that framed the music of Fela, The Coup, and Mos Def. Black music in particular countered the dominant ideology that was posed through "popular music" (Levine 2007).

Describing the "staying power" of popular white musical forms during the early part of the twentieth century and its continuity with dominant ideology, Lawrence Levine offers the following analysis:

> However deeply their [white composers] wit could cut through the sentimentality that marked most popular music, their songs have endured with the generations that grew up with them because they reinforced deeply inculcated dreams and ideals in a world which daily disproved them. In a period when divorce rates were rising, family stability declining, pastoral styles disappearing, bureaucratic impersonality and organization increasing, popular music constructed a universe in which adolescent innocence and naïveté became a permanent state. Men and women (often referred to in the songs as boys and girls) dreamed pure dreams, hopefully waited

for an ideal love to appear (the gift of some beneficent power that remained undefined and unnamed), and built not castles but bungalows in the air complete with birds, brooks, blossoms, and babies. Adults were being socialized to a world constructed out of childhood fantasies or, more accurately, adult views of childhood fantasies. (Levine 2007, 273)

Levine elucidates the process by which dominant ideological formulations of culture mask the reality of social and economic instabilities. Further, they reproduce racialized heteronormative formulations of life that are key to the foundation of the capitalist enterprise. Counter to the dominant ideological forms, Levine argues that "Negroes shared many of the assumptions and dreams of popular music. But they had recourse to another music [the blues] which differed markedly from the larger society's popular songs . . ." (Levine 2007, 273). The blues, Levine posits

insisted that the fate of the individual black man or woman, what happened in their everyday "trivial" affairs, what took place within them, their yearnings, their problems, their frustrations, their dreams—were important, were worth taking note of and sharing in song. Stressing individual expression and group coherence at one and the same time, the blues was an inward-looking music which insisted upon the meaningfulness of black lives. In these respects it was not only the more obviously angry work songs but the blues as well, that were subversive of the American racial order. . . . (Levine 2007, 269–70)

Building upon the work of Levine, Tricia Rose provides a similar analysis of the formulation of hip-hop and its development out of the material conditions of massive disinvestment of social services and capital from racialized centers within New York City (Rose 1994). Additionally, she posits that the struggle of Black people against police repression and racialized violence by the state is key to hip-hop as a Black cultural form. According to the work of Levine and Rose, Black music is dangerous to dominant ideology in that it disrupts normalized constructions of work, violence, and existence.[22]

The second method utilized by the state to remove the threat of alternative culture formulations is to denigrate them as uncivilized, degenerative, and morally corrupt. Through this process, alternative cultural expressions become naturalized as deviant. Robin Kelley poignantly labeled this type of attack against Black culture in particular as the "Culture Wars." Kelley states that the term is vital because it describes the "ongoing battle over representations of the black urban condition, as well as the importance of the cultural terrain as a site of struggle" (Kelley 1997, 8).

It is within this framework that the students in Mr. Frank's class operated. Harassed and subjugated by the police, the students were defined as the bane of social existence. However, given the opportunity to engage with the protest poetry of the Harlem Renaissance, the students immediately placed themselves within a larger struggle against structures of violence and domination. The threat to the dominant ideology was made real when the students were able to link historical struggles of racialized oppression to their current lived experience. With the poetry of Claude McKay as a conduit, they inverted the constructions of their communal spaces of gathering from spaces of immoral behavior to sites of racialized terror and discipline that are fundamental characteristics of the prison regime.

The power of ideology can never be overemphasized. The school as a site of social indoctrination of state ideology functions prominently within the prison regime. The ability of the school to promote dominant narratives of being while silencing others is crucial to the white supremacist U.S. nation project. Ruth Wilson Gilmore's analysis of the power of ideology is critical, because it molds the lives of students. In the name of ideology, Julio could be added to the list of Black and Brown soldiers killed in the violent occupation in Iraq, or he may be employed to brutalize the thousands of souls resting in INS detention centers. Yet, as a struggle against these processes, the daily experiences of the students such as Humberto placed them squarely within a larger cultural genealogy that posits alternative forms of reality in the effort to eliminate the prison regime.

CHS thus served as a site of indoctrination and preparation. The indoctrination provided the rationale to readily accept the inscribed hierarchies within society. By process of omission, CHS purposely did not teach historical and contemporary accounts that countered multiple forms of oppression and threatened established forms of power. The preparation was for a social arrangement based upon subjugation. This was achieved through the shaping of students to desire particular jobs that were key to the maintenance of the prison regime. The affinity to these jobs was based upon the attainment of political, social, and economic capital; however, such desire was directly complicit to the reproduction of racialized, gendered, and sexual violence. CHS's implementation of punishment and control mirrored the technologies of control that were central to the processes of indoctrination and preparation. In the face of massive amounts of financial and human resources that were utilized to implement the harsh ideological practice of imprisonment within public education, the question begs: What was it about Black folks that demanded they had to be ushered into or work for a massive network of proverbial and literal cages?

Bringing the conversation back to the relationship between the STPP and ideological enclosures, a severe limitation of the STPP framework is its failure to grapple with the aforementioned inquiry. As a result, developed solutions for example do not analyze core issues that fuel the connections between prisons and education. There has been a normalization of Black oppression to the prison through ideological enclosures via curriculum development, pedagogical practices, and discipline policies that have constructed a particular type of Blackness that is void of history, politics, and agency. An inability to consider these processes has led to local, state, and national discussions of the STPP focused on racialized discipline policies, but also on Black student behavior as a central cause of Black youth being funneled into prison. Across the country there have been hearings, public forums, and panels at which nonprofit organizations, politicians, and philanthropic agencies gathered to discuss the STPP. Without fail, a major component of these hearings are the marching forward of Black youth who testify that because of their reckless behavior they were suspended and/or expelled from school. Akin to asking for penance, they state that they know what they did was wrong but they did not deserve such a harsh penalty for their actions. In addition to being a racialized spectacle, the framing of the STPP as somehow being connected to Black student behavior completely belies the point that Erica Meiners brilliantly points out: within the current ideological enclosure of the prison regime, Black students have a "right to be hostile" (Meiners 2007). The trumpeting of Black behavior as a problem thus feeds into the very same ideological enclosure that legitimates Black confinement. It is the hostility to the prison regime by Black students that upsets the balance of perceived power. However, hostility and anger are the only logical responses to such a paradigm that demands Black subjugation. Counter to commonsense renderings of the STPP framework, the STPP framing actually reproduces the same ideological agenda that it claims to refute and the critical question still lingers: Why have Black people been rounded up into sites of enclosure during the past forty years (both within prison and within their communities)? Building off the work of Meiners, I argue in the following section of the chapter that a key aspect of ideological enclosures has been in a violent response to the ability of Black people to organize and mobilize hostility into action. Counter to narratives such as that presented by the STPP, it is crucial for us to change our framing of power as a top-down synthesis upon helpless Black people and begin to wrestle with the heavy weight of ideological contestation.

Total Control, or Fear of a Black Planet

In his text on the formation of Black education in the United States, William Watkins stated the following regarding the centrality of ideology in the nation building process:

> Ideology is not left to chance. Modern industrial society sought out ideas that supported it. Hence, ideology becomes the currency of those dominating the culture. Ideology is imparted subtly and made to appear as through its partisan views are part of the "natural order." The dominating ideology is a product of dominant power. (Watkins 2001, 9)

Thus, understanding the ideological apparatus at play within schools and prisons allows us to see the motives and intentionality behind the implementation of repressive policies. Yet, resting within the vile underbelly of the beast is not enough; rather, what is crucial is to gain perspective upon the rudimentary actions of the beast. That is, does the beast attack in order to assert dominance or are such attacks launched out of deep-rooted insecurities of impending demise? In the case of Black folks' relationship to schools and prisons, such perspective provides a blueprint by which to understand whether the ideological work that undergirds "order and function" is done in a proactive manner or is performed to prevent the explosion of a bubbling consciousness.

Much of the scholarly analysis of order and control is often attributed to postulations of discipline located within Michel Foucault's theorization upon political anatomy. Although Foucault has dominated the realm of order and control, his failure to grapple with the position of race as an integral component within the dialectical struggle pertaining to freedom has proven his analysis incomplete. At the heart of Foucault's theorization of political anatomy is the incessant need to control the body; this in turn renders the body "docile." Arising at the height of empire building and colonization, control over the docile body was required in order that the body may be "subjected, used, transformed and improved" (Foucault 1979, 136). Foucault posits that discipline over the body was enacted through the construction of society as a mechanism and the body as a representation of that mechanical framework. Thus, rules and regulations that disciplined the body were invented and enacted through the development of rules that governed society. As nation-states consolidated power and gained social legitimacy, the disciplining of the body also intensified. As an example, the legitimacy of colonial empires was largely predicated upon their military strength. However, such military strength could exist only when there was social legitimacy granted to the need of a military. The rhetorical inflection as to the need of the military ranged from that which protected "us" from "them" to the military as the active facilitator of civilization.

Key to the rhetoric is the tacit social agreement that discipline was needed to maintain a successful military. This discipline requires that the body become disassociated from inane subjectivity and render itself docile to a greater power. Foucault theorizes that these techniques "defined how one may have a hold over others' bodies, not only so that they may do what one wishes, but that they may operate as one wishes, with the techniques, the speed and the efficiency that one determines" (Foucault 1979, 138).

Ironically, rather than a form of extreme force, the military within the schema of empire building has been sanctioned as a pacifying good for society. Hardt and Negri argue that the rise of empire and imperialism coalesces with the enactment of the military by particular social groups as a means to keep "peace" (Hardt and Negri 2001).[23] The ability to pull off this sleight of hand is facilitated by those within society who are attempting to attain power and maintain privilege that is associated with the ideological thrust of military intervention. Thus, the power associated with the military (also the police) is key to the reproduction of one's social, economic and political capital, or biopower. Building upon Foucault's conception of biopower, Hardt and Negri claim that:

> biopower is a form of power that regulates social life from its interior, following it, interpreting it, absorbing it—every individual embraces and reactivates this power of his or her own accord. Its primary task is to administer life. Biopower thus refers to a situation in which what is directly at stake in power is the production and reproduction of life itself. (Hardt and Negri 2001, 24)

However, a lack of a racial analysis with respect to Foucault's theoretical orientation renders his conceptualizations of political anatomy, docile bodies, and biopower insufficient. His framing presents the state as an all-encompassing force that has the power to dictate the parameters and jurisdiction of human existence. Such an analytical framework flies in the face of the historical relationship between the state and Black people. Rather, it has been the effectiveness of Black mobilization, organization, and radical movements that has kept the state "on its toes" and continually changing strategies in an attempt to maintain the fragile façade of power.

Perhaps there has been no greater evidence of this dialectal engagement than the abolition of Trans-Atlantic slavery. Whether in England, the United States of America, or Brazil, the demise of slavery has all too often been written as a benevolent act, or accomplished by the hands of "radical" whites (Robinson 2000).[24] Yet, with just a little digging through the historical record, a far different and much more upsetting narrative is depicted. In both England and the United States, the abolishment of slavery was marked by the conspicuous rise of industrial capitalism. Although the titans of northern capital such as Andrew Carnegie, George Peabody, and John D. Rockefeller were credited with the establishment of philanthropic organizations and new economic models that brought an end to slavery, such action attempted to save capitalism. Watkins argues:

> Although not all of the new elite were visible in public life, most supported a reordering of society, a redistribution of wealth, and a new economic power base in society. Those who got directly involved in political ideation, such as Rockefeller, Carnegie, and others, most often who spoke for the new class of plutocrats. The subsequent corporate ordering of society would subjugate and/or influence the legislation, cultural, and social dynamics of the entire nation. (Watkins 2001, 14)

The key for Watkins in this process was the development of philanthropic agencies and foundations that were able to circumvent normal political routes in order to protect the interests of a new capitalist class (Watkins 2001, 18–19).[25]

Within this discussion it is necessary to note that the inability of colonial agents and planters alike to control Black culture and humanity in the United States, Western Africa, Caribbean, Central and South America brought forth the end of slavery. Slavery as an economic model simply ceased to work. Cedric Robinson documents:

> By 1838, slavery in the British Empire had been officially abolished
> by a Parliament now "reformed" to enhance the power of industrial
> capital. "The slaves," Mary Reckford reports, "had demonstrated to
> some at least of those in authority that it could prove more danger-
> ous and expensive to maintain the old system than to abolish it."
> And similar moments were to occur in the United States in 1863
> and 25 years later in Brazil. (Robinson 2000, 164)

As a means to try to wrestle power away from liberated Black folks, industrial capitalists introduced new enclosure models in an attempt to contain a radically democratic people. New enclosures marked by the advent of waged labor and rural sharecropping in turn gave rise to forms of disciplining technologies that sought to maintain and in some instances exceed slavery-induced profit margins.[26]

Similarly, within the current moment, the technologies of discipline that are utilized within a failed industrial economy such as that of California represent a desperate attempt to counter the moral weight of Black humanity. Just as within slavery, the weight of the industrial model paled in comparison to the fortitude of Black freedom movements. Arising out of the tradition of the League of Black Revolutionary Workers in the North and Fannie Lou Hamer in the South, organizations emanating out of California, such as the Los Angeles chapter of the Black Panther Party, refused to trade Black humanity for the trappings of industrial capitalism. As noted by Danny Widener, "Los Angeles produced one of the country's largest and most influential chapters of the Black Panther Party, in part because the Los Angeles branch faced challenges that made it perhaps even more representative of the national conditions faced by the party than the

Oakland headquarters" (Widener 2010, 12). Built upon a model that was antithetical to capitalist exploitation, demands were made to address fundamental grievances against both the industrial class on one hand, and government actors, facilitators and policies on the other that advanced the desires of the capitalist interests. Within the ten-point platform, for example, the Black Panther Party asserted, "We want an end to the robbery by the capitalists of our black and oppressed communities." Putting their demands into action, the Black Panthers implemented systems that poked gaping holes into the myth of the United States as a democratic nation-state.

Akin to Black laborers in South Carolina prior to and after Reconstruction, the Panthers realized freedom was to be earned on two fronts: the first was the appropriation of material resources from the state and the second was the establishment of independent systems of governance that were free of elite white manipulation.[27] It was out of this realization that the Black Panther Party simultaneously created autonomous educational and health centers that did not rely upon support from the state or federal government or philanthropic organizations and also demanded that the federal government hand over control of economic, political, and social resources to Black communities.

It was for this reason that the Panthers were highly targeted by agents of the state (Churchill and Wall 2002). Heads of state and capitalist organizations alike feared Black radical organizations such as the Panthers, because on a fundamental level they rejected the fallacy of capitalism as a legitimate system of social and economic relations.[28] Such action stymied the development of capitalism on two levels. First, a demand for the reallocation of financial resources and redistribution of wealth within the nation meant that capitalists would lose the ability to manipulate the public financial coffers. Second, the formation of a truly democratic society would undermine the goals of the white elites who very well understood that the establishment of a broad-base collective movement would represent the end of capitalism.[29] In light of such fears, it cannot be of any surprise that federal, state, and local government (and Los Angeles in particular) attacked the Black Panther Party with such brutal force.[30] With blood spilling in the streets and casualities mounting on both sides, industrial capitalism in the United States had reached its zenith. Similar to the plutocrats, the capitalist class realized that the system was becoming far too expensive to manage and had no choice but to retreat to another form in order to maintain any semblance of control. Thus, it must be read that out of the inability to successfully co-opt Blacks, the system was once again proven broken and unable to shape the course of Black humanity.

Thus, rather than the power of the systems of perceived control, the technologies of discipline and punishments currently utilized in the modern era are merely developments of prior failed attempts to enclose humanity. Writing in response to Craton's argument that "formal Emancipation was little more than a hegemonic trick. New forms of slavery were instituted by importing Asiatic 'coolies' or simply wage slavery," Cedric Robinson pushed to situate capitalist development in relation to the failure of Black culture to be co-opted or subsumed under any structure. Robinson stated:

> The list, of course, should not have ended with wage slavery. It properly should also include peonage, sharecropping, tenant farming, forced labor, penal labor, and modern peasantry. Nevertheless, we must also remind ourselves that whatever the forms primitive accumulation assumed, its social harvest would also include acts of resistance, rebellion, and ultimately, revolution. In the peripheral and semi-peripheral regions of the modern world system, at least, Gramci's [*sic*] hegemonic class rule was never to be more than a momentary presence. (Robinson 2000, 165)

Robinson's analysis of capitalism reshapes the terms of the dialectical debate and argues for the paradigm to be shifted from the power of the capitalist elite to affect Black freedom to rest upon the fear that Black radical movements have to completely undo capitalist systems of governance. Within the postindustrial capitalist epoch, the analytic framework needs to address the threat that the Black community in particular poses to the newest iteration of capitalist response to revolt and rebellion. Further, within the context of a postindustrial model of education that is dominated by the enclosure of the prison, Robinson's shift allows us to resituate the position of the Black community from passive subjects to active agents. The formulation of legislation and social policy was in direct response to the mobilization of Black people who demanded a truly democratic form of governance that would begin to address the vast economic divide between the corporate and land-owning class within Southern California and everybody else. Similar to other reactionary moments of the past (that is, Black

Codes), the State of California passed legislation that attempted to reach the entire spectrum of Black people, regardless of gender or age. Thus, policy formation not only targeted Black adults, but paved the way to criminalize Black youth as young as elementary-age students. It is within this purview that we have to remember that the youth of CHS are not only the children and grandchildren of the original targets of violent, racialized laws, but have themselves endured the same type of social doctrine that has attempted to enclose their freedom. Thus, it is incumbent upon us to change the nature of ideological debates pertaining to Black youth that are currently dominated by invented problems such as the achievement gap or lack of moral or ethical standards to an analysis of just how and why prison and education policy have become two sides of the same coin of Black education.

Further, it is vital to move away from solution models such as the STPP that do not address the ideological enclosures that have formed in response to Black libratory movements and practices. A major fault of this brand of solutions is that they depend on a particular strain of anti-Blackness that leaves Black people without history, agency, and power. Whether as a willing party to Black subjugation or as a liberal move to reform structural apparatus through policy initiatives, history has proven that the result of the reliance upon these models is a negation of Black demands in order to fulfill the demands of a particular elite class (that is, industrial capitalists). Solutions ranging from industrial education to the policing of Black education have been developed only to stymie the efforts of Black people to utilize education in order to develop a more just world. At the heart of these processes, ideology is critical in making the grotesque palatable and the hideous attractive. Similarly, ideological enclosures must be reinvented (often building upon previous iterations) in order to remake Black subjects as the purported enemy or problem. Within the current moment, schools figure prominently over the struggle of ideological enclosures as they did during the late nineteenth century. Through curriculum, discipline policies, and pedagogical practices, they demand that Blackness be muted in order to make normal a system of racial, gendered, and sexed hierarchies. As an ideological enclosure, the prison regime works to (re)make these hierarchies appear normal and resistance against it as an imminent threat to the collective well-being. Such work is needed in order to justify the violent brutality and trauma that is inflicted upon Black people on a daily basis.

It is here at the intersection of ideology and violence that the connections between schools and prisons manifest in its most readily identifiable linkage: punishment. The following chapter explores the development of a multilayered punishment apparatus that fueled the physical enclosure of public education. Analysis and ethnographic data in the chapter probe the dissonant inner workings within the State of California, a state known for bureaucratic autonomy, suddenly worked in a harmonious union. Government entities from the local level to the county level to the state level seamlessly instituted mandates that normalized harsh punitive measures within the daily practices of educational management of Black students.

3
_____

Land of Smoke and Mirrors

The Meaning of Punishment and Control

Analysis of discipline, punishment, and coerced control within state structures such as public education often center on the ability of such entities to wield seemingly limitless power against aggrieved population(s).[1] As argued in chapter 2, such an analytical framework is especially true of the School-to-Prison Pipeline (STPP) discourse. As a consequence, the STPP research and much work upon Black populations in the United States often depicts the state in an offensive posture in relationship to a fledging, reactionary group of helpless people. However, what if the looking glass were reversed? That is, what if technologies of punishment and control were utilized by owners of capital, political leaders, and their ilk out of fear of what power relationships would look like in a society that was not built upon massive wealth disparities, racial terrorism, and sexual violence? To the converse, what if our analysis portrayed the strength and ability of Black people to transform society in the face of bitter oppression? Although the dialectical relationship between Black people and those in positions of power has had a long historical trajectory, the era from the civil rights movement to the present is marked by a distinct utilization of public education as a strategic tool on the part of radical organizations to dismantle white supremacy.[2] For it has been during this time period that the mobilization of extreme force and repression against Black communities, in direct response to Black demands, led to intense forms of enclosure marked by the rapid development and maintenance of the prison regime.

A brief aside about enclosures: enclosures have been a key mechanism to limit the mobility and freedom of Black people. In particular, owners of capital in conjunction with bourgeoisie sympathizers (that is, political officials, junior partners) have implemented various modes of enclosures in response to Black demands for cultural, social, and political liberation (Woods 1998; Woods 2009).[3] However, what was quite remarkable about the expansion of the prison regime as an enclosure was the extent to which a harsh physical, punitive system became intertwined with the daily function of Black existence. In order to remind of us of the totality of the system, Michelle Alexander notes that there are more Black men within the clutches of the prison regime than were in the bondages of slavery prior to 1850 (Alexander 2010, 175). Although the presence of police and representatives of the criminal justice system have had a sordid past in the lives of Black people, the type of repression that was ushered in during the late 1960s and early 1970s and enhanced during the 1980s and 1990s was formerly relegated only for moments deemed "states of emergency" (that is, riots, massive political demonstrations). Yet, in this new epoch, the extreme and excess became normalized as a continual presence within Black communities. Pam Oliver comments:

> The apparatus of coercive repression was ramped up in response to the Black urban riots and other social disorders, including disorderly antiwar protests on campuses. But policing and coercion in Black communities stayed high, even after the disorders died down. . . . In fact, social control expenditures continued to rise and the U.S. started escalating policing and incarceration. Police funding in the 1970s was increased more in cities with larger black populations and that had strong civil rights movements. . . . In the 1980s and 1990s, these same surveillance operations were put in the service of the drug war, the major source of the mass incarceration of Black people after the mid-1980s. By 1990, the United States was effectively a police state for its Black citizens, and to a lesser extent, for poor Whites, as well. The crucial thing to understand is that a repressive strategy initially triggered by massive urban unrest and other social movements was maintained and expanded long after the riots abated. It was not aimed at preventing unrest by repressing riots; it was preventing unrest by repressing potential rioters. (Oliver 2008, 10)

Key to Oliver's analysis is the extent to which the presence of the coercive arm of the state became a mainstay in the day-to-day lives of Black folks as an attempt prevent the further development of dissension within Black communities. It is only after one seriously wrestles with this issue can one develop a firm understanding of the extent to which policing and agents of repression have been integrated into Black communal institutions from grocery stores to parks to churches. Yet, taking Oliver's point a step further, although the Black community as a whole was targeted, even more evident was the intentional attack upon those ordinary and everyday spaces that had proven to be fertile in the development of Black culture, resistance, and organized dissension: schools.

Punitive Enclosures and Schools

Two distinct periods mark the punitive enclosures of Black education in Southern California. As discussed in chapter 2, the first was during the 1960s following the 1965 Watts Rebellion. The coalescence of the Los Angeles Police Department (LAPD), Los Angeles City Council and the Los Angeles School System ushered in an era of mass policing in the city that signaled the birth of the prison regime. Although a time stamp for the second period would seem to be the 1992 rebellion following the Rodney King trial, the moment of distinction predates the mass action. 1992 was very important because it marked a rupture of politics as usual in LA, yet it was events such as rampant police killings and general Black subjugation throughout the 1980s that brought forth the events of 1992. I argue that in addition to looking at 1992, we should analyze the 1984 Olympic Games in Los Angeles as a pivotal point in the development of a heavily militarized LAPD and the intensification of brutal punitive enclosure upon Black communities. Against the backdrop of the Cold War and the conjured threat of the USSR in conjunction with the events that unfolded at the 1972 Munich Games, LA city officials and the LAPD successfully lobbied the federal government to provide funding to expand the LAPD workforce and attain some of the most sophisticated military weaponry on the face of the planet (Klein 1985; Warnick 1985). However, after the games were over the LAPD did not have to return its new arsenal or scale back its labor force. The threat was merely changed from an outside terrorist force (that is, Russian Communist) to a domestic force: the hyperviolent, drug-peddling, gun-toting Black criminal.

Although much of the attention, and rightfully so, has been given to the affects of the War on Drugs upon Black communities, what has not been discussed is the manner in which in cities such as Los Angeles policy was crafted that intensified the punitive enclosure of Black people via a strike upon schools. In addition to ramping up the police presence on school campuses, new coalitions formed among school districts and the criminal justice system to create and enforce laws targeting Black youth and their families that would severely affect the economic, political, social, and overall well-being of Black communities across the region. Similar to the 1960s, the focus on schools was a strategic effort targeted at collective organizations such as the Bloods and the Crips. Although depicted as a menace to society via popular media (that is, news programming and entertainment), these organizations were slowly organizing into a united force throughout Los Angeles County and had very specific demands about the education of Black Angelinos. The punitive enclosure that ensued was of epic proportions; it essentially removed all doubt that Black schools were nothing more than sites of urban containment. In addition to a layered policing force that included formal policing, school districts employed staff members to police the schools and many followed the model of the Los Angeles Unified School District (LAUSD) and created their own school district police. In addition, LA County initiatives sprung forth that provided funding via the state coffers to arrest and issue citations and/or misdemeanor offenses to youth for fighting or being late to school.

The genius of public education as a strategic site is the very ordinariness of its structure. In light of state laws that require mandatory attendance until the age of eighteen, a direct connection to the community, and its readily organized assembled body, schools became a natural site of Black consciousness and cultural expression. Thus, during the past forty years, public education has become the most significant arena that has been long neglected by scholars of prisons, Black resistance, social movements, and repression. The extent to which the daily structure of public education has become a very ordinary and grotesquely normalized site of hyper-criminalized surveillance and sheer repression is quite astounding.

It is within the context of post-1984 that I draw upon the development of the prison regime as both a physical site of containment and an institutional device to enforce manifestations of punishment and control within public education by corralling counter-knowledge formation and radical demands upon the state. Given the growing public awareness of prisons in the United States, and California in particular, I rely upon the work of prison abolitionists, scholars, and activists who posit that the prison regime has a long-ranging political, economic, and social repressive impact that extends beyond the physical site of the prison. In this vein there must be a question of the racialized underpinnings that allow the institution to flourish. If such an oppressive and brutal regime is granted social credence, what are both the intended and unintended auxiliary ramifications that ripple through society? In a related manner, we are forced to grapple with the possibility that there are certain sectors of society (and perhaps deep within us) that comprehend the primary function of such a punitive enclosure. That is, to open the gates would in fact unleash bases of knowledge formation that would radically alter society. It then becomes imperative to study how technologies of punitive enclosure are currently utilized outside what is commonly considered the prison—that is the physical site of the prison—and important, why they are vigorously enforced. The following sections of the chapter detail the development of the punitive enclosure of Black education through the workings of policy formation and state propaganda that relied upon racialized fear tactics to legitimate Black containment in an effort to circumvent Black collectivity. These analyses give way to ethnographic renderings of the current state of education within these enclosures and I hope shed light on the heinous conditions that are produced by a punitive enclosure system.

Prison/Public Education Policy

On August 3, 2004, Los Angeles County District Attorney Steve Cooley wrote a letter to the Los Angeles County Board of Supervisors regarding the appropriation of financial resources (Cooley 2004). Written in bullet-point format, Cooley urged the supervisors to cede a block grant of funds in the sum of $200,000 from the State Bureau of Corrections to the Los Angeles District Attorney's Office to implement a program entitled Abolish Chronic Truancy (ACT) within the cities of Long Beach and Paramount. Affecting the Long Beach, Paramount, Little Lake, and Los Nietos School Districts, the newly acquired money would in part fund two new positions, designated as District Attorney Hearing Officers (HOs), who would oversee the day-to-day implementation of ACT. Outlined within the letter, the establishment of the HOs and utilization of the block grant had four primary objectives:

1. Initiate contact with students who were deemed as excessively truant to school and their parents or guardians in order to explain the legal ramifications of continued truancy and establish a legal basis

for this process with the execution of contracts among the school, student, parent, and HO.

2. If truancies continued, the HO would place the parent and student under the jurisdiction of the School Attendance Review Board (SARB), consisting of probation, law enforcement, and mental health officials.

3. Under the watchful eye of SARB, if the student had at least fifteen unexcused absences, the student and parent or guardian were brought to a SARB hearing attended by both the HO and a deputy district attorney wherein all parties signed a new contract.

4. Based upon the SARB contract, if there was no improvement in truancy, a Penal Code 272 case would be brought against both the parent and student and forwarded to the Los Angeles County Superior Court for prosecution.

Although much of the concern pertaining to ACT rightfully addresses newly funded ways to criminally prosecute youth and their families, Cooley's letter highlights something much more powerful that has taken place in the State of California. Under the mandate of ACT, a seamless tapestry has been woven into the State of California Department of Corrections, Los Angeles District Attorney's Office, Los Angeles County Board of Supervisors, Los Angeles County Sheriff's Department, and the Los Angeles County Probation Department, all in an attempt to control public education within Los Angeles County. The magnitude of these connections cannot be overstated, especially since none of these state entities has either specific educational expertise nor was founded to govern the day-to-day practices within public education. Given the coalescence of such vast and financially powerful punitive institutions, the question has to be raised: Why and how did agents of the criminal justice and prison systems become such instrumental players within public education and specifically the schooling of Black people?

Abolish Chronic Truancy (ACT) was first introduced in Parmelee Elementary School in 1991 in South Central Los Angeles by Deputy District Attorney Thomas Higgins (Mozingo 1998). At the time, South Central Los Angeles was a majority Black section of Los Angeles, with Black people making up 55 percent of the population (Myers 2002). Rather than an isolated occurrence, ACT has to be placed within a larger context of draconian legislation and social policy that specifically targeted Black communities throughout Los Angeles and Los Angeles County.

The development of ACT is located within a pivotal moment in California legal policy, whereby the California constitution was amended in order to incarcerate Black folks and in particular Black youth throughout the state. In 1988, the California State Legislature created Senate Bill 1555, better known as the Street Terrorism and Prevention Act (STEP). STEP had two objectives: the first was to create a policy to criminalize "gang" members, who during this time were being publicized as the moral and social pariah of California. Key to this distinction were enhancements associated with STEP that enabled prosecutors to place additional charges that carried an exorbitant amount of prison time (Sigal 2010). If any offense were proven to be gang affiliated or gang related, the state could legally add time to the sentence on top of the original charge. Thus, it is not uncommon for those charged under the STEP Act who are proven (even in the most vague of terms) to have any gang affiliation to face hundred of years in prison because of sentencing enhancements.[4]

SB 1555 amended Penal Code 272, which was originally utilized as a tool to protect children from violence at the hands of adults. The amendment of the code created a misdemeanor charge if parents did not take responsibility for the proper control and care of their children. If found guilty under the amended law, parents would face a fine of up to $2,500, one year in county jail, or a combination of both (Clements 1995).[5] One of the key tenets of "control" was for all children to be in school during designated hours. It was this application of the law that led to the Abolish Chronic Truancy policy, which through a mythical façade of increased crime, was implemented within public schools in South Central Los Angeles.[6] The key to the creation of the "criminal truant" was perhaps the most powerful cultural institution in the Southern California, which for more than a century had done the bidding of the landed corporate class: the *Los Angeles Times*.

The *Los Angeles Times*: Maintenance of Law and Order

Amidst a contrived "moral panic" about the correlation among truancy, juvenile delinquency, and gang activity, the Los Angeles District Attorney's Office and the Los Angeles Police Department drummed up pandemonium regarding the threat of young high school students who were causing mayhem throughout Los Angeles County.[7] Utilizing the *Los Angeles Times* as their mouthpiece, the Los Angeles County District Attorney's Office and its main proponent, Tom Higgins, who by 1995 had moved into a new capacity over the Juvenile Justice Division of the District Attorney's Office, rallied for the passage of legislation that placed the District Attorney's Office and the police over the purview of truancy and schools.[8] Yet this was not the *Times*'s first foray into the realm of public persuasion. Rather than an anomaly, such was the historic and contemporary modus operandi of the *Los Angeles Times*. Key to the attempted transformation of Los Angeles and the surrounding area into an open-shop, white supremacist paradise, the *Times* was the medium of choice for the white, wealthy capitalists of the region.

The paper was established by General Harrison Gray Otis in 1881 and was intended to substantiate a particular type of truth that would serve to legitimate the desires of the white financial elites of the region, in particular Otis and his descendants, the Chandler Family.[9] The significance of the *Los Angeles Times* can be traced back to the 1888 economic collapse, which similar to the Great Recession, was the result of a dramatically overinflated housing market and gross land speculation on the part of a burgeoning financial sector. In the midst of unfortunate circumstances, General Harrison Gray Otis saw the economic crisis as a golden moment to establish the paper as the centerpiece of a three-pronged attack upon the masses who struggled mightily in the face of economic uncertainty: promote the interests of private capital, crush any sentiment of labor organizing, and propagate the evils of any economic system that remotely mentioned an equal distribution of economic, political, or social resources.[10] To this end, Otis used his power and financial influence to transform the police department into a violent tool of oppression against workers and support public policy that attacked the public (Davis 2006, 295; Halberstam 2000, 156).[11] Most notable of this sort were the continual attacks that the *Times* editorial staff, at the behest of the ownership and their partners, made against public housing in Los Angeles. This was exemplified by the 1951 forced removal of a predominantly Latino community from Chavez Ravine and the subsequent elimination of a plan for a massive low-income housing complex in order to provide a stadium for the newly arrived Dodgers baseball team (Davis 2006, 122–23).[12]

The paper that Otis developed near the end of the nineteenth century was further refined throughout the twentieth century by his son-in-law,

Harry Chandler, and future Chandler clan, into an all-encompassing space to establish Los Angeles as a site of racial terror and economic disparities in order to maintain large private property holdings and the economic leverage that was associated with land ownership in Southern California.[13] David Halberstam writes:

> The friends of the Chandlers were written about as they wished; their enemies were deprived of space, or attacked. What was not printed was as important as what was printed. The *Times* sanitized and laundered the operations of a rich anti-labor establishment and its politicians; it repeatedly used red scares to crush any kind of social-welfare legislation. It gave its enemies no space and no voice. If a newspaper at its best reflects and hears all factions of the community, letting them play their will out as openly as possible, examining the legitimacy of each case on its merits, trying to limit the emotions and passions, then the *Times* was a manifestly unfair newspaper; it appealed to ignorance and prejudice and it fanned passions. (Halberstam 2000, 167)

Although the ideological mapping of the *Times* remained strongly indebted to the capitalist class, the ownership of the *Times* made a strategic change during the Black Power era of the late 1960s and early '70s. In 1969, the *Times*'s governing board swung their support behind a young Black former police officer, Thomas Bradley, in the race for mayor of the city. Such a move would have been unthought of twenty years prior. However, the owners of the *Times* realized the threat posed by radical Black organizing throughout the city. The very tactics that the *Times* supported for more than fifty years of violent police repression had unleashed a furor of unabated protest and resistance typified by the 1965 Watts Rebellion. Police repression alone was not sufficient to protect the interests of the city's power brokers. Employing a new tactic, the *Times*, under the direction of Dorothy Chandler, incorporated a small percentage of reformist-oriented Black, Jewish, Asian, and Latino representatives into the fold to further discipline the masses of poor throughout the city (Davis 2000, 1992). The pinnacle of this new model was Tom Bradley. Although Bradley lost his initial mayoral bid, with the *Times* support he formed a broad wealthy base and won the following election, serving in the post for more than twenty years. Bradley's tenure was emblematic of the *Times*'s philosophical shift during the same time period—a bourgeois ethos of upward mobility that both castigated and held ill regard for millions of poor Black and Latino residents throughout the city. Building upon the Bradley model, the *Times* highlighted the success of racially diverse junior capital partners such as the mayor himself while simultaneously publishing stories on the death of the "Black ghetto" (Davis 2006, 302).

The affect of this shift was a new *Los Angeles Times* that intimately connected upward mobility and success with racialized politics of anticrime and moral values, both of which were central to the rapid incarceration of Black Angelinos. Building upon the *Times*-generated Bradley model, new civic "Black leaders" such as Bernard Parks represented a model type of proper negro. With a sleight of hand (and out of direct fear of Black power movements), the leadership at the *Times* attempted to configure the police, state bureaucracy, and private capital as no longer viable targets of Black resistance, but rather as spaces of enviable employment and the epitome of civic engagement. Thus, those who remained steadfast against and demanded radical change within the very structures (that is, public governance, police, public education) that were being lauded as acceptable channels of mobility were quickly demonized as both foolish and criminal. It is within such a social milieu that the *LA Times* became a larger and louder bullhorn of new "law-and-order" regimes that were increasingly violent in actual implementation (that is, the police beating of Rodney King) and policy development (that is, Three Strikes legislation).

Given the intimate link between public education and the prison system, it was no surprise that the *Times* frequently wrote about new draconian efforts to suppress the nonwhite student population throughout Southern California. In June 1995, the *Times* ran a series, "L.A. School Truancy Exacts a Growing Social Price," on the supposed problem of truancy within public schools. In line with the passage of legislation that criminalized a wide range of acts from drug utilization to loitering, the series followed the lead of the LA City Council, which just a month prior had paved the way for the criminalization of truancy. Authored by Beth Schuster, the piece connected school truancy to drug usage and future criminal endeavors. Adopting the rhetoric of the LAPD, Shuster wrote in the entry column:

> Daytime crime rates are rising in part because growing numbers
> of students are skipping school and committing crimes, said
> LAPD spokesman Lt. John Dunkin. When Los Angeles Police

Department officers in Van Nuys this spring conducted a rare, three-week-long school truancy sweep, shoplifting arrests fell 60%. Other youths spend their unsupervised days scrawling graffiti on garage doors, storefronts and office buildings. A report compiled by the Los Angeles County Office of Education on the factors that contribute to juvenile delinquency concluded that school absences are "the most powerful predictor" of delinquent behavior. Children who are truant are at a higher risk of being drawn into behavior involving drugs, alcohol or violence. Studies show that chronic truants are more likely to use drugs; in one study, half of the truants admitted smoking marijuana in the prior six months, compared to 29% of their non-truant classmates, and nearly one-third of the truants said they took two or more drugs on the same day. (Schuster 1995a)

As a model to corral the concocted problem, the series outlined the positive impact of a New York City truancy program that unabashedly criminalized youth. In an effort to further substantiate the strategic attempt to link crime with truancy, Shuster stated:

Giuliani blames truants for contributing to the city's escalating daytime crime rate. "Our problem was a major one so we needed to do something pretty decisive," Giuliani said in an interview. "This, we believe, is helpful in reducing crime but also in protecting kids. The fact is you can't ignore the problem." So far, police have picked up about 40,000 students and recovered 488 weapons, including 88 guns, since the beginning of the school year. (Shuster 1995b)

Yet, Shuster's analysis of truancy was not complete until she was able to create a mythical world reality whereby Black and Brown students were the locus of deviance and criminal activity associated with truancy. Given that she focused her analysis on William Taft High School, located in the Woodland Hills area of Los Angeles (a majority white enclave of the San Fernando Valley), she spoke to the linchpin of racial integration within Los Angeles Unified School District. Near the end of her column on Taft, she commented, "Like other suburban campuses, Taft has a large contingent of bused students—some of whom take the bus to campus only to connect with friends and run the streets, returning to Taft in time to be bused back home" (Shuster 1995a). On the surface, such a statement might go unnoticed if not for the racial politics concerning bussing within LAUSD. Spearheaded by Bobbi Fielder and Barbara Weintraub (who later became president of the LAUSD Board of Supervisors), white resistance emanating from the San Fernando Valley during the 1970s and '80s rivaled that of virulent white opposition to bussing programs in Boston during the same time period.[14] The focal point of white angst regarded the bussing of Black students from South Central Los Angeles into predominantly white neighborhoods and the resultant bussing of white students into Black neighborhoods to comply with desegregation mandates set forth by the federal government. It must be noted that much of the concern and anger pertained to the control of land and resources that were associated with public education. Given that land and home values have long since been determined by race, many white residents within the Valley wanted to ensure their economic and political privilege associated with whiteness (Massey and Denton 1993; Shapiro 2005). Building upon this legacy, Shuster invoked the known racial hostility signified by bussing in order to make sure that the readers of the LA Times knew who were the criminal instigators of this new type of crime that was supposedly ravaging their communities.

In order to strengthen the race-baiting propaganda, the Times ran another part of the series that was disseminated only throughout the San Fernando Valley.[15] The column tells the travails of a young white student Jarid Mels, who is a characterized as "master ditcher" (Shuster 1995c). Yet, counter to other parts of the series, there is no mention of crime, police, or punitive measures. Rather, Jarid, through the urging of his English teacher, mother, and hyper-intelligent "strawberry blonde" girlfriend, becomes a success. Counter to discourse pertaining to Black youth during the same time period, there was no dysfunctional castigating of Jarid's mother as a single parent raising a male child, no state-based intervention programs, or the incessant need to remove youth like Jarid from his neighborhood in order to reduce crime. Rather, the model appears rather simple: develop community support between the school and the residents to reduce truancy. Yet, throughout the series, such an alternative is applicable only to white youth, while Black and Brown youth had to face the wrath of the criminal justice system.

Such irony was not lost upon the nonwhite population that were opposed to the new truancy program from its inception. Despite assurances from the chairman of the city council public safety commission that police would not target nonwhite populations, Black communities in Los Angeles knew that such promises should be taken with a grain of salt.[16] Perhaps more infuriating to activist and community members alike was the fact that Black and Brown schools such as South Gate High School (located in the city of South Gate, which is near the center of the Los Angeles County, with a 98 percent Latino student population) had effectively stymied the tide of truancy to the tune of 95 percent student attendance without the utilization of the police and other punitive measures (California Department of Education 2009; Shuster 1995a).[17] Yet, in the face of such evidence of community-based, non-punitive measures that proved highly effective, the *LA Times* chose to publish a major series that lauded the city council efforts to criminalize poor Black and Brown youth.

During the twenty-year period since the LA City Council legislated the issuing of truancy tickets in Los Angeles County, it became clear that both the LAPD and the Los Angeles School Police Department have focused their efforts on Black and Latino residents of Los Angeles County. In a massive undertaking, the Labor/Community Strategy Center collected all truancy tickets issued between 2004 and 2008 and found that of more than 47,000 tickets issued during the time period, more than 88 percent were issued to Black and Latino students (Criollo, personal interview with author, August 4, 2009). Extremely punitive in nature, the tickets are structured on a progressive fine system, whereby each ticket that is issued carries an increased financial burden. Although the first ticket carries a $250 charge, additional tickets carry fines in excess of $900; further, if students are unable to pay the fines, their only recourse is to pass the financial burden on to their parent or other family member. However, until paid, the fees will continue to follow the individual via the Department of Motor Vehicle database (Adler 2009).

Fear of Freedom: Policy and Enclosures

Both the ACT program and the issuance of truancy tickets illustrate how policy mandates have constructed punitive legal, social, and economic enclosures in an attempt to maintain control over Black Los Angeles. The formation of policies such as ACT and those that enabled the implementation of a racialized draconian police force has to be placed within the context of a communal organizing that had a radical social, political, economic, and important, education agenda for Black life in Los Angeles. It was in this era, post-1984, that policy was explicitly utilized to form punitive enclosures within Black communities in order to prevent the establishment of a unified front of Black collective organizing such as the coalescence between the Crips and the Bloods. The establishment of the threat of the Black criminal through propaganda spouted by reputable media outlets such as the *LA Times* was done to both counter the demands of the organizing efforts and also provide legitimacy for policy initiates that inserted the prison regime as the solution to issues of economic, health, political, and education disenfranchisement. Thus, the buildup of the enclosure was in order to remove Black communal response to issues of state terror and violence and replace it with policy-led programs that would further entrench Black communities into the control of the state apparatus. It has to be remembered that Black Angelinos were not clamoring for their loved ones and fellow neighbors to be placed within the clutches of the prison regime. Rather, these policy initiatives that were established from the 1980s onward were presented as the only solution. This section of the chapter explores these policies and the Black communal organizing that they were attempting to enclose.

A common strategy that was used to sell these very harsh policies to the public was the utilization of seemingly benign rhetoric to mask the real intentions of the initiatives. The language of initiatives such as ACT has been written specifically as an "early intervention" and "prevention" programs. The reality is that such wording has been used in order to further build up an enclosure apparatus of Black youth throughout Southern California. The District Attorney's Office in 2007, under the guise of a gang task force initiative, proposed expansion of the policy in the form of a parcel tax to fund an estimated $50 million, to extend the ACT program into middle schools (McGreevy and Hymon 2007). The gross irony of the proposed tax is that, as an extension of the "tough on crime" discourse, it further intensifies the oppression of Black people; Black people are paying to have the state prosecute and monitor them and their children on a more comprehensive basis.

As a part of the conflation of the prison and public education systems, ACT is a piece of a larger paradigm that levies suspensions, expulsions, and arrests against Black students at an outrageous level. In particular, although during the early 2000s Blacks represented only 17 percent of the national public school population, they represented 26 percent of the suspensions and expulsions (National Center for Education Statistics 2003). During this time period, 24.2 percent of all Black males in public schools had been suspended, although only 14.4 and 12.2 percent of Latino and white males respectively had been suspended. In expulsion rates, the statistics are equally skewed: 6.7 percent of Black males in public education were expelled from school, while 1.9 and 2.2 percent of Latino and white males respectively were expelled (U.S. Department of Education 2003).

Heralded and intensified over the past twenty years, "zero-tolerance" (that is, automatic suspension or expulsion) programs have proven to be ineffective in stemming the tide of crime or deviance in public education, nor have they served to increase rates of academic success (Fuentes 2003). A reflection of the minimum-sentencing guidelines instituted by both federal and state governments, the zero-tolerance movement is largely racialized whereby Black students are disproportionately affected (Browne et al. 2002).[18] Integral to the zero-tolerance policies in Los Angeles has been an extreme emphasis placed on policing. In the middle of the decade, the city released a comprehensive measure to address the "problem of gangs" in Los Angeles. This measure includes the coordination among the City of Los Angeles, Los Angeles County, the FBI, the Bureau of Fire, Alcohol, Tobacco, Firearms, and Explosives, the Drug Enforcement Agency, the U.S. Attorney's Office, and school districts throughout Los Angeles and Los Angeles County. A major component of this measure is the increased policing and state intervention within public schools. Although the measure has received much fanfare and news attention, community activists and academics alike warn that such measures have been enacted in the past and have proven to be both highly ineffective and function to push students out of school (Browne et al. 2002).[19] Yet, rather than back away from the ineffectiveness of such policies, school districts throughout Los Angeles County envision them as the great savior.

The history of such measures is commonplace within the urban terrain of Los Angeles and Los Angeles County. As an example, Operation Hammer, implemented by then–LAPD Chief Daryl Gates during the 1980s, is a prime example of the oppressive tactics employed by the state. Under the guise of gang "clean up," police officials routinely arrested, beat, and logged the names of thousands of Blacks throughout Los Angeles (Kelley 1996).[20] The result of these policies was that by 1991 "one-third of all young black males (20–29) living in Los Angeles County had already been jailed at least once in that same year" (Miller 1996, 5). In light of these figures, Jerome Miller argues that "the absolute majority of young black males in Los Angeles could expect to be dragged into one or another of the county's jails, detention centers, camps, or prisons as they traversed the years between adolescence and age 30" (Miller 1996, 5). Massive corruption, exemplified by the Rampart Scandal during the 1990s, brought to light the systematic and institutionalized racism and violence inherent within the Los Angeles Police Department (Winton and McGreevy 2007).

Clouded by the "success" of Operation Hammer was the City of Los Angeles's ability to extend the LAPD into multiple facets of Black life. Founded in 1983, the Drug Abuse Resistance Education program, better known as DARE, introduced for the first time en masse police officers on the campuses of predominately Black public schools. Piloted in Los Angeles, the program placed LAPD officers not only on campuses as a "security" apparatus, but also within the classroom to teach classes (ironically, one of the primary areas that the officers taught classes on was violence prevention). In spite of the fact that DARE failed to stem drug abuse, the program was expanded across the country (Clayton, Cattarello, and Johnstone 1996; Ennett et al. 1994).[21] This was compounded by the fact that both state and federal governments, as a condition of the 1986 Drug Free Schools and Communities Act, were mandated to allocate all of their anti-drug resources to a program that failed to "keep kids off of drugs" in order to receive any federal funding.[22] Further damning, Melody Lark's 1995 study of implementation of DARE within California public schools found that

> the federal and California state government developed drug policies that generally are not compatible with the perspectives of the education administrators or the experiences of the target group—students. Furthermore, drug policies incorporated only a small portion of drug causation that theorists, researchers, drug experts, public officials, and community representatives and leaders identified. Moreover, federal and California state government established expectations that education administrators believed school drug prevention programs could not fulfill. Under these conditions, the relationship between federal and California state drug policy formation, causation, and California school drug prevention program implementation has little potential for reducing student drug use. (Lark 1995)

Although DARE and similar programs such as "McGruff the Crime Dog" and "This Is Your Brain On Drugs" campaign contained slick advertising, the truth of the matter was that such policy served only to further incarcerate Black youth. As an example, soon after the establishment of DARE, the federal government passed the Drug-Free Schools and Communities Act Amendments of 1989. Bolstering the 1986 policy, the 1989 legislation established Drug-Free School Zones that increased prison sentencing for drug transactions made within 1,000 feet of public schools. Given the fact that communities within Los Angeles contain several schools, the probability that a drug transaction would be committed within 1,000 feet of a school led to the long-term incarceration of thousands of Black men and women who were the targeted population of the new legislation. Similar to DARE, the establishment of the 1989 policy and the massive financial resources that accompanied it and subsequent policies proved to be ineffective in reducing drug use among youth (Gorman 1998). Conversely, as the presence of police on school campuses and the criminalization of drugs intensified, rates of drug usage among youth increased (Gorman 1998, 127).

In the face of a litany of research and studies that proved the ineptness of punitive state and federal policy, city and county governments continued to pour the bulk of their resources into these failed programs. One must question the logic behind the insistent implementation of programs that clearly failed to meet their stated objectives. Yet, what if the objectives were other than those stated on a grant application or government memorandum? Utilizing Pam Oliver's thesis and evidence that demonstrates that the repressive actions against Black communities are an attempt to dampen resistance against a fundamentally unjust system, the development of programs such as DARE is a part of a larger tactical approach to resist Black freedom. What is understated is that formation of racialized legal policy was in direct response to, and fear of, the coalescence of Black youth during the late 1980s leading into the 1990s. Within this paradigm, the hyper-militarization of the police is enacted out of the same type of fear that brought violent action against Black radical movements two decades prior.

Yet what is often obscured within the narrative of liberation movements in the post–Black Power era is that Black communities never stopped fighting for freedom. Similar to the efforts of Bunchy Carter and the Los Angeles chapter of the Black Panther Party two decades prior, organized members of the Slausons and other communal groups (Michael Zinzun, for example) were instrumental in the organizing of Black youth throughout Los Angeles under the moniker of the Gang Truce during the 1980s and '90s. Originating out of the Nickerson Gardens, Imperial Courts, Jordan Downs, and Hacienda Village Housing Projects in Watts, the Gang Truce was a youth-based movement that challenged the power structure in Los Angeles County through a massive alliance of organizations throughout the region. Zinzun, a former member of the LA Black Panther Party who founded the Coalition Against Police Abuse (CAPA) in 1975, became a key ally of Black youth who faced continual repression at the hands of the LAPD and other law enforcement agencies throughout Southern California (Zinzun 1997). Rather than merely an attempt at reconciliation, the Gang Truce placed demands upon the local power structure and directly challenged the legitimacy of elected officials and owners of capital to dictate social and economic policy. It is within the contestation over resources that the attack upon Black youth is understood as a reactionary strategy to counter the demands issued by the Gang Truce.[23] In response to their efforts of police and city and county agencies to undermine the Truce, Zinzun stated:

> It's a threat to them to have young people working together,
> demanding jobs, demanding justice. They've never come out and
> supported the truce. In fact, the city has recently expanded the
> anti-terrorist division to eliminate probable cause necessary to in-
> vestigate a crime. This means I can call and say I think you're doing
> something wrong and they can spy on you for six months and tap
> your phones without any other evidence. . . . And we believe the
> first group they're going to target is the youth. By assuming they're
> gang members and may be storing guns and drugs, they can actu-
> ally tap people's phones and spy on them for up to six months
> with a warrant extension for another 90 days just on a tip. (Zinzun
> 1997, 260)

Much more than lip service, the Gang Truce, via the established networks Zinzun had developed through his membership with the BPP and years of work with CAPA, became a national model employed by youth to both organize themselves and directly assert their authority as stakeholders within the governance of their communities.[24] Speaking about linkages that were being made throughout the country, Zinzun, in a 1995 interview with Paul Burton, responded to the fear on the part of police and elected officials regarding the Truce:

> I think it's all part of the whole attack on Black youth, Latino youth—justification for the rousting, the harassment, moving in military weapons and so on. You see, if you look at the L.A. Uprising you can see the kind of fear they had. They have this fear of these young people. . . . I think that they're afraid of the gang truce. They're always hollerin' about "We need to stop all this violence," and then all these young people start joinin' the gang truce and the first thing the police do is attack. The establishment attacks the truce, which is in fact what they said they would like to see. In Chicago they had all these young El Rukins and Vice Lords and all the gangs registering people to vote and it scared the hell out of the whole country. They had 10,000 people registering people. These big, buff gang members talkin' 'bout, "Are you registered to vote?" That scared the hell out of the establishment because they know that the unity that we are attempting to bring about can only be part of their downfall. And the gang truce is reflective of that— initiated in Watts out of the baddest housing projects on the west coast. And here they are now leading the charge and it's impacting all the rest of the country. Can't beat it. (Burton 1995)

Speaking to the seriousness of the youth involved in the Gang Truce, a physical document entitled the "Multi-Peace Treaty-General Armistice Agreement" established a written guide. Stylistically based upon the 1949 United Nations–endorsed peace treaty between Egypt and Israel, the Agreement contained four articles and two annexes. In addition to laying the groundwork for acceptable relations among gangs throughout Los Angeles County, it set forth demands made upon city, state, and federal structures. Key were the following mandates:

1. Eliminate the national gang database which currently gives youth a permanent record for simply being detained for "suspicion of being a gang member," even if the youth is later released for lack of evidence. What must happen is changing state legislation to erase the records of any individuals unjustly detained or

arrested and permanently recorded. This record often prevents them from being employed.

2. Eliminate federal programs such as "Weed and Seed" that target whole communities as being non-rehabilitatable, subject them to repressive law enforcement programs and place service monies under the jurisdiction of law enforcement agencies.

3. Eliminate illegal searches and gang sweeps.

4. Stop police abuse and their "US Against Them" attitude. (Vargas 2006, 190)

Additionally the Truce called for the establishment of a Civilian Police Review Board to oversee the actions and future direction of the LAPD. The document stated:

1. The Review Board will judge complaints of unnecessary force, false arrest, harassment, tampering with evidence, abuse of authority, violation of civil rights, illegal surveillance, abusive language, gay bashing, racial or ethnic slurs, etc.

2. The Board will have the power to review and alter police procedures and policies concerning the abuse areas.

3. The Board will have the power to discipline (ranging from censure to suspension without pay for up to six months) and fire police officers. It will also have the power to recommend criminal prosecution and to award civil damages up to $50,000.

4. The Board will also have an independent staff of investors with full subpoena powers, plus immediate and unrestricted access to shooting areas.

5. A special Prosecutor will be elected whose job will be to handle cases of misdemeanor criminal charges against police officers.

6. Any police officer who threatens, harasses or discriminates against another officer of the LAPD who witnesses an act of police abuse and reports it to the Civilian Police Review Board shall be subject to penalties as outlined in the Review Board Initiative. (Vargas 2006, 190)

The Truce was informed by an ideological framework that grappled with the tension between the violence and repression developed within a capitalist paradigm. At every turn, the document addressed the multiple forms of exploitation associated with capitalism and especially those emanating from the Rebuild Los Angeles plan, which positioned corporate investment within Black communities as the sole solution to issues raised in the 1992 rebellion after the Rodney King trial.[25] In addition to providing an in-depth analysis of housing, health care, and employment, the framers astutely argued against the established public education system within the city.[26] Vargas notes that the Gang Truce "demands our constitutional right to education." It appeals for an end to "racism, sexism, and White supremacy in education, in teacher training, in curriculum . . . , and in the classrooms" (Vargas 2006, 191). As a whole the Gang Truce directly countered the heavy weight of the landed capital class that sought to continually reinscribe the subjugation of Black life. It is in this spirit that framers sought a new form of governance and economic relations. The document stated:

> Our concept of progressive economic development centers on meeting people's basic needs, people being able to get a sense of satisfaction from their work, and being able to provide their loved ones with a quality of life in which they have access to and can enjoy all the benefits this society has to offer. . . . We also believe that progressive economic development must be based on a sense of individual and collective responsibility for one's community and the world. Rather than economic development that pits one person against the other, or one group against the other, we believe that economic development should advance the individual and the community. . . . So instead of enterprise zones, we call for cooperative zones, which promote social and economic justice, and are free of racism, sexism, and other forms of oppression. (Vargas 2006, 193)

It is within this framework that the implementation of legislation to criminalize dissent, reinforce a system of racial capitalism, and unleash the viciousness of police violence has to be understood as a reaction to the radical assertions on the part of Black people in Los Angeles. The result of these policies, of course, can be found not only within the myriad of prisons that are scattered throughout the state, but within the very fabric of state life (that is, schools, parks, health services, housing). In light of the massive response to Black resistance against repression, what must be considered are not only the mechanisms behind the technological apparatus, but the racialized ideological imperatives that fuel the beast.

Policy Meets Ethnography

As a means to analyze the full scope of the prison regime and the effect of policy formation upon Black radical formations, the subsequent pages draw upon my ethnographic research at CHS and offer insight into the underpinnings of punitive enclosures within education. After working at CHS for a few months, it became quiet clear to me that the overtly punitive measures utilized by the school to govern its population formed an enclosure apparatus that produced only one logical conclusion: to withdraw. Either physically or mentally, the only viable option was to dissociate oneself from the school because the daily violence enacted upon the students was beyond reproach. Although some stopped attending school, others showed up with the intention of just making it through the day until the final bell rang. The enactment of policy initiatives that had placed several forms of policing on campus in addition to the strict parameters by which students could engage with each other and teachers had erased any notion that anything of educative value was occurring at CHS.

Perhaps the most frightening aspect of my observation was that the lockdown model that had been established during the 1960s at Jefferson High School in LA had been refined to the point that it operated as the status quo in enclosure of student action. Whether or not police were physically present in the classroom or particular location, every facet of the school apparatus operated under the philosophical framework of a lockdown. Student movements were continually patrolled, punitive measures were allocated for conjured-up infractions, students had to follow the strict letter of the school law, and the punitive enclosures, marked by an elaborate system of fences and gates upon the student body, were spectacular in scope and range.

Prison or School?

Driving toward County High School on the broad avenue, the marker never ceases to amaze me: an extensive network of forged iron and concrete that extends for what seems as far as the eye can see. Staring at its enormity in relation to the multitude of youth who walk beside it, I know that I have just entered the school zone. Moving parallel to the massive steel black fence that reaches roughly nine feet in height, I often question how long this powerful enclosure has stood around the perimeter of the school. Stopped at a red light, I wonder what the community members who reside within the many apartments and houses that border the school think about the gate. I begin to think about the possibility of everything in this neighborhood being enclosed in the same manner as the school. Gas stations, small grocery stores, strip malls, and restaurants wrapped behind twisted, metal cages. I don't have to think too hard—to my left, I notice that some of the businesses in the community have adopted the school model and are in fact blocked from entry or exit by elongated bars. The light turns green and as I continue, so does the fence, sprawling down the street, rounding the corner south, and continuing yet again into perpetuity.

As I make my way toward the main entrance for faculty and staff, I try to imagine the disposition of a student who has to begin the morning by walking alongside and then through this structure in order to "learn." It is difficult enough to reconcile the existence of one massive gate, but I know that steel conglomerate is a strong symbol of what is to come once entry is granted. I follow the iron trail in my car and slowly turn along the street and wait to be signaled in by one of the security officers on campus. The flow of students passes in front of the entrance to the parking lot and the security officer waves me through the gate. I turn into the lot, my eyes scanning for a parking spot. Locating a good spot that is directly in line with the main entrance, I swing my late-model Japanese import through the maze of automobiles and park in a spot squeezed in between two other much larger vehicles. I place my substitute teaching badge on the dashboard and gather my lunch, weekly planner, and the book that I hope to crack open during conference period. It is only much later in the school year that I realize that I have become desensitized to being enclosed on all four sides by chain-linked and steel bar fencing that itself is encircled by the much larger albatross located a few feet from the parking lot. Once inside the parking lot, teachers and students alike have entered the second layer: a fortress that is tightly controlled and intensely secured.

The steel barriers that enclose the parking lot have one pedestrian entrance that is open during the morning rush to class. A tributary of drivers is funneled alongside an ocean of students walking onto campus. From the east and the west, large groups of students pass through bars and enter the school grounds. Stepping beyond the boundaries of the patrolled parking lot, I join the masses and approach yet another barrier: a tall, steel-rod fence that is patrolled by a staff officer. The officer's sandy brown hair and faded caramel complexion suggest that she has spent much of her time at this post in the sun. She sits in front of a podium that is covered by a brightly colored umbrella. Wearing dark sunglasses and standing at about five feet and five inches, she checks all students who have been absent to verify their readmittance into the school. Without verification of absence from school, students are sent along another path, directly to the assistant principal's office.

The staff member is flanked to her right by another security officer. A middle-aged black man donning even darker sunglasses than his counterpart, he fits the stereotypical look of "security." Wearing shorts, a white shirt, and a blue hat, his feet are covered in beige construction boots. An orange fluorescent vest affirms that he is a security officer. As students approach the gate, identification cards must be displayed in order to reach yet another level of security. He is, in essence, the proverbial gatekeeper. He yells phrases such as "All right now" and "Let's have a great day." All the while, the irony of his verbal rhetoric is not lost upon the students.

I nod to the security guard, show him my substitute badge, and as he recognizes my face I am granted passage into the school. Walking through the fence, a soft voice calls my name. "Hey Mr. Sojoyner, are we going to have you for Language Arts?"

The voice is coming from Ashley Davis. Ashley, a young black woman and very self-assured twelfth-grade senior, desperately wants to attend college away from home in the fall. I tell Ashley that I wish I was, but today I have been assigned World History and Government. "Alright Mr. Sojoyner, see you later," she calls back as she catches up with friends who are waiting for her about twenty feet from where I have to make my first stop of the day.

Just a few paces from the initial security apparatus, I veer to the left and enter the main administration building that houses the school principal, three assistant principals, administrative assistants, four academic counselors, and a deputy of the Los Angeles County Sheriff's Department. Briefly engaging in superficial dialogue with the administrative assistant, she hands me my teaching assignment, keys, and roll sheet and repeats the routine with another teacher who is waiting behind me. I retrace my steps back to the door and exit out of the building. Turning to the left and filing in with the mass of young adolescents who are making their way through the entrance, I begin my journey to the south end of campus. Passing through an open corridor buttressed by the choral room to the right and the 100 Building to the left, I slowly come to what is considered the quad region of the school, which houses an outdoor eating area. Students gather together in groups as large as ten at every corner of the small area that is bordered by the cafeteria to the north and a student snack store to the east. The gymnasium, which displays an overdrawn, colorful depiction of the school's mascot, is directly west of the quad. To the south, white one-story buildings are intermixed with once temporary hollowed, underground aluminum-siding bungalows. At this point I have gained permanent status, becoming a part of the grass and concrete tattered landscape. Clustered among each other, students have very little space to fit comfortably, and they make do by sitting on bench tables and standing on the small walls that enclose the dry flowerbeds located in front of the white buildings.

I navigate through the sea of young faces and am amazed by the sheer number of students who are able to fit within the small space. From my vantage point inside the human conglomerate, it appears that the school is far too small to house all of these students. Yet as I walk south, just beyond the clusters of Black and Brown faces, it is clear that the school is built upon on an abundance of land. Although it is not as big as some newly constructed high schools in the area, there is clearly enough space so that students can congregate among the vast swaths of open land that separate the buildings from one another. Taking a few paces, I look immediately behind me, just beyond the sea of students, and notice that there is a perimeter that has been established around the students. This outer ring is patrolled by members of on-campus security personnel and administrators who do not permit students to move beyond their imposed boundaries. The security forces stick out on campus; they wear loud orange or sand-washed gray shirts that are accompanied by relatively rough scowls across their faces. They are strategically placed at all points of access and within the center of the student mass. Communication is transmitted through walkie-talkie devices.

Turning back around, I head down one of several walkways that extend like arteries from the main administration building through the quad and disperse throughout the campus. Aside from the main administration building there is only one other two-story building, which is located in the southeast corner of the school. As I walk down a long path that leads toward the 700 Building, I see a few students, mostly grouped in couples, who have broken out of sight of the security forces, sitting along walls of the 200 Building. The 700 Building is located near the southernmost point of the school. Standing atop of the stairs that lead to the second-floor classrooms, one gains a great perspective. To the east, the campus is separated from a major avenue by the steel monstrosity that greets students and community residents alike. To the west, a long, rustic, gray chain-link fence separates the academic buildings from the physical education fields. In the southeast direction, there is yet another chain-link fence that prevents entry from the southern parking lot, which is enclosed within another steel-rod fence. The football practice field, located southwest of the 700 Building, is blocked off by another fence that separates the field from a series of train tracks that run along the rear of the school. Within the campus, I notice that there are several breezeways that connect the individual pathways that extend from the 100, 200, and 600 to the main administrative building. However, these paths are closed off by gates that prevent access to their use unless opened by a member of the security staff who continually patrol the school grounds.

Although the feeling of enclosure is somewhat normalized throughout the daily ritual of attending school, it is not lost among students that limits are placed upon their movements. Peering out into the sea of coercive control, I remembered a brief conversation just prior to the beginning of class that I had with a young Black male. He had transferred from another school that was located in a predominantly white, affluent community. We talked about his experience thus far at County and I asked him a question about the differences between CHS and his previous school. He stated, "The biggest difference are the fences. Over there you had more freedom, but here there are fences and gates everywhere."

Such a lockdown framework has to be placed in contradistinction against schools in predominately white neighborhoods such as those touched on in Beth Schuster's racially dichotomous rendering of truancy tickets. Not only does such a framework not exist, but students are encouraged to explore and learn by tapping into their natural curiosity. Instructed early on in the educational philosophies that promote student freedom, such as the Reggio Emilia or Waldorf methods, the notion that one would have to surveil or legislate student behavior and action is absurd. Yet, just a few miles away, this is not only the expectation of nonwhite students, but it has been framed as the only way that these Black and Brown students can be educated. The result is that the lockdown model as apart of the punitive enclosure has extended beyond what we would consider traditional sites of punishment and implemented as a daily pedagogical practice. The subsequent two ethnographic sections of the chapter detail this process and the horrific normalization of student enclosure as teaching practice.

Silence Is Golden

I made my way into the second level of the 700 Building in an attempt to check in with the Language Arts teacher for whom I was supposed to substitute later on in the month. I tried to catch her prior to the start of classes because she was very popular and her class was always abuzz with the voices of youth eager to ask her advice on everything from clothing styles to the development of a persuasive argument. I had formed a deep level of admiration for her teaching style, the generosity that she offered her students, and the passion that she brought to teaching. At least once every two weeks, I made it a point to meet with her as she was dealing with an illness with a close family member and we had developed an inter-dependency upon one another—me a willing and eager listener and she a mentor teacher. Briefly catching up, I informed her that I had to hurry off to teach economics that morning and I was a little nervous because this was the first time that I had taught this class. She provided strong words of encouragement as I made my way out of her class and headed back down the stairs on my way to face the unknown.

Walking slightly north, I moved with purpose, because I wanted to make sure that I arrived to class early in order to get mentally prepared for the day of teaching. Approaching the band room, I made a sharp turn to the right and snuck in between the bungalows to make a beeline for the economics classroom. I hurriedly walked alongside the band room and government classrooms and looked out at the empty space that would soon be swarming with students with the ringing of the morning bell. I finally reached the cluster of classrooms where I had never taught before. Leaning on the doorknob, I took a deep breath and pulled open the door.

"Good morning," he stated. The well-lit room was alive and boisterous with colorful newspaper clippings and artwork on his walls. At 7:30 in the morning, Mr. Keynes was clearly at his best. Having already developed his lesson plan for the day, he invited me in and gave me the lay of the land. The background ambience was supplied with early 1970s rock, and the *Los Angeles Times* was spread across the large beige counter that faced a multitude of desks. As with many of the classrooms at CHS, the room no longer served its original purpose. Marked by a large faucet atop a deep steel basin inside of a faux Formica countertop and a spacious surplus storage closet, it appeared that the room was originally designed as a science lab. Mr. Keynes had masterfully revamped the space and utilized the massive lab closet as an office and lunch room and the countertop as a podium.

"Alright, so when the kids come in, usually I have them do a warm-up assignment. I keep the music on for about ten minutes and then cut it off when the majority of students have finished. Following the warm-up, you can lead in with the material for today. What was your degree in?," he asked. "African American studies," I replied. "Great," he responded. "Today we are discussing the economic system of market forces. The mechanisms that drive supply and demand."

He explained the material and gave me a packet of overhead projector sheets that displayed the assigned notes for the day. "I have all economics classes for the day and a teacher in training comes in during fourth period to teach. You can place your stuff in here in the back room and if you need to use the refrigerator please go ahead." I placed my lunch sack and books in the rear storage room and made my way back to the counter where Mr. Keynes was looking over the newspaper. A middle-aged white man, he seemed very comfortable with his job. Wearing a tropical-style shirt that bore wonderful arrangements of floral prints, he wore sand-washed jeans that gave the appearance of being extremely relaxed.

His room was immaculately clean. Across all four walls were materials related to economics. There were depictions of the laws that dictated the parameters of the capitalist system as well as faux-newspaper clippings that discussed the New Deal and the Great Depression. All of the desks were neatly arranged within rows and columns facing each other. Mr. Keynes inserted a perfect bisection in between the rows, similar to the British Parliament, where he placed his projector and examined the room as he lectured during the day.

So, I have pretty great classes today. I usually don't have any problems with them. You shouldn't have to say much of anything to them. I have a basic system that is dictated upon points. They all understand this and none of them want to lose any points. If they chew any gum, they lose fifty points. If they have their head on their desk, they lose twenty points. Like I said, you don't have to say anything, they all know this. All you have to do is this.

He moved the roll sheets to the left and opened a black binder to reveal another internal roll/grade sheet that many of the teachers used to keep track of student progress during the year.

Once you have finished taking roll, just peruse the room with your eyes. If you look in their direction and see that they are chewing gum, then just place a dash by their name on this sheet. The same goes for head on the desk and any other infraction such as talking without being called upon.

I was very skeptical that his plan worked as smoothly as he described, but his calm confidence made me very intrigued. "Okay, I am going to be here for just about all of the first period. After that you can take over. You are welcome to sit in the back and read the paper. Here is today's edition," Mr. Keynes stated. He handed me the paper, and I began to look over the assignment as he gathered his lecture materials for the day. Although we both waited for the bell to ring, I made my way behind the counter into the storage room. I sat at a table that had been erected for lunchtime eating and conference period breaks. The bell rang and I made my way back to the counter as the students arrived for first period. The music quietly played through the mounted speakers in front of the class, and Keynes placed the warm-up assignment on the overhead projector.

The students proceeded to take out sheets of paper and began the warm-up. Mr. Keynes began to go through his roll-call ritual and placed the roll sheets to his left and revealed his black binder. Slowly his eyes glanced throughout the room and the students slyly looked back to make sure that they had the appearance of working. He completed surveying the class and wrapped up the warm-up assignment.

"Is everybody just about finished?," he questioned the class. As the class's silence signaled a consensus, Mr. Keynes made his way back to the head of the classroom. "So yesterday we spoke about the economic system, the forces that pull and push on supply and demand. Today we are going to further that discussion."

He took out the handouts that he had shown me prior to class and placed them on top of the overhead projector. Turning off the lights, he began lecturing verbatim from the words that were illuminated on the screen just above the white board. En masse, the class took notes from the screen. He stopped in the middle of his lecture and looked up to check the time.

"Alright class, as I stated to you yesterday, I am going to be leaving early today. You all have a substitute teacher, Mr. Sojoyner who will take over and will require your full and undivided attention." With that, he collected his materials and made his way to exit the classroom. Taking over from his lecture notes, I went through all of the slides in a very slow pace. It was obvious that the students couldn't care less about the content on the white screen; rather what mattered was that they had written down all of the content. I finished the discussion as the bell signaling the end of the class period rang. In between periods, I decided to use a different approach to teach Mr. Keynes's lesson plan.

The next group of students made their way into the classroom and greeted me with silent head nods or faint smiles. The first change that I made was to the music. I ducked under the counter and quickly turned the station away from the classic rock channel. I turned the large silver knob back and forth on the late model radio until I picked up a good signal from the only jazz station in the area, KKJZ 88.1 FM. Raising myself back up from underneath the counter, I recognized a familiar face in the class, Rasheed. I quietly acknowledged Rasheed and then placed the warm-up assignment on the overhead projector.

Walking back to the desk, I began to take roll in the class. I was instantly struck by the amount of power that I had over the class. The students understood right away that Mr. Keynes had spoken to me about the deduction of points. Equipped with an immense amount of power, I gave Keynes's control device a test and was amazed by its effectiveness. The instant my eyes started to look over the class, the students all sat up straight in their desk. Students who were chewing gum quickly clinched their jaws and froze dead in their stance, hoping that I did not catch them. Those who had lain their heads across an outstretched arm along their desks quickly popped to attention. It was remarkable and profoundly sad all in the same moment.

I pulled the four-legged wheel cart that held the overhead projector away from the main lecture counter and placed the slides in the center of the screen. Asking one of the students in the class to turn off the lights, I clicked the black switch of the projector down, and the brilliant light filled the screen above the whiteboard. Just as soon as the light hit the screen, the students began writing in their notebooks. Talking through the main points of the lecture, I went on about the forces that affected supply and demand. Luckily, the dim sunlight that peeked through the darkly tinted windows facing the opposite side of the main entrance provided just enough light so the students would not fall asleep as I presented the material.

Although I sensed that the students had mastered the art of copying notes from a projection screen, I was not sure if they actually understood the material. Placing my hypothesis to the test, I engaged them in a few questions about the economics lesson that they were learning. "So since we are talking about supply and demand," I started, "can anyone give me any examples of how it works?"

The room fell completely silent. "Okay," I thought to myself, "maybe the question was too vague."

"Tell me then," hoping to get the conversation started, "how many of you work jobs after school?"

About half of the class raised their hands and I knew that we had something going. Asking them where they worked, they stated Starbucks, Foot Action, and Footlocker, to name a few.[27] "So at your places where you work, what drives supply and demand?" I asked. Thinking that I had an inside track into an instant conversation, I had failed again. The students looked puzzled and bored, so I probed a little deeper. "Alright since some of you work at Footlocker, why does a pair of Jordan's (brand-name tennis shoes) cost one-hundred and twenty-five dollars?" Still there was nothing but silence.

Very frustrated at this point, I finally exclaimed, "Why don't you guys ever talk? I don't get it. You just write and write, but do you ever think about what you are writing."

Rasheed raised his hand and as he began to speak, I realized that I had just crossed a few boundaries that maybe I should have taken the time to explore rather than assume. "Well, Mr. Keynes doesn't really allow us to talk in class. So we don't talk. No one wants to lose points by talking, so we just sit here and take notes on the material that he has on the board and allow him to do all of the talking."

The Cold Hard Truth

I was not ready to handle the magnitude of Rasheed's explanation. The students were being instructed not to talk and, more important, not to think or question the authority of those in power. Rather, in an odd twist, they were being rewarded for being docile. I stood in front of the students, trying to contain an emotion that bordered on a mix of embarrassment and anger. Getting through the rest of the lesson, I told the students that as long as I was in the class they should feel free to dismiss Mr. Keynes's rules, because I was not going to penalize them for speaking their minds. Unfortunately, despite my best intentions, the limited time that I had with the class could not undo the punitive measures that Mr. Keynes had enforced during the course of the school year. I tried the same tactics with the students in the following class period and was similarly rebuffed. Discouraged, but not dissuaded, I looked forward to the lunchtime break that was approaching where I could reassess my futile attempts at teaching economics.

As the period came to a close, I gathered my small plastic bag and headed back toward the break room. Reaching for the peanut butter and jelly sandwich, I sat at the table and was able to slowly decompress from the morning session. Opening the bag, I thought of Sidney and wondered how he was faring in light of the events that he had disclosed to me as we ate lunch together one bright and sunny day during the last month. Usually well composed and possessing a calm confidence, on this particular day Sidney's voice was somber, yet resonated with great clarity. "I shouldn't really be here. This is not a good school. The stuff that I am learning here, I am like a year or two behind where I was." He sat eating his food with a flat expression across his face and asked, "Man, did you hear about Ms. Fox?" I told him that I had heard some talk floating around the school, but I was not sure of the details of what had happened. I reminded him about the time I substituted for Ms. Fox's class, and, as we went through the metaphorical process in a poem by Emily Dickenson, the students commented that they did not understand the proper usage of a metaphor. Sidney chimed in that they did not understand any of the poems that they were supposed to have mastered by the time of my arrival to the class.

"Well yeah, Ms. Fox is racist." Although I had heard these stories from students before, Sidney's pain and anger was unmatched.

"So, she likes telling these racist jokes. At least she calls them jokes in class." At this point I was a little worried and asked what types of jokes she was telling. He continued

We were in class one day and this one Latina girl asked a question about the work and said that she did not understand what was going on. So Ms. Fox said that it was okay because she was going to be working with a mop and a broom once she got out of school.

Then a Latino dude asked for help and she told him that it didn't matter because he was going to be working outside of the Home Depot soon.[28] "What made her jokes worse was that she tried to then make jokes about being white and would say, "See, I am not racist, because I talk about myself too."

However, all was not lost. One of the lessons that I learned very quickly is that students are very astute in the fine art of resistance. Once Ms. Fox's racially motivated commentary had reached its peak, the students decided to strike back.

Sidney relayed the events of the story to me with an odd mixture of elation and disgust across his face:

Well, we were in Language Arts class and she was trying to play this CD. So, she had her CD player on top of the desk and wanted us to listen to this song or something. And my friend Antonio— he likes to talk and stuff—he was talking real loud when she was trying to play the CD. So then she just stopped and looked at him and shouted, "SHUT THE FUCK UP!" The whole class just got real quiet. We didn't know what to do. So then there was this white girl in the class who also talked a lot. So then she started talking. Then Ms. Fox just lost it. She yelled at the whole class, "I SAID SHUT THE FUCK UP." She then slammed the CD player on the desk and stormed out of the room. When she came back in the room, she said that she had to walk out of the classroom because she lost her cool and had to curse. She said that she had to go to the office, but then looked back as she was walking, and she had a smile on her face. So then we found out that she was suspended for a week from school. She told us before she left that she was under a lot of stress because her stepfather or somebody was sick, but I ain't buying that. She deserved whatever she got.

Although the actions in the class may not be understood as a premeditated form of rebellion, once the students found a method that would potentially provoke Ms. Fox, they fully rose to the challenge. It was clear that Ms. Fox understood the limits to her actions. Following that conversation, Sidney searched me out and, with an indifferent smirk, told me that Ms. Fox had completely changed once her suspension was lifted. She was real quiet and cut out those racial jokes. She even apologized again and said that she was not racist. He confided in me that he still was not buying into her tactics and could not wait to get out of her class.

At this point, I completely understood Sidney's anger, which was further compounded by the fact that according to Sidney, Ms. Fox hated black people. In a hierarchical ranking, he explained, Black students were on the bottom of her list.

So I have to turn in my final assignment for her class and my computer would not allow me to save my work, so I couldn't print out the paper. I went to her, but she wouldn't let me print out the assignment. But then this Latino guy ask her if he could turn in his paper late because he couldn't upload it to the "turnitin.com" site. And she lets him. I couldn't believe it, but that's how she is, just racist.

It would be all too easy to dismiss Ms. Fox as a rogue teacher whose teaching style was indicative of a forgone era marked by blatant racial hostility. However, I found that silencing at CHS took many forms. Although berating students the way Ms. Fox did was abhorrent, just as insidious were techniques that conflated student silence with academic achievement. Such was the case with Mr. Keynes, who barely raised his voice and yet was much more effective than Ms. Fox in removing student agency and power from the classroom.

A key aspect that should not be lost in both Ms. Fox's and Mr. Keynes's ability to enclose upon student action and thought were the firmly established policy directives that had been developed over the course of the previous twenty years. It was not lost upon the students at CHS that going against the grain of a teacher would not only result in a trip to the principal or counselor's office, but face to face with the formal law personnel or campus security who often flexed their power in much more visceral ways than did the formal police. Likewise, it was not lost upon teachers that they had this power at their disposal. Thus, it should not be seen as a surprise that Ms. Fox exhibited the behavior that she did, because not only was there recourse for student complaint, but the current culture of education supports such display of ostentatious disrespect in the education of Black youth. The final two ethnographic segments provide insight into the exact nature of how Keynes and Fox were able to maintain their power. The enclosure of Black youth was reinforced by a two-pronged approach that reified the punitive enclosure of the students. On one hand, the coalescence of the criminal justice and the education system at CHS meant that students could be arrested and charged with "crimes" on the school grounds. On the other was a strategic response to criticism launched at schools such as CHS that had high rates of suspension and expulsion. During my time at CHS, there was a slow push that culminated in schools being rated in part upon the number of suspensions and expulsions that they issued. In response to the exhibiting of "inappropriate behavior," students were sent en masse to in-house suspension, or simply referred to as in-house. During my brief experience while working in the in-house unit, I quickly gleaned that although the critique of suspensions and expulsions was valid, the response by schools such as CHS heightened the enclosure process and reinforced the school's attempt to wield unrestrained power over the students. The result was a system in which students were demeaned, disrespected, and treated with utter disdain under the premise of just punishment.

School Orientation

Given the extreme hierarchal administrative and punitive structure of CHS, the actions of both Mr. Keynes and Ms. Fox could exist only within a space that granted legitimacy to their actions. By the time I had taught in Mr. Keynes's class, I fully understood that not only did the school approve of these methods, but they were tame in comparison to the technologies of repression that were at the school's disposal. During the second week of classes, I quickly learned just how far the school would go to try to control the youth. Assigned a math class that was south of the main administration building, just behind the economics classroom that I had taught in for Mr. Keynes, I found myself in cramped quarters. Running out of room on campus, the school had carved a small niche that appeared to be a former portion of the staff parking lot located in the immediate rear of the campus. A bustling group of tenth-grade students stared at me with a collective eager gaze as I entered the room. Although the students thought I was there to instruct math, I was not teaching anything this morning. Together we were about to learn about the specific type of education that was administered at CHS. After taking attendance for the day, I was charged with accompanying the tenth graders to the school auditorium for orientation. Snaking from the depths of the school's underbelly, one group of thirty students walked from the rear of the school to join the multitude that slowly headed north. Chatting along the concrete path that eventually led to the main administration building, we walked into the general meeting space that could be considered underwhelming at best.

The school auditorium was dimly lit save for a single spotlight that had just enough energy to call attention to the wooden plank stage. Given that the population was well over 2,000 students, such a space seemed better equipped to handle an elementary school rather than the district's only high school. As the mass of tenth-grade students made their way through the spring-hinged seats, a well-dressed, middle-aged white male took the stage. It was clear that he garnered respect from all of the faculty in the room, and his nonchalant attitude indicated that this was not the first time that he had given this speech. Having the build of a former athlete, it was evident that though he still had the same caloric intake, it seemed like it had been a long time since he conducted wind sprints or heard the buzz of a treadmill.

As the students came to comfortable positions in their seats, the presentation began. A projector from the middle of the room kicked into high gear. The ebb of excitement in the room was instantly drained by the words upon the screen: Rules and Regulations. The students who were initially excited about missing class now slowly became withdrawn and almost collectively sunk in their seats.

The middle-aged man introduced himself as the principal and welcomed the students to another year of "learning and excitement." The only caveat was that success was determined by an ability to follow the rules. What followed was as predictable as watching a bouncing ball come to a slow halt. The students in turn reciprocated the dull intensity in the room by engaging in conversation with their friends. Methodically, the principal went through the list of counselors in the school followed by a brief description of their functions. Just as he got to the last counselor, the students had reached the peak of their attention span and he commanded the students cease all talking.

As he drudgingly made it through his presentation and passed the baton to one of the three assistant principals, the students became restless. The thought of sitting through another ten minutes, let alone another thirty, was a bit much for me. As the assistant principal concluded her presentation, which was relatively brief and covered what classes and tests should be taken for college entry, I was mildly hopeful that the rest of the presentations would not continue in a similar vein.

A woman with a dark brown complexion and long flowing extensions took the stage. I was hoping that her position as a Black woman would provide some connection to the largely Black, Mexican, and Salvadoran student population. I was being a little too naïve . . . for she was the enforcer. Her role as assistant principal was to ensure that all students adhere to the attendance policy. It was clear to me, however, that she was fighting a losing battle. Yet the more intriguing aspect was that it was she, a representative of the state, who willingly presented the policy as a confrontation between the school administration and the students.

From her initial introduction of the attendance policy, it was clear that the students were in fact targets rather than beneficiaries of an educative process. She went through the attendance rates of four other schools in more affluent areas of Los Angeles County and detailed the drastic difference between their attendance rates during the first two weeks of school. What followed as she broached the subject of truancy clearly drew the line between the state apparatus of the school and the objects of oppression: the students.

In a stern and unforgiving voice, she mandated that the students could not be truant to school. She then detailed that at each level of truancy the consequences became increasingly dire. The first offense was an automatic one-hour detention after school whereby students would have to pick up the trash from the school grounds. The next truancy was a mandatory "Saturday School," when students once again had to spend half of the day attending to the sanitary needs of the school. The third offense marked a suspension for the student, and the final offense mandated an intervention by the District Attorney's Office. She then explained to the students that their parents, under penalty of the law, would be charged by the prosecutor's office and the student would be sentenced to Los Padrinos, the local branch of the California Youth Authority. She ended the segment by commenting that the school would be taking a field trip to Los Padrinos in October.

Surprisingly, the students were not the least bit fazed by her threats. As the cadence in her voice began to trail off, the students took their cue and went on with business as usual. Rather than be "scared" by the policy, the students had long since become normalized to the antagonistic relationship between the state and themselves.[29]

The concluding presentation of the afternoon was from a middle-aged Black man who had the expression of "I am the law" written across his hardened muscles and in his intense stare. Wearing a straight-billed baseball hat and transition eyeglasses that had not yet dimmed from brightness of the sun, he marched upon the stage wearing construction boots, a reflective vest, and a serious demeanor. In a very confrontational tone, he barked out, "SB [Senate Bill] 650," and then again, "SB 650." He certainly had my attention. He then explained the grave consequences of SB 650 for the students. Any student or students who have the appearance (not the action, but the appearance of the action) of engagement in a physical altercation are immediately placed in the custody of the school district police. These school district police are actually Los Angeles County deputies whose offices are located between those of the attendance clerk and the principal within the main administration building. The deputy then issues a citation along with a $395 fine. Additionally, the student and his or her parent or guardian have to attend a court hearing and anger management classes—which cost an additional $300. Furthermore, the student must purchase the texts for these classes—yet another $300. Although preventive detention measures are draconian in their nature, SB 650 is representative of a comprehensive policy that simultaneously enacts several state institutions (that is, school, police, courts) upon the youth under the guise of public safety. The presentation concluded and the students were ushered out of the auditorium by class. I walked into the bright sun, not sure what to make of the experience, but I had a sinking suspicion that the orientation was merely a primer for the repressive structures of domination that attempted to limit the actions of these youth.

In-House

Unfortunately, my intuition was proven correct on many occasions during my time at CHS. However, none could have been more poignant than the brief time that I spent with students in the in-house suspension center (IHSC). Adjacent to the auditorium and physically located in the main administrative building, IHSC was prime real estate—in arm's reach of the deputy's office and within very close proximity to the principal's headquarters. Although the physical design of the classroom was representative of the cold harsh confines of prison and jail holding facilities, the more disturbing correlation was the violent, abusive, and inhumane nature of the staff's interaction with the student population.

Upon learning of my assignment in ISHC during the afternoon time slot, I walked into the administration building, where I was told I could find the room. Unaware of its existence, I questioned the administrative assistant as to the room's location. Taking the very short trip across the hallway, I was directed to a door that was located at the northeastern-most location of the school. Crossing along the faded white tile, I walked over to Room 001 without any expectation as to what awaited me. Immediately, two startling images caught my attention. First, not one of the several students in the room spoke, gestured, or even dared to utter an audible phrase as I entered. This was a rarity at County High School, where students generally had something to say at any given moment. The second, but no less troubling image, was the loud phrases that were written in bright red ink across the white marker board: "NO TALKING, NO MOVING, COMPLETE SILENCE." Similar to the eyes of a still portrait that follow the observer across the room, the eyes of the roughly twenty silent, docile bodies followed me as I walked over to introduce myself to the regular "teacher," Mr. Guggiana.

During some part or maybe a steady progression of his entire life, it was obvious that the man's face had been overexposed to the sun. The wrinkles and permanent red markings along the ridge of his cheekbones and beneath his eye sockets erased any true telling of his age. Looking to be in his mid-fifties, the tall, white, strongly built man clearly had mastered the inner workings of his job. Arriving early to the room, he finished typing some words on the computer and glanced in my direction.

"Just go ahead and have a seat and I will be right with you. You are a little early, but that is good. I can finish this and get out of here."

As I placed my day planner, book, and white plastic grocery bag that contained my lunch on the floor adjacent to the chair that I sat in, I was trying to grasp the meaning and purpose of the room that, until that day, I never knew existed. Peering around the room, I noticed that he had almost finished typing.

"Okay, this is what we have. These students here will be leaving at the end of the period." As he pointed to the left column of the sheet that he had, he verified the names of the students with another list.

"So, these students here will be leaving at the end of the period. Now the rest of the students will stay until the end of the day. You can give them a break when the bell rings after lunch to go to the restroom, but other than that they are not to get up or move at all during any part of the day."

His voice remained in a nonchalant tone as he indicated that if I wanted to use the computer, it was at my disposal. "Do you have any questions?" As I signaled that I did not, he resumed collecting some papers and doing some last-minute typing. As I sat and made eye contact with the students in the class, I continued looking around the room trying to figure out what was going on in Room 001. The stale coldness of the room reinforced the general gloom that was floating throughout the space. Four small 2 × 2-foot windows provided the only natural light. Given the fact that the small windows were horizontally arranged directly beneath the ceiling, there was a strong indication that the room had been built to minimize contact with anything that did not have to do with the room.

Instead of natural lighting, the bright ambient glow of florescent lights filled the space. The lights were arranged in distinct quad-style patterns along the ceiling. Their brightness highlighted the stale appearance of the room. The ceiling, walls, floors, and writing board were all adorned in a dull shade of white. As I sat in the chair observing the students observing me, the coldness of the room once again crept upon me. I then noticed that the majority of the students, in particular the girls, were trying to provide themselves with any form of warmth possible. Although some had snuggled their arms within the confines of their shirts, others had bundled themselves in coats and sweaters.

Completely unfazed by the brisk air, Mr. Guggiana turned to me as the lunch period bell rang. "Alright, let's see what we have here." As he uttered those words, I took my little plastic bag that held my cold lunch and moved to a seat closer to Mr. Guggiana.

Checking over the list, he carefully read the names on his sheet as he verified the names on the students' identification (ID) cards. As each student approached, he looked at his or her ID card and then back at them and then at their ID one more time. After going through just about all of the names, he called the name of José Munoz. No one replied. He called again and received the same response. It was at this point that the students responded that he was sleeping in the back. "José!," Mr. Guggiana yelled. Apparently awaken from a dream that had nothing to do with being in this room, José awoke with a dead and confused look upon his face. Quickly realizing where he was, he slowly gathered his belongings and begrudgingly approached the front desk. José took his ID card, gave a cold glare over the room, and left through the door.

As José left the class, Mr. Guggiana informed me that he was leaving and to watch over the class until the security guard came to relieve me. He exited the door and for about five minutes, there was an unnerving silence that moved throughout the room. These brief moments were the testing ground. The students were trying to figure out what type of culture and tone I was going to set in the class. They were hesitant to talk right away because that would break all of the rules all too soon. Yet as the teacher, I did not want to be the first to speak, as that was the common manner in which they interacted with figures of authority on campus.

So I sat there Internet surfing across the *LA Times* website, looking at the "Prep Sports" section. As I perused through the scores of the local high school basketball games, one of the female students decided that it was time to break the silence. Rather than ease into the test, she immediately put the rules of engagement on the line.

"So, how old are you?," she asked. I had received this question quite frequently during my time at County. I had soon figured out that the students wanted to know my age in order to understand the rules of engagement. If I was considered young in their eyes, then they would interact with me in a similar manner that they would with their peers. Given that I looked considerably younger than many of the teachers on campus, it was also a test to figure out whether I was going to be strict in the class.

Realizing that the test had been issued, I responded with a common reply. "Why do you want to know? Do you think I can't teach here?" This achieved two things. The first was to switch the focus from my age and the second was to move the focus onto their own thoughts. Asking my patented question, the young girl responded with a comeback that I was not prepared to answer.

"No it is not that, I just figured that you were young and I couldn't figure out why you would want to teach here." Thinking about her response, it was a deep insight into the psychological violence that takes place at public schools. Although she was clearly articulating that teaching at an institution such as County is not worth the time and energy that teachers get paid, it also tapped into something much more profound. If students understood the school to not be worth teaching at, then what was that saying about their own self-worth and value of education? I was awestruck by the level to which the students were systematically dehumanized by the violent, racist, and oppressive structure of which they were forced to "learn."

Given that I spoke to the young girl, in contrast to the normal instructors of the room, the other students looked to join into the conversation. I asked the young woman why she was in the IHSC. "Because of this girl in my PE [Physical Education] class. We were playing volleyball and she clearly didn't want to play, so she kept messing up for the whole team. So I got upset and cursed her out and the teacher heard and I got sent over here."

Without even having to ask, a young Black woman sitting directly behind her commented with a similar story. As she began to tell the story, the anger in her voice became apparent in her bodily motions. Although her voice became increasingly louder, her body lifted higher and higher until she was almost out of the chair.

Yeah, this school sucks. I am in here because of that racist Mexican woman at the front of the school. Everybody knows that she don't like Black people. So I am coming into school in the morning and the lady says something like "Have a nice day," but you can tell that she is being real fake and don't mean it, so I curse at her. Then I get a referral and am in here.

Amazed by these stories, I almost lost sight of the fact that one of the young women in the front row had raised her hand. Almost shivering, she asked if I could lower the air conditioner temperature in the room. Getting out of my chair, I went over to the thermostat and attempted to change the temperature controls. I could not find any buttons to push and the temperature control device appeared to be locked shut. A young, burly, brown-haired white male sitting near the thermostat spoke up, "You won't be able to change it. It can only be changed from outside of the room."

"What do you mean?," I asked him.

"The only way you can change it," he responded, "is from the district office."

Not wanting to believe that he was right, I tried to twist and prod the gauge open, but could not succeed. I looked back at the young man and told him that he must have been kidding. He just shrugged his shoulders and went about his business of looking straight ahead at the board. As I returned to the desk, I asked him why he was in the class. He responded that he had been truant to school on numerous occasions. Another young lady in the class responded that she had also been truant and that is why she was in the class.

As the members of the class went into explanations as to why they felt they were in the class, I did a silent rough count while they were talking. Of the fifteen students in the classroom, only two of the class participants were in the class for what could be described as violent behavior. Two young women were brought into the class for fighting with one another. Ironically, given that the previous teacher had separated all of the students based upon their ID cards, these two young ladies were within three chairs of one another.

As these young students sat in the class, they simply had nothing to do. The rules of the class were that there was to be no leaving the room, regardless of the reason. Given this fact, if the students did not have their books or assignments with them, then they simply had to sit and just look aimlessly at the white walls that enclosed their existence.

The coldness of the room continued to permeate when one of the students approached requesting assistance with her geometry homework. A young Latina girl with a bright smile and wearing a hopeful look upon her face, she brought her book to the desk where I was seated. Placing the book on the desk, she explained that she needed help with the last few questions of her assignment. Given that I had recently substitute taught for a geometry class, I knew that I could assist the young lady because we had just finished going over the assignment that she was completing in her class. As we went over her first three questions, we were interrupted by a campus security officer opening the door.

As he entered the class, the security officer, a middle-aged Black man, wore a stern scowl that was indicative of his upset disposition toward the spatial arrangement of students in the classroom. He immediately barked out, "Alright, the party is over. Everybody listen up. Ya'll know the drill, everybody to the left side of the class."

As one young lady began to talk, he yelled out, "It is not that type of party. No talking. Everybody to the left." He pointed to the left side of the classroom and all of the students, in a timid and begrudging manner, gathered their belongings and moved toward the door.

The security officer continued. "I want two rows. If you are outside of these two rows, then you are in the wrong seat," he commanded to the students.

The young lady and I looked in amazement as the relaxed demeanor of the room instantly changed. "Alright," he said, "I got it from here."

As I gathered my lunch sack and belongings, he began moving toward the desk. The young geometry student stood before him. "May I help you?," he asked.

"Can you help me with my homework?," she responded.

He looked very perturbed by her question. Then in a very quiet tone, as if it was a secret between them that no one else in the room could hear, he said, "Well normally I don't do this, but if you want I'll let him stay in here and he [referring to me] can help you with your work, but I am not going to help you." Looking confused by his behavior, she stood motionless in front of him.

Having absolutely no patience, he looked at her and, in a verbal manner that implied she did not understand English, he talked in an extremely deliberate and far too loud tone: "YOU HAVE TWO OPTIONS, HE CAN HELP YOU OR YOU CAN GO BACK TO YOUR SEAT!"

At this point, the young woman was completely dumbfounded by the security guard's actions. Her mouth slightly open and her eyes bewildered, the extreme hope that I saw as she approached my desk ten minutes prior had completely vanished. His patience completely gone, the security guard decided to go in for the kill.

In a very powerful and over-the-top tone he yelled at her, "Alright little girl, here it is one last time. You can either get his help or sit down." All of a sudden, his tone completely changed from power to lust and slyness. "Or maybe the two of you guys weren't really doing any work at all." He looked directly at me, then looked back at her and told her to go sit down.

I knew this could not be happening. At that moment, I was filled with a rage, anger, and frustration that I had a rarely felt in my life. This man, who clearly did not care about these students, was inferring that the young woman and I were having some sort of inappropriate, intimate encounter.

Before I could even utter a response, he looked at me and said, "It's too real for the kids. It is just too real." I shook my head at him in disgust and walked out of the classroom.

Unfortunately the situation at CHS was in fact too real. Rather than an isolated incident, the intense level of discipline found in the in-house suspension center was dispersed throughout the school. Perhaps most troubling was the manner in which such incidents unfolded in the day-to-day reality of the "classroom." Counter to the mythology of the classroom as a sanctum of intense learning, it was the first line of defense that sought to rebuff the vast coffers of knowledge that the students brought with them to school.

The containment of such radical thought is the perhaps the ultimate goal of the enclosure process. Viewed from this lens, we can clearly understand that rather than a School-to-Prison Pipeline, the education of Black youth is itself a punitive enclosure. Students are not being trained for prison; rather, as previously documented at CHS and by policy initiatives such as DARE and ACT, Black students have a firm understanding of the technologies of control that we would normally associate with prison. This reorientation of the centrality of the prison regime as the primary enclosure model forces us to shift our gaze away from reformist means to "fix" schools and to address the locus of the problem: the processes of forced enclosure that foregrounded the expansion of prisons and mirror the most draconian forms of prison domination emanate from public education (Sojoyner 2013). Thus, as an aside, the movement to abolish prisons needs also to incorporate the abolishment of the enclosure of public education of Black communities.

Building upon the powerful impact of both policy and direct action in the enclosure of Black freedom, chapter 4 explores the construction of a particular type of Black masculinity. Specifically, the chapter analyzes the enclosure of what is considered proper masculine behavior. Specifically, the problematic assertion of a heteronormative, upwardly mobile, Black masculine subject in contrast to the deviant Black criminal has created a litany of problems within Black communities, the number one being unmitigated violence upon Black women. Further connecting policy to processes of enclosure, the chapter discusses the grave impact that occurs when policy formation becomes wed to gender construction and is utilized as the primary solution.

4

Troubled Man

Limitations of the Masculinity Solution

I have always hated alarms. The jarring awakening from much-needed rest has never sat well with me. Six o'clock in the morning and I was already looking forward to when I could return back to my slumber much later that night. Today was going to be a challenge unlike many others that I had experienced since I began teaching. A longtime family friend who had spent many years in the classroom told me that teaching was a burnout job, and her words were becoming prophetic. Setting aside the creation of lesson plans and grading, which as a long-term roving substitute I did not have much of, the mental energy required to engage 160 fifteen- and sixteen-year-old students during the course of the day is beyond draining.

By the beginning of fifth period, which is right around 1:00 PM, your legs begin to give way to fatigue and you search for any opportunity to relax your weary body. The mind, having been pulled in so many different directions by different personalities in different situations, demands that you close your eyes and allow it to recharge for at least five minutes. Yet you have to summon the energy to teach another group of forty sugar-propelled adolescents who need you to be at your best. As the students trickle into the classroom, bright smiles and the cheerful glee of youth provides needed motivation. Slowly, the sometimes cheesy quotes that you have read on social media memes and greeting cards fill your head: "Be at your best, the children need you." "The children are the future; show them the way." "Be the difference you want in the world." As the last few students make their way through the door, the motivation is working and you can feel a modicum of energy return to your legs. Knowing this is the time for action, you slowly make your way off that stool, chair, or desk that provided that brief moment of comfort. The rest of your body follows, and now that you are upright your mind begins to pick up steam and you know that you have just enough stamina to give these students the best fifty-six minutes of instruction that they have ever had. You know that as soon as the next bell rings, you can find a quiet place to rest and begin the process of decompression. There might be one or two students who stop by after school for assistance, but you look forward to those moments. That is why you got into teaching in the first place—the ability to see that "click" in a student's thought process when you have made the brain stretch that much more. But somehow you have wound up at this point—going over asinine material required for a standardized test that has long since been proven unable to measure anything of substance.

These thoughts pour through my head as I lay in bed in a moment of reflection, and the clanking of the second alarm lets me know that it is now 6:05 AM. I look at my alarm with disdain and a hatred that is at a low simmer, because today is going to be an especially long day. After fifth period, I have to attend a meeting that I have been dreading since the moment I placed it on my calendar. The assistant principal needs help. It seems that in a categorical breakdown of the student test scores, young Black males have consistently performed the worst out of every subgroup on campus. This is particularly troublesome for the assistant principal because, as I have been told, the Black males are bringing down the collective weight of all of the test scores on campus and the school is on the verge of once again falling below the state benchmark. Her job is riding on these test scores, because if the state intervenes and takes over the school, she is more than likely out of a job. Hence, she has scheduled a meeting after fifth period.

The meeting will consist of myself, the assistant principal, and members of an organization that I have been working with that assists Black youth in navigating through school. I am not perturbed about the meeting itself. What disturbs me is that I have a pretty good idea of what is going to take place at this meeting, and specifically what phrases will be uttered in the name of assisting Black males. For a brief moment I consider calling in sick for the day and find comfort in the warmth of my pillow. But alas, I am in my car by 7:15 AM and begin to make my way along the tapestry of freeways that are littered with eighteen-wheeler trucks, SUVs, and school buses. I have the radio tuned to 90.7 FM, a listener-supported news-based station that provides information ranging from presidential campaigns to police abuse at the Los Angeles County jail facility. I often use the tidbits of information as "jumping-off" points for class discussion. Taking in the news, I prepare myself for the extended nature of the day. Pulling into the parking lot, I go through my usual ritual and call upon the ancestors to give me the strength to make it through fifth period. It works, and at the closing bell, I am forced with the reality of having to make my way to the assistant principal's office.

Walking through the long open-aired corridors, the usual fast-paced nature of the school has dramatically calmed down. The vast majority of students have been ushered off campus through the guided surveillance of the on-campus security force. I enter into the main administration building and I see the members of the organization that I have been working with sitting in the lobby waiting for the meeting to begin. The assistant principal comes from around the corner and greets us with a warm smile. She leads us to her office and we sit down for a discussion. "So we have a problem. These Black boys are struggling." She takes out several sheets of paper that contain a range of statistics and bar-graph data. Pointing to the standardized test score section, she states:

> As you can see, over the past five years, the Black male students
> have been doing quite bad. They are doing worse than the ESL
> (English second language) kids. Math, science, history, language
> arts—it doesn't matter—our boys are suffering. I do not know what
> is going on, but we have to do something. This is beyond sad. There
> is not even one Black male who has been eligible to apply to a Uni-
> versity of California or Cal State University school. And you know
> what happens once they get to community college. How many of
> them transfer from Southwest or El Camino into a four-year? It
> is just thirteenth grade. And these kids did not do well in twelfth
> grade, so how are they going to do in an environment that is more
> of the same. We need changes across the board and we need it now.

This is the point where I sense the conversation is about to shift away from education per se and to one focused more on the nature of being a man. And almost right on cue she adds:

> I don't know what is going to happen to all of these boys. I mean,
> these are supposed to be the future leaders of the community
> and they can't score at a proficient level on this test. We have to
> teach these boys what it means to be men. They walk around here

with their pants hanging below their waist, smoking weed and doing everything but what they are supposed to be doing. What happened to all of the real men that would teach these boys how to be men. These boys need some role models to come in and teach them how to become real men. Now I know that most of them are being raised by mothers, aunts and grandmothers who are doing the best that they can, but you and I know that a woman cannot raise a boy to be a man. These boys in here are headed straight for jail if we do not do something. Do you know how many of these boys I have seen everyday? And it is not for letters of recommendation. They are always getting into some kind of trouble. Either the teachers can't control them, or they are not coming to school or they are late and all drugged up when they get here. Straight to jail, if they haven't been there already, straight to jail.

This is where we come in. Because of the low performance on the state standardized test, the state has allocated a pool of funds that can be used to assist students to perform better on the test. In addition to these financial resources, the assistant principal has learned about the possibility of external funding through private philanthropic organizations. She states, "I also know about these grants where Black boys are mentored by strong and successful Black men in order to become men. We can work together and make this happen. These boys need our help." For the next thirty minutes, she takes us step by step through a plan she has created though which the organization would provide college students and recent graduates to serve as mentors and tutors to Black male students at County High. She informs us that she has buy-in from the administration and was given the green light to roll out the program as soon as possible. The program director of the organization informs the assistant principal that she will carefully go over the proposal and get back to her by tomorrow.

We leave the office and make our way to the parking lot. Once there, I ask the question: "So what are you going to do?" The program director replies;

Now Damien, I know how you feel about the whole thing and you know I how feel about all the talk about mentorship. All of these grants on mentorship just want to have you come in, give a talk to some boys and then you have "mentored" somebody. And you know that these boys need more than just some drop-in visitation. They need constant support and nobody has the infrastructure to provide that. We are talking about problems that are much bigger than what is going on here. Stuff that is going on at home, what happens to these kids once they leave here and you and I both know what type of education that they are getting here. I swear I see more police here after school than teachers. And that woman [the assistant principal] knows that her job is on the line. You and I both know that is why she called that meeting. But we have an opportunity and I think we have to run with it.

I get what she is saying. We both understood the realities of the nonprofit world and that windfalls of money don't come knocking at your doorstep everyday. She continued, "But you know that money would really help us and we can really help these Black boys." I felt defeated, in large part because I was exhausted beyond belief, but also because I did not have another solution. I did not have access to a magic money tree and I knew from working with the organization that funding for Black males was laden with all kinds of restrictions and strings attached. I replied with a simple, "I know."

We exchanged good-byes and I returned to my car feeling beat down and wondering how things could be "fixed." The conversation brought to bear a series of ironies. How is it that these Black boys are all failing at school, but they are all that you see on the basketball and football teams? I knew of two young Black men who were on the verge of failing out of school but were stars on the sports teams and were playing every game day. Given that the principal was at one time on the football coaching staff, I wondered whether he was the type of "man" that was supposed to be created. I also knew of another young man who was ostracized by his teammates at the insistence of his basketball coach, who was also a respected man on campus. The student, Rashad, had made a carefully thought-out decision to focus more on his classwork than endure the long hours before and after school required for practice and games. In response, the coach chose to emasculate him through virulent language and used Rashad's decision as a model to showcase of what it meant "not to be a man," but rather a "quitter" (Schnyder 2012). Further, what about all of the money that was going to build a state-of-the-art sports facility while all of these Black males students were supposedly failing at school? I'm sure that if thought of in a collective manner, those millions of dollars could have drastically altered the experience of all Black students at County High School. And why was it that the school security staff was all Black men? In a school that had virtually no Black men as teachers, how did it work out that the entirety of the security staff was Black men? Was this the type of manhood that was to be achieved?

There was also the glaring irony of the role of policy in the education of Black male youth. The buildup of policies emanating from a non-perfunctory, racially coded test-based platform and vicious, draconian discipline measures had effectively situated young Black boys at the bottom rung of the proverbial educational ladder. How was it that the same framework that was utilized to position Black males within such a paradigm was now going to help them achieve? In addition to having an abnormal focus on Black males' behavior, these policy initiates invoked a particular set of middle-class-based norms that denigrated poor and working-class Black people, who made up the majority of the Black population at County High School.

At the time I did not know how to posit an alternative, but I was 100 percent sure that mentorship and "respectable" men teaching boys to become men was not the answer. Nor did I think the problem lay with the alleged fact that "women could not raise boys to become men." The logic in that statement reified the marginal status of Black women within the Black community as, on the one hand, unfit mothers because their inability to parent was the supposed reason for rampant Black male deviance, and, on the other hand, trapped in a gendered position that placed them within the liminal position of having the sole responsibility of rearing the Black youth (that is, nation). To counter such logic, I saw at County High School that the intense focus on Black male behavior obfuscated violence enacted upon Black girls. From witnessing security guards "hit-on" Black girls to hearing from a former security guard stories of sexual assault of Black girls, there seemed to be a blatant denial and omission of the real issues.

There were problems for sure at County High School, but the meeting that I just took part of seemed to add to the façade rather than provide space to critically think of viable solutions. I looked at the clock in the car and was surprised to see that it was almost 5:30 PM. The sheer exhaustion of the day took a toll upon me, and all I could think of was returning to the quiet solace of my bed.

Policy as Gendered Enclosure

The conversation with the assistant principal reflected a drastic change within twenty years in both the attitudes toward Black youth and the means by which solutions were developed. From the 1990s, marked by the Gang Truce, to the middle of the 2000s, the discussion had changed (even within Black communities) from a structural analysis of education to one that placed the locus of blame upon the individualized failure of Black males. Key to the transition was the development and refinement of policy solutions that informed a gendered enclosure model. The gendered enclosure model imposed very strict confines on proper masculine expression and behavior that served to mute multiple forms of oppression experienced by Black women. At the core of gendered enclosures were the utilization of formal (that is, governmental) and informal (that is, philanthropic) policy mandates and recommendations as a means to control and redirect the framing of issues pertaining to race, gender, and sexuality.

Beth E. Richie describes the shift within the discourse as a key component in undermining demands that exposed the root causes of structural conditions such as poverty, racism, and sexism that were key to the buildup of a prison nation.[1] Richie comments, "The disinvestment and subsequent concentration of disadvantage that establish the foundation for the buildup of America's prison nation required the manipulation of the progressive social values that dominated public sentiment in the 1960's and 1970's." Richie adds that in order to achieve this shift in discourse, "the architects of disinvestment strategies needed to refocus the prevailing social analysis of conditions that lead to inequality from blaming structural conditions the ones that focus on individual failure" (Richie 2012, 109).

It is at the point of manipulation and diminishment of Black communal demands during the prison regime that policy became critical to the rearticulation of purported solutions. Controlled either by the financial dictates of philanthropic organizations or the power structure of the state and/or city bureaucratic structure, policy-driven solutions enabled the reproduction of oppressive forms of violence while seeming benevolent. Culling through the social movement literature, Richie states:

> When the goal changes from structural transformation to accessing resources, establishing bureaucracy, or policy reform, the potential for lasting change is threatened. In particular, when social

change movements depend on third parties for financial support, the potential for changing social arrangements is diluted, resulting in factions, co-option, and backlash. Furthermore, work that does not challenge ideological positions and unequal institutional relationships will not lead to structural change. In the end, social movements that do not remain outside of established political mainstream organizations, that do not seek to change society but rather seek assistance from the state in creating a more sympathetic moral version of the current society become static. (Richie 2012, 75–76)

Thus, the articulation of a problematic gendered discourse by the assistant principal is not an isolated incident by a misguided administrator. Rather, her analysis is developed within the milieu of a gendered enclosure model that demands adherence to specific racialized, class-specific, gendered norms. The gendered enclosure model has maintained the legitimacy of these norms by reinforcement of three specific policy driven frameworks that build upon each other. The first has been centering the conversation of societal failure upon an individual ethos and morality claims. Once this framework was established, a path was opened to locate the Black criminal as the core problem of the Black community. Rather than address issues of poverty and resource abandonment, this framework quite simply stated: if you can remove the Black criminal, you can solve the problem of Black communal suffering. The second is the investment into a particular type of respectable, upwardly-mobile, heteronormative, Black masculine subject. The construction of this Black masculine archetype proved valuable in order to counter to the deviant criminal and also provide the perfect "role model" for young Black boys. The third has been the reinforcement of patriarchy through the diminishment and silencing of violence against Black women through emphasis placed upon the supposed needs of Black men. The development of this framework has had devastating impacts upon Black communities; as argued by Richie, counter to popular rhetoric, the construction of the prison regime has not squarely been the burden of Black masculinity, rather it has been built upon violence enacted upon Black women.[2] The subsequent pages in this chapter further expand upon these three frameworks as key contributors to the gendered enclosure model and provide insight into the Black communal movements that the model has attempted to silence.

STPP, Policy, Gendered Enclosure, and the Black Criminal

Given the high rates of incarceration of Black men over the past twenty years, an abundance of solution-oriented briefs, reports and policy recommendations that have emanated from nonprofit, government, and philanthropic agencies directed at the "plight" of Black men.[3] Although explicit focus has been placed upon Black men, during the past ten years there has been an increasing amount of attention paid to the development of young Black boys into proper Black men (Hyman 2007; Toldson 2008). The general logic that undergirds these solutions is twofold. First, situated within a politics of individual respectability, the locus is placed upon training Black boys to become better citizens. The solutions that are generated from this approach include teaching Black boys how to become proper fathers, get jobs, and adhere to the rules of heteronormative behavioral practices. These reformist constructions of Black masculinity are particularly harmful because the implementation of these policies stands in direct contradiction to Black feminists critiques of the capitalism and the construction of masculinity within the framework of a capitalist ethos that propagates violence onto Black women. These critiques are important, because adherence to heteronormative, male-dominant, policy-driven frameworks reproduces gendered and sexual oppression within the Black community.

Second, the construction of Black masculinity through these narratives follows the problematic arc of the School-to-Prison Pipeline (STPP) (NAACP 2011; Office of Juvenile Justice and Delinquency Prevention 2009). As a point of departure, the STPP does not locate the fundamental problem as enclosures of Black people; rather there is an intense focus on how to keep Black youth out of the physical site of the prison. Although the distinction may seem minor, these two frameworks produce totally different forms of analysis and consequently, vastly variant solutions. One major distinction between the two is the manner in which the STPP encapsulates prisons into binaries that reinforce hierarchies of power and difference. Much of the literature and arguments within the STPP pertain to the behavior modification of Black students in an effort to prevent them from having to endure disciplining mechanisms that could potentially lead to their imprisonment. Similarly, there are general calls to equalize the types of punishment that is meted out to students. For example, many of the proponents of stopping the STPP argue that Black students

are overrepresented in categories of harsh disciplining procedures (ranging from suspension to arrest), though non-Black (often white) students
who commit similar types of offenses are afforded options that are much
less punitive in nature (that is, detention, counseling). In order to provide
an analysis of the limitations of the construction of Black masculinity and
policy, it is best to begin here, with the problematic linkages between the
STPP and Black masculinity.

A major problem with policy work pertaining to Black youth in school
is that it is predicated upon binary notions of proper versus improper.
Much of the policy work argues that by changing the behavior of Black
youth, said youth will be saved from the clutches of a harsh disciplining
system and ultimately prison. Yet this discussion is absent of both history
and proper social context. Although the attack upon Black behavior has a
long history dating back to the enslavement of Black people, for the purpose of my argument, the time period of the 1960's is important, as it is the
foundation of the current model of severe policing and violent repression
regarding the education of Black people.

The time period of the 1960s within public education in Los Angeles is
a watershed moment, because in response to Black radical community organizing, policy shifts occur that place police officers on Black high school
campuses throughout Los Angeles (Sojoyner 2013). As stated in previous
chapters, from this moment forward, police officers not only served as
bastions of disciplinary force, but also as educators. Police officers were
instructed to teach Black students how to be proper citizens (that is, docile and subservient) while simultaneously propagating the authority of
the state as the sole dominion of power. That is, the state in the forms
of the criminal justice, judicial and legislative systems, were the proper
and, important, only avenues to garner justice. In this framing, those not
adhering to such a system of justice were not only deemed to be criminal,
but were implicated as being "the problem." Such logic flowed very elo-
quently from President Richard Nixon's vice president, Spiro Agnew, who
blamed the uprisings on college campuses during the 1960s upon Black
radicals (Franklin 2000).[4] Yet, such reactionary posturing revealed the
fragile nature of ideological systems of maintenance that were bursting at
the seams. It is within this context that public education was a key site of
doubling down with counter ideology programming that reinforced binaries of difference. The construction of the criminal in juxtaposition to
the good citizen justified the enactment of racial forms of terror and at-

tempted to shift the conversation from a radical form of democracy back to an Aristotelian democratic tradition that legitimized Black subjugation and demanded docility.[5]

By the 1960s, with the enclosure of Black schools underway, a new ideological model was developed that rationalized the extreme disciplining and surveillance of Black youth. With not so subtle rhetorical devices such as militants, gangs, and terrorists already situated within the lexicon of the Los Angeles propaganda machine, Black youth were firmly positioned as the perpetuators of violence and civic mayhem (Manes 1963; Welfare Planning Council 1961). With each major crisis ranging from the 1965 Watts Rebellion to the 1968 Jefferson Student Strike to the 1969 LAPD attack upon the Los Angeles chapter headquarters of the Black Panther Party, the idea of Black menace was placed into action. These strategies proved to be vital in discrediting the revolutionary roots of Black organizations such as the Crips and the Bloods during the 1970s. Coupled with state intervention via the police infiltration and importation of guns and drugs into Los Angeles, the rhetoric of the violent criminal was dialed up to full capacity. By the 1980s, both Operation Hammer and CRASH, under the guise of ridding the city of gang violence, justified the manner in which violence was meted out against Black Angelinos (Kelley 1996). As stated by Dr. Ernest Smith, who operated public health programs for Black Angelinos, this was not a war on gangs; rather this was a war on Black people (Holland 1995).

It is out of Smith's analysis that we begin to understand the intent of policy. Rather than focusing on the actions of police as the end point of the discussion, there has to be an intense focus on the policy that placed "boots on the streets." My point here is to focus on the manner in which policy was developed *to create criminals.* This becomes very critical as the fissures produced by acts of resistance across Los Angeles within Black neighborhoods and across high schools exposed the illegitimate claims of morality that were being touted by the likes of Presidents Richard Nixon and Ronald Reagan. The reactionary response by state policy was both spectacular and yet, mundane. The first step in this process was to put forth measures that would attack the efforts of Black movements for liberation. The spectacular nature of these policies was marked by the utilization of military grade weapons such as assault tanks and persistent surveillance bus helicopters that patrolled and hunted down Black youth throughout Los Angeles County. The sheer craziness of militarizing Black neighborhoods was noted by Black artists such as Toddy Tee in his 1985 classic Los Angeles anthem "Batterram" and former N.W.A. member Ice Cube's 1993 hit "Ghetto Bird" (Cube 1993; Tee 1985). Toddy Tee commenting on then–Los Angeles Mayor Tom Bradley's endorsement and support of using assault tanks commented, "Mayor of the city, what you're trying to do? They say they voted you in in '82. But on the next term, huh, without no doubt, they say they going vote your jackass out. / Because you must of been crazy or half-way wack to legalize something [assault tanks] that works like that" (Tee 1985). Tee's analysis of Bradley's role in the destruction of Black communities in Los Angeles elucidates the disastrous consequences created by the binary framework of criminal/citizen.

Bradley, elected in 1973, was the first Black mayor of Los Angeles and the second Black mayor of a major metropolitan city in the United States. In the wake of radical actions undertaken by the Black community during the 1960s and 1970s, Bradley has to be understood as a disciplinary force in the lives of the Black community in Los Angeles. I spoke with a Black Angelina woman who as a sex worker had several run-ins with Bradley during his tenure as a LAPD officer and she in no uncertain terms commented, "He [Bradley] was a chicken-shit cop and he was a chicken-shit mayor" (Phyllis Jenks, personal interview with author, July 1, 2005). Although hailed as a peacemaker following the 1965 rebellion and a key political figure that brought the 1984 Olympics to Los Angeles, in reality, Bradley's regime ushered in some of the most violent forms of permanent urban Black repression that the country had witnessed. As stated in chapter 3, the 1984 Olympics provided a perfect backdrop to complete the militarization of Black communities. Given the rhetorical nature of the "War on Drugs," these killing machines became the visual representation of the moniker. Ranging from infrared technology to long-range automatic assault rifles to urban compatible tanks, Black people throughout Los Angeles were under attack from technology developed by a U.S. military apparatus that had spent the better part of the previous forty years perfecting weapons systems during the Cold War.

Although the buildup of the militarization of Black Los Angeles is key, it is necessary to understand the ideological underpinnings of Black repression. It is here where Thomas Bradley became a central figure. Bradley represented and propagated the three-headed hydra of reform, respectability, and policy. As a reformist, Bradley consistently undermined the radical workings of Black organizing. His efforts are best exemplified in his attempted co-optation of the Black youth organization, the CRIPS, during the 1970s. While commonly known as a violent Black youth gang, the history of the CRIPS belies a radical past that Bradley desperately tried to dampen. As told by the writer of the CRIPS constitution, Danifu, the original acronym of the CRIPS stood for Community Revolutionary Interparty Service (Sloan 2005).[6] Trying to get a step ahead of Black organizing, the Mayor's Office offered financial assistance and other resources in exchange that the CRIPS change their mission from revolutionary to reform. According to Danifu, "They [the mayor's office] took the R which was revolution and took that definition off and put reform. You had people coming with programs and trying to teach them [Black youth] that they should be trying to get into the system instead of change the system . . ." (Sloan 2005).

Utilizing the CRIPS as a model, the Mayor's Office became proactive in developing counter-revolutionary, reformist mobilizing by developing organizations whose explicit intent was to deradicalize Black youth. However, part of this reformist agenda was also to construct gangs as the scourge of society, which would both demonize Black youth but also buttress the coffers of the city programs. As told by Amde Muhammad, "Gangs was a proposal. You can make money off of them. The police department got new cars, new computers, new helmets, bigger guns. All of this, gangs was profitable to everybody who dealt with them" (Sloan 2005).[7] In order to ensure the profitability of the gangs, city officials denied access to these government programs to individuals who had a history of radical based politics. In addition, the government granted all funding to reform-based individuals and organizations who either pocketed the money or developed programs that did not address the core issues of worsening economic inequality between Blacks and whites and the removal of public infrastructure (except for forms of policing) from city governance (Sloan 2005).[8] The irony was that without any analysis of the root causes of Black revolt, violence within the Black community worsened while reactionary economic resources were filtered into Black Los Angeles.

The centerpiece of Thomas Bradley's early tenure as mayor was to manage the drastic and swift transformation of industrial South Central Los Angeles. As the majority of working class jobs departed from Black Los Angeles to either the growing white suburbs or out of the country, Black unemployment skyrocketed (Davis 2006; Gilmore 2007). In part, Bradley was pushed forward and elected in order to deal with the ramification of massive Black unemployment, just as Blacks had gotten access to those very jobs. The fear of city leaders and planners during this moment of economic and social crises had to be the rise of radical organizing. Given that the core of Black communal organizing centered on autonomy and internal development, as a strategy, it was incumbent that Black radical thought be made irrational. As stated above, a major aspect of this management process was the intense militarization of Black Los Angeles. However, a more subtle and insidious tenant of this process was the management of a Black middle class that would serve as the ideological and material disciplinary force for the masses of poor Blacks. Following in a long tradition of racial uplift politics, the gendered enclosure model, through education, invoked the construction of a proper type of Black masculine subject who would conform to the parameters of a racial capitalist structure in order to squash the demands of Black communal organizing.

Respectability, Gendered Enclosures, and Radicalism

Similar to the brokering of Black education during post-Reconstruction, Black education became important to the development of class in the midst of crisis. Higher education was used by Black communal groups such as the Black Panther Party to access resources and also recruit Black students into radical forms of communal organizing. As articulated in chapter 3, the state decided in no uncertain terms this had to be stopped. The case of Stanford University exemplified this shift in philosophy. Following the trend of many colleges and universities in the wake of the passage of civil rights and affirmative action legislation, Stanford began recruiting Black students to be in accordance with federal government policy. Drawing Black students from schools located within Los Angeles and Alameda counties, the students brought with them the cultural ethos of resistance and renewal that was prevalent within their neighborhoods during the time. Rather than accepting the educational and social curriculum at Stanford as fact, the newly arrived Black students reshaped Stanford in particular ways. With the establishment of the Black Student Union, the climate at the institution quickly changed. In 1968, at an emergency forum hosted by the school president, Richard Lyman to address issues brought to the fore by Black student organizers, members of the Black Student Union (BSU) interrupted Lyman's speech, grabbed the microphone from the hands of the president, and took control of the meeting. Following the model of organizing that was set forth by communities and neighborhoods that these students came from, the Black students presented a list of demands that included the hiring of more Black faculty, admitting more Black students, and laying the foundation for the establishment of a Black Studies Department under the leadership of the Black radical scholar St. Clair Drake (Phillips 1990).[9]

In line with the political action in 1968, Black students at Stanford set out to develop institutions that would speak truth to power. The Black student newspaper, *The Real News Mutherfucker*, was established in 1969 followed by the Black Student Participation Center in East Palo Alto during the same year and the Committee on Black Performing Arts in 1971. In many respects, 1971 was a pivotal year as Black students proved their effectiveness in organizing. In response to the unjust termination of Sam Bridges, a Black worker at the Stanford Hospital, the BSU formed a coalition with the Latino student organization Movimiento Estudiantil Chicano de Aztlán (MEChA) in protest of the denial of tenure of a Chicano doctor at the hospital. Following a series of sit-ins, protests, and rallies, the hospital administration called in the riot police, who subsequently beat and tortured students with mace and batons (Phillips 1990, 27).

The event led the BSU to issue "Black Reparation Demands" to the Stanford administration. The Demands linked students', workers', and the Black community of East Palo Alto's struggles together against the collective weight of Stanford's flagrantly racist actions. Specifically, the Demands called for the establishment of an Institute for Black Studies that would include an undergraduate and graduate component, a complete overhaul of human resource policies at the Stanford Hospital, endowment divestment from corporations that exploit Black labor in West African countries, and the need for Stanford pay reparations to Black community members in East Palo Alto for gentrification efforts and employment discrimination on the part of Stanford expansion (Phillips 1990, 26).

In response to Black student action, Stanford developed a two-pronged approach to counter Black mobilization. The first tactic was to cut back on funding to Black student organizations throughout the decade of the 1970s, which effectively put the students in a situation of having to increasingly worry more about money than organizing. Second, Stanford fended off the call for the establishment of a Black Studies Institute and left the entity as a program (the distinction is enormous, but for our purpose, as an institutional entity it could not hire faculty nor enroll graduate students). Because of its weak structural status and against the vehement opposition to previous chair, Professor Sylvia Wynter, Stanford was able to subsume the program into a larger "multiculturalisque" department, which removed even more autonomy than the little it was initially granted.

The diminishment of Black studies had a particularly devastating effect upon Black student efforts. First, Black studies was the main organ that connected Black students to organizing within local Bay Area communities and was also proactive in the recruitment of particular types of Black students. Second, Black Studies was one of the lone academic institutional forces that lent its efforts to challenge student efforts ranging from demands to affirmative action adherence to endowment disinvestment from apartheid South Africa. Thus by clipping the wings from the program, the university made genuflections to a developing diversity policy model that stood in direct contradiction to the programmatic vision set forth by St. Clair Drake.

The thrust of the burgeoning diversity policy model was to sprinkle Black and Brown faces throughout the growing chorus of finance and military capital that had gained traction as the economic model of development within the United States and California in particular during the 1970s and '80s. Working in tandem, departments such as political science and economics praised decentralized governance and neoliberal economic plans, while the sciences and engineering departments developed cutting-edge technology to be utilized within an ever-expanding military industrial complex. Recruiters from multinational finance capital such as Morgan Stanley and Goldman Sachs, as well as the private defense sector such as Hughes Aircraft and Boeing, descended upon Stanford into welcoming arms as the university pushed Black and Brown students to further extend the tentacles of U.S. power.

What cannot be forgotten in the aforementioned process is that the demands of the cadre of Black students in the late 1960s and the original formation of Black studies stood in direct opposition to the very education that would come to mark Stanford as innovative and diverse. The key to the subtle yet violent dampening of Black radicalism was the struggle over ideology—a struggle that was waged within the volatile terrain of education. The events that unfolded at Stanford provided a quick glimpse into a larger confrontation that ensued throughout California. Similar models of student action took place across the state, marked by the infamous student and community takeover of San Francisco State University during the 1968–69 academic year. In response to these victories, there was a vicious counter response. UCLA students and Black Panther members

Bunchy Carter and John Huggins were murdered on the campus of UCLA on January 17, 1969, by FBI provocateurs while they were in conversation about the ideological direction of the Black Student Union.[10] The same year, Angela Davis was infamously removed from her teaching post at UCLA. With then–Governor Ronald Reagan leading the mob, he vowed that Davis would never teach again in the University of California system.

The attack upon education within California was key in challenging the formation of an educative system put forth by Black mobilization that demanded a radical democratic rendering of the past and future. Although there was an explicit attempt to silence Black liberation movements, a major component of this strategy was to replace Black radical ideology with a reformist policy agenda that would redefine visions of success. These new visions included the co-optation of small portions of the Black community into management positions of the burgeoning warfare state. This new form of Black leadership, and in particular Black male leadership as exemplified by Thomas Bradley, would function in part to discipline a rapidly growing number of Black poor and dispossessed within in Los Angeles County. Central to this process were the enclosure of radical ideology through removal and the criminalization of dissent. Specifically, the criminalization of dissent as marked by Bradley's tenure would function to legitimate both policing as a natural function within the Black community and utilization of formal channels of the state bureaucracy (that is, policy and legislation) as the only viable solution. The effects of the reformist-led vision of leadership proved too dangerous to the Black community. Following on the heels of the Moynihan Report, this new form of leadership became the centerpiece of a Black masculine reclamation project that further oppressed Black women in order to gain access to power (Hull, Scott, and Smith 1982). Specifically, this enclosure model provided the rationale to round up "nonrespectable," criminal Black males and simultaneously extended the clutches of patriarchy (that is, returning the Black man to head of the household) that effectively silenced serious concerns about rapid rates of violence levied against Black women.

Gendered Enclosures, Policy, and Violence

During a typical fall night in 1988, when the warmth of summer in Los Angeles was replaced by a cool and gentle breeze, Enietra Margette, a young Black mother of two children who had recently separated from her husband, walked toward her best friend's home. Lynda Lewis lived with her husband and children near the intersection of 91st Street and Normandie Avenue. Enietra had made plans with Lynda earlier in the week to attend a party together, and they had decided that the meeting location would be Lewis's home. Making her way down the street, she was approached by the driver of an orange Ford Pinto who asked her if she wanted a ride. Initially rebuffing his overtures, she was intrigued by his charm and verbal wit, and she stayed as he continued to flirt with her. Impressed, she got into the car with him and they drove off through the broad Los Angeles streets. Within seconds, his demeanor changed and he called her by the name of a well-known sex worker in the neighborhood. He then pulled out a gun, shot her in the chest, and sexually assaulted her. Margette blacked out, but was awakened by the flash of a Polaroid camera. Startled out of unconsciousness, she jumped and tried to subdue the man. They struggled and she demanded to be taken to a hospital. The man stopped on a street and beat her repeatedly with the gun before dumping her out of the car and onto the street. Amazingly, Enietra was able to walk back to Lynda's house before collapsing on her porch after no one answered the door. Lynda, thinking that Enietra had decided not to attend the party, went with her husband. Returning home at 1:00 AM, they were shocked to find Enietra battered, bruised, and shot on their doorstep. Via ambulance, she was raced to the University of California, Los Angeles Medical Hospital in Torrance where the doctors were able to remove the bullet from her chest. She remained in the hospital for three weeks as she teetered between life and death. Making a full physical recovery, Enietra was the first and only survivor of a man who systematically hunted and killed Black women throughout South Central Los Angeles from 1985 until 2007.[11] Given the moniker of the "Grim Sleeper," he had been seen only by Enietra, who could provide in-depth detail about him. Yet, similar to the violence against and murders of Black women that had preceded her ill-fated night, the investigation was handled very haphazardly and nothing was uncovered (Pelisek 2009).

Although there have been newspaper articles and television news accounts about the Grim Sleeper, the work of anthropologist Juli R. Grigsby (2014) is the first to provide much-needed detail and theorization that connects issues of race, class, gender, sexuality, conceptions of crime, and violence. Grigsby asserts that there was an eerie normality and particular silence around the death and disappearance of Black women during the late twentieth and early twenty-first centuries in South Central Los Angeles. Silence around the fact that during the 1980s, aside from the killings associated with the Grim Sleeper, more than fifty Black women in South Central Los Angeles, many of whom were sex workers, were killed (Grigsby 2014). Silence around the fact that as crack cocaine hit the streets in Los Angeles, its impact on Black women was most profound. Silence around the fact that as federal and state policy sliced away at much-needed welfare programs, Black women suffered mightily without resources that were critical for daily survival. Silence around the fact even in the midst of cries and pleas of family members to both police and elected officials, the lives of Black women were not taken seriously. Silence made by the rhetoric devices of "welfare queen" employed by presidential candidates that placed a gruesome façade upon the multiple forms of violence that Black women faced. Yet, there is nothing natural about Black women's oppression. A deeper look into the details of the killing of Black women in South Central Los Angeles reveals an intense level of disdain and disregard of Black life that cut along lines of race, gender, and class.

On July 7, 2010, police arrested Lonnie Franklin Jr. at his home on West 81st Street in South Central Los Angeles. Ironically, Franklin Jr. was arrested only after his son Christopher Franklin was booked on illegal weapons charges. Christopher's DNA, after a highly controversial and contested measure of DNA swabbing, proved to be a familial match to the evidence of a string of murders of Black women ranging back to 1985.[12] In a sting operation, the LAPD were able to attain the salvia of Franklin Jr. from a slice of pizza and made a positive match to the murders of ten women. Yet, when detectives searched the home that Franklin Jr. shared with his wife and children, the LAPD came face to face with a troubling reality. Police found more than 180 photos, from a period dating back at least twenty-five years, of primarily Black women in very compromising positions. Unbeknownst to his wife, in the same manner that he had snapped a Polaroid photograph of Enietra Margette in 1988, Franklin Jr. had taken and collected photographs of Black women, many of whom he sexually assaulted and murdered.

The photographs stunned the LAPD. Although they were confident that they could link Franklin Jr. to ten murders that took place between 1985 and 2007, they were overwhelmed by the possibility that he was responsible for the murders of more than a hundred women. Having limited alternatives, the LAPD made a very uncharacteristic move. In an effort to identify the women in Franklin Jr.'s photography collection, the LAPD released the photos to the public in search of answers. In addition to placing billboards in predominately Black neighborhoods within Compton, Carson, Watts, Long Beach, and Los Angeles, the LAPD also released the photos to various news media outlets and relied upon concerned family members and friends for assistance. Very quickly, the number of victims associated with Franklin Jr. jumped from ten to more than forty, with police still unsure as to the total number of Black women who were slain. In 2012, the police turned to social media and released the photos of an additional forty-plus women onto the social media outlet Twitter, hoping to find more clues into the lives of women who were still unaccounted for.

Given Franklin Jr.'s immense photography collection and his apparent hiding in plain sight, two interconnected questions arise: (1) How could more than fifty Black women disappear and/or be killed and the police not uncover anything in the way of leads or clues? (2) How is it that within the Black community, Franklin Jr. did not raise any "red flags" about his violent actions toward women? Although the former question is an all-too-common query that has also been posed by many family members, I focus my argument upon the latter. Through my research in Black Los Angeles, there is a common joke that although everybody in the neighborhood knows who is causing "trouble," the police target their gaze on everybody else.[13] However, in the case of Lonnie Franklin Jr., neighborhood instincts did not identify him as a potential threat to the safety of the community. Living in a close-knit Los Angeles neighborhood for more than fifteen years and being an active participant within the lives of many residents, how could he be so gravely misread? Although an easy response would be that Lonnie Franklin Jr. was some sort of criminal mastermind who understood how to hide his transgressions in a very covert manner, I argue that something much more insidious provided a cloak of anonymity: the powerful interplay between masculine ideology and policy formation. That is, rather than the neighborhood misreading signs, they in fact correctly followed all of the social cues and read Franklin Jr. not as a problem but rather as valued member of the community. These two issues are not inherently mutually exclusive: there are numerous examples of individuals who may "appropriate" resources not merely for themselves but as a means to better their neighborhood. However, there is something particularly problematic with linkage between the assertion of proper forms of masculine performance and gendered forms of violence that go unchecked and unseen.

Upon the arrest of Franklin Jr., many neighbors and longtime friends expressed a sense of shock when the man who they had come to respect was accused of such heinous acts. Franklin Jr. displayed all the norms of proper heteronormative behavior that afforded him immense admiration. Having a background in auto mechanic technology, within the neighborhood Franklin Jr. was known as a "jack-of-all-trades" with cars. According to friend Lydia Kam, who along with her husband lived close to Franklin Jr. for the better part of a decade, "This man was an A-1 mechanic. He didn't make mistakes on how he fixed cars. He was a good man to know" (Watkins 2010). Another neighbor, Eric Robinson, stated, "He was a nice guy. Everyone thought he was nice. He was a real genuine grease monkey for sure—loved them cars" (Simon 2010). Cynthia Robinson, who had been good friends with Franklin Jr. for more than two years, recalled, "The Lonnie that I knew of was a nice guy. He worked on my car maybe three or four times. Every time I'd see him he'd wave" (Simon 2010). Applying the logic of bettering the community through a variety of means, most of his neighbors knew that Lonnie had attained car parts and other items through the informal economy. However, there was also the understanding that the local Black economy was in shambles. In this context, Franklin Jr. was read as continuing in the collective tradition of Black people providing for each other when the official state apparatus refused to give Black people their rightful due. Rather than hoard his talents and goods for himself, Franklin Jr. was lauded for sharing with his neighbors. Beyond working on cars, Lonnie was known as an all-around upstanding man within the community. He brought birthday gifts to elderly neighbors, taught his children the value of hard work, and provided for his family. As stated by neighbor Yvette Williams, "His family didn't want for nothing. No one in the world is an angel. But I could admire someone for taking care of his family and his home" (Becerra and Gold 2010).[14]

Yet, on the flip side of "respectable masculinity" is the construction and maintenance of the feminine—and proper feminine performance. A true embodiment of proper masculinity, Franklin Jr. often spewed unfiltered vitriol about women and specifically women whom he deemed as not upholding specific moral standards. In particular, Lonnie would not hold back his feelings regarding the ills of sex work and that the women who were involved in the profession deserved to die (Watkins 2010). His neighbor, Mark Tribble, commented that Franklin Jr. "would have violent fantasies. He was putting the girls down . . . saying someone is going to kill these girls, saying they were going to end up dead" (Watkins 2010).

It is this aspect of Franklin Jr.'s bold assertions of violence against Black women that is very troublesome. It is alleged that Franklin Jr. had been killing women as far back as 1985 and did so in a very limited geographical and racial scope. Rarely straying beyond a five-mile radius, Franklin Jr. terrorized the lives of Black women with very little intervention from the police. The very convincing and historically informed argument has been made that if the women were not Black, the investigation and public outcry would have been much more pronounced.[15] Adding to this argument was the not-so-subtle framing of sex work as minimizing and in some aspects legitimizing the killing of the Black women. Although the case is now infamously coined the "Grim Sleeper," it is important to note that the original name of the case was dubbed the "Strawberry Murders" (Pelisek 2008). The term *strawberry*, or *berry* for short, is a pejorative phrase used during the 1980s and 1990s to refer to women who traded sex for goods, most commonly drugs.

However, as the pieces came together in the case against Franklin Jr., it became apparent that the women whom he had killed were not a homogenous group. They were students, some held employment in local establishments in the area, some struggled to find work. That is, although some had addictions to drugs and some were sex workers, the women that he targeted represented a large swath of the Black population in South Central Los Angeles. They were mothers, daughters, and sisters. Yet the police in a very dismissive manner disregarded the lives of these Black women. The gendered and sexed ideology that undergirded the "Strawberry Murders" gave the police the leverage to not fully investigate the murders. This was made evident by the harrowing tale of Enietra Margette. Margette's story does not end with her survival, but rather what did not happen once she mended from the physical wounds. It was not until nearly twenty years later that she was contacted by detectives about the case. Following a long hiatus after his attack on Margette, it is alleged that Franklin Jr. resumed his killing of Black women in 2001. In Christine Pelisek's 2009 extensive interview with Margette, it was revealed that she was never questioned by investigators in the connection to the string of murders that had taken place in her neighborhood. Pelisek writes, "In the fall of 2006, Margette, by now a full-time student taking classes at a local college to become a pharmacy technician, was paid a visit by two Los Angeles County Sheriff cold-case homicide detectives who were investigating the shooting death of 22-year-old Lachrica Jefferson in 1988—the same year Margette escaped her attacker" (Pelisek 2009). Pelisek describes how shocked Margette was to learn for the very first time, eighteen years later, about the possibility that she was the intended victim of a serial killer. According to Pelisek:

> The detectives had a possible suspect in mind, and they wanted Margette to look at a "six-pack" of photos to see if any of them resembled the ranting gunman who had shot her inside his tricked-out Pinto so many years ago. They came back to me and said [my assailant had] started back" attacking women again, she says, a look of amazement on her face. Yet until that moment, "no one told me he was a serial killer." For years, she thought she had been attacked by a man confusing her with a local prostitute—a belief that had left her feeling, if not safe, at least not threatened. . . . The feisty lady with the nerves of steel began to think back: Was that stranger on a bus who gave her the creeps years ago the serial killer? What about the day she thought she saw that same man from the bus walking by her and asking, "Do you know me?" She had retorted, with a load of attitude, "Why? Am I supposed to know you?" Would she act that way toward a stranger today knowing what she knows now? (Pelisek 2009)

The case against Franklin Jr. was much more than a botched investigation. There was particular intentionality into why the attacks upon and deaths of Black women were not taken seriously. The 1987 investigation into the murder of Barbara Ware is indicative of the investigators' flippant attitude toward Black women. Police investigators were tipped off about the location of her body by an anonymous caller who provided not only the place, but also the license plate number and type of vehicle that was used by the reported assailant. Equipped with this information, police were able to locate the vehicle, a van belonging to a local church in the neighborhood. The van, still warm to the touch, was found in the parking lot of Cosmopolitan Church located on Normandie Avenue, in the same neighborhood where Black women's bodies were increasingly being found in dumpsters and under mattresses in neglected alleyways (Coolican 2010). Yet the police did not follow up on any of these leads. The police did not question members of the church, of which Franklin Jr. was a member, nor did they take evidence from the van that was used in the killing of Ware.

It is in this regard that the actions of the police have to be understood as something more than merely a botched investigation. These Black women, having been constructed as "strawberries," were read as not upholding the proper moral feminine performance as constructed through a masculine gaze. Further, as argued by Erica L. Williams, the masculine, pornographic sexual gaze upon Black women is always present. Set in Bahia, Brazil, Williams writes that she, as a Black woman conducting fieldwork, was approached on several occasions by men who assumed that because she was a Black woman she was a sex worker (Williams 2013).[16] Rather than an anomaly, Williams details that construction of Black women as sexual objects by male tourists was the norm. Williams's argument can assist us in understanding the masculine construction of Black women in Los Angeles. That is, although the construction of Black women has become integral to the male sex tourist imaginary in Bahia, the construction of poor and working-class Black women in South Central Los Angeles has been constructed within a heteronormative masculine framework of immoral sexual deviance. Thus, regardless if any of the women were actively involved in the sex work in South Central Los Angeles, the fact that they were Black women in South Central Los Angeles placed them in a particular type of deviant sexual norm that then relegated their exploitation as normal.

It was within the commonsense logic of Black women's abhorrent sexual mores that Franklin Jr. was able to operate and kill in such a violent fashion over a long period of time. The ubiquity of this logic was not only found within the inner workings of the police, but also of the media coverage by the likes of the *Los Angeles Times* and CNN, which asserted that the women whom Franklin Jr. killed were "prostitutes" and "lived on the margins of society" (Dolan, Rubin, and Landsburg 2010; Simon 2010). The irony, of course, is that Black women were forced onto the margins of society. What these publications failed to account for were punitive social welfare policies during the 1980s that in conjunction with the withdrawal of the manufacturing sector resulted in a planned model of abandonment that would shake the core of Black Los Angeles (Davis 2006; Kelley 1997). The effects upon Black women were especially devastating. Budgets for clinics that had been established within housing projects throughout South Central Los Angeles and offered vital women's health, prenatal, and pediatric services were cut (Holland 1995). The collapse of these auxiliary clinics in turn placed immense burden upon the primary health care facility in South Central Los Angeles, Martin Luther King Jr.–Charles Drew Hospital. King–Drew (as it is referred to in Los Angeles) did not have the capacity nor was it designed to intake all of the needs of South Central Los Angeles.[17] The closure of clinics and the steady demise of King–Drew was of particular significance given that the withdrawal of the manufacturing sector forced many Black Angelinos and women in particular into low-wage jobs that were not accompanied by health care or retirement benefits (Kelley 1997).[18] Juli R. Grigsby documents that with the collapse of the health care and employment infrastructure within South Central Los Angeles, Black women's overall health fell precipitously. In particular, she notes that Black women's rates of infant mortality, sexually transmitted disease and infections, and forms of cancer mirrored that of women in nation-states that lacked a viable public health infrastructure (Grigsby 2014).

It is within this moment during the 1980s that the influx of crack cocaine within South Central Los Angeles has to be placed into context. Specifically, given the lack of resources for mental and physical health care, Black women in South Central Los Angeles occasionally turned to readily available drugs as a form of self-medication. Yet, unlike the coddling discourse pertaining to white men's illegal utilization of prescription drugs such as Adderall in order to maintain levels of performance in school or maintain their focus in the face of economic crises, Black women were subjected to a harsh rhetoric of moral impurity (Melody 2013; Schwartz 2013). However, what is omitted from such accounts is that Black women did not have access to psychologists or mental health professionals, and when they did it was within the limited scope of government programs that had been drastically cut. Unlike white men with economic and cultural resources, Black women were forced to exist within a drug economy that placed them within continual peril. Given that the drug trade was and continues to be dominated by men, Black women were and are placed in liminal situations. Often relying on abusive male partners or engaging in dangerous sex work, Black women were faced with a cruel duality. Although the policing of sex work explicitly targeted Black women, there were very few formal protections for these same women to guard against violence and abuse by male consumers (Radatz 2009, 1).[19]

This cruel duality women sex workers in Los Angeles experienced was exacerbated once sex work became a target of reform by policy makers and the nonprofit sector. A very telling social fact about the policy is that though it does very little to readdress issues of oppression, it often adds tremendous weight to the burden of the oppressed. In the case of the murders of Black women in South Central Los Angeles, the focus and target soon became Black women themselves. By 2006, the killing of Black women along the Western Avenue Corridor continued at a methodical pace. At the same time, Community Coalition, a nonprofit organization founded in 1990 by U.S. Representative Karen Bass, sought to intervene into the nature of violence and crime of South Central Los Angeles. With a mission to "help transform the social and economic conditions in South LA that foster addiction, crime, violence and poverty by building a community institution that involves thousands in creating, influencing and changing public policy," Community Coalition focused its efforts on the betterment of Los Angeles (Community Coalition 2013).

With an explicit focus upon public policy, Community Coalition forged close relations with the mayor of Los Angeles, city council members, and city planners. Through these relationships, Community Coalition dedicated its staff and resources to lobbying city officials either to enforce already existing public policy or create new policy. In the early 2000s, Community Coalition strategized in earnest to rid South Central Los Angeles of liquor stores, hourly motels, and recycling centers. The rationale espoused by Community Coalition was that a major contributor to crime in neighborhoods throughout South Central Los Angeles were drug users and "prostitution." The aim of their strategy was to focus on the supposed key sites of proliferation of both drugs and sex work. Recycling centers were a target because, they argued, drug users would collect recyclables (that is, plastic bottles, aluminum cans, cardboard, metal) during the day, turn them in to the centers, and utilize the money to purchase more drugs. Liquor stores were key locations for both alcohol and drug transactions, and hourly motels were sites where sex work most frequently occurred (Jeong 2011).

By 2006, Community Coalition had effectively lobbied the Los Angeles City Council and City Planning Office to get policy placed in the voting docket. Liquor stores, recycling centers, and hourly motels were sites of organized Community Coalition-led demonstrations and rallies. By 2008, Community Coalition, in conjunction with City Councilwoman Jan Perry, developed the Nuisance Abatement Ordinance (NAO) that was passed by the City Council. NAO provided the City Council with the legal means to vigorously enforce public nuisance ordinances within South Central Los Angeles (Community Coalition, 2009a; Community Coalition 2009b). Although Community Coalition touted the passage of the NAO as a victory, the on-the-ground reality of the policy was anything but celebratory for the Black residents of the South Central Los Angeles. With the passage of the NAO, the city used its enforcement powers to increase policing of Black communities. As told to me by Ms. Sweet, a longtime resident near the Manchester Square region of South Central Los Angeles, "Before 2008 you would always see people walking up and down Vermont, but after the police came down and starting cracking heads, everybody disappeared." Nat, a seventeen-year-old from the same neighborhood, corroborated Ms. Sweet's account of what took place in 2008: "The police just come down here and do what they want. They will pull up on a group of us and start patting us down for drugs, guns, and everything. As a matter of fact, they took my phone once and just threw it against the ground and broke it, for no reason. But I know why, because they didn't want us taking any pictures or taping what they were doing."

The passage of the NAO had a profound impact upon the Black community, but specifically women sex workers. NAO placed the gaze of police surveillance upon the one place—hourly hotels—that sex workers felt some modicum of safety to conduct business. The irony is that though the stated goal of NAO was to provide safety for the Black community, its passage effectively pushed Black sex workers further into the margins and made them even more vulnerable to either incarceration or brutality at the hands of male clients. It is within the dueling models of community action versus policy intervention relating to the "safety" of Black women that the problematic policy-based initiatives come to fruition.

Specifically, policy-based strategies have to invest and rely upon a politics of masculine respectability in order to have the support of lawmakers and city officials. Such a political stance means abiding by a constructed set of moral standards that have nothing to do with the lived conditions of Black people. Black women in South Central Los Angeles were not being killed because of the presence of hourly motels or liquor stores. Yet, it is easy to rest the blame upon the moral proclivity of Black people in order to avoid addressing the need for radical change. Such posturing is merely a façade that masks the root causes of violence.

An interview with Kusema Thomas, an organizer with Community Coalition, exemplifies the fallacy of moral claims that are inherent within policy-based strategies. Speaking about the need to get rid of "prostitution" and drug use from South Central Los Angeles, Thomas spoke about his vision of the future. He stated, "I grew up here and want to see something different. When I was growing up, it was a community with rich culture with middle-class families. We can go back to that. The 80's changed this neighborhood a lot. Bars were going up around the buildings. There are car alarms. But I believe we can change that" (Jeong 2011).

There are two glaring problems that emanate from Thomas's argument (which replicates the logic of many policy-based solutions). First, the reason that Black middle- and working-class families were able to flourish for a brief moment in time in South Central Los Angeles was the presence of a vast manufacturing sector that had just opened the doors of employment to Black people during the 1960s. However, by the late 1970s, those jobs had either moved out of the country or into the growing white suburban enclaves that sprouted up around Los Angeles (Davis 2006). As mentioned earlier, the removal of an economic infrastructure in tandem with the complete dismantling of the welfare state by Presidents Reagan, George H. W. Bush, and Bill Clinton left the Black community in a state of peril. Analyzing the effect of the dismantling of the welfare state and the buildup of the prison regime, Beth Richie states:

> Criminalization of poor women through welfare reform works in America's prison nation to the extent that women lose their rights to privacy and are forced to make information public that might put them at risk of abuse, they're vulnerable to moral judgments and criminal sanctions because their social position is understood as a part of their moral failing, and then are ultimately left to fend for themselves once they experienced male violence. It is tantamount to policing of woman's obedience to society's gender laws—laws that are part of the broader project of conformity to hegemonic roles—and criminalization of those who threaten or deviate from them. (Richie 2012, 113–14)

Second, there is a hyperbolic tendency to romanticize earlier moments of Black Los Angeles as utopic progress. To the contrary, however, Black Los Angeles was a city built upon strict racial segregation and exploitation (Davis 2006; Johnson 2013). Further, Blacks in South Central Los Angeles throughout the 1950s and '60s wrestled with internal class discords created by the influx of Black immigrants primarily from Texas and Louisiana who were deemed as socially and morally backward for holding on to their southern traditions (Welfare Planning Council 1961; Woods 1998).

Thus, the reason for the decline of Black communities within South Central Los Angeles cannot be attributed to a failing Black morality. Rather, the structural conditions of planned racial and economic segregation followed by the development of economic and social abandonment models are at the crux of the problem. Policy-based strategies relating Black urban communal failures to moral and class norms (such as NAO) must be placed in context of a set of consistent rhetorical, ideological, and applied attacks upon Black communities and specifically Black women. Ranging from the Moynihan Report during the late 1960s and early '70s, to the construction of the welfare queen during the 1980s and early '90s to the dominant narrative of sexual deviancy embodied by the black prostitute during the late 1990s into the 2000s, the locus of the blame has been placed upon the dysfunctionality of Black women.[20] At the core of these policies is the legitimatization of the masculine subject through the denigration of women. Although the Moynihan Report and the archetype of the welfare queen reinforced the notion that Black women were preventing Black men from taking their rightful place as leaders of the family, "black prostitution" provided for the resurrection of a respectable type of masculine performance in relation to an abhorrent black feminine sexual discourse. The latter is perhaps best understood in the proliferation of nonprofit organizations in Los Angeles that have argued for the betterment of the community through a platform of social and economic uplift of Black men. This could only be achieved, however, through "cleaning up" the community in order to attract large private corporations into the Black community; at the heart of the cleaning-up process is the removal of immoral drift: "prostitutes."

The gross irony that belies the gendered enclosure model is that the lived conditions for Black women have worsened and Black communal support for such strategies has further reproduced Black oppression. Black men who wholeheartedly buy into these policies (and urge Black boys to abide by such logic) fail to understand that the development of such work is rooted in an ideology that willingly exploits the social construction of Black sexual and gender roles in order to legitimate repressive economic and political legislation. For example, the flip side to the construction of the welfare queen was George H. W. Bush's framing of the Black male criminal through the infamous Willie Horton marketing strategy during the 1988 presidential campaign.[21] While the welfare queen functioned as a smoke screen to implement cuts to social welfare, Willie Horton served to undergird the expansion of prisons throughout the United States. Similarly, the Moynihan Report, although attributing matriarchy to the demise of the Black family, did not take into consideration the fact that housing projects designed for Black people, such as the Pruitt-Igoe Housing Projects in St. Louis, disallowed Black men from living with their families

(Freidrichs 2012). The failure in the case of Pruitt-Igoe reveals that the economic calamity within Black communities had nothing to do with Black men being "leaders" of their households, but rather that because of social and economic policy, Black families, if fortunate, were reliant upon one source of income. Further, Black families were prevented from accessing government programs (that is, access to home loan programs) to build wealth that would buffer against declines in employment income (Lipsitz 2011; Shapiro 2005).

Perhaps most damning was the fact of the Grim Sleeper case itself. The respectable, policy-driven strategy of Community Coalition paradoxically placed Black women in more harm rather than create safer neighborhoods. Through an intensification of policing and targeting of venues to conduct sex trade, Black women were forced further into the periphery, exactly where their bodies collected behind dumpsters and under dingy mattresses.[22] As a solution, and as argued by Black feminists, we have to look at strategies that place the violence against Black women at the center of the analysis.[23] It has to be a politic that squarely locates the most vulnerable, such as Black women sex workers, at the center of the analysis. Further, as argued throughout *The Color of Violence: The Incite! Anthology* the goal cannot be reform that will ensconce Black people into a repressive system through a series of policy initiatives; rather there must be a politic that seeks to build safer communities by bringing an end to violence against women absent of policy formation that would ensure oppressive tactics such as policing, surveillance, and incarceration (Incite! 2006).

The role of formal policy within the complicity of Black oppression is not a new phenomenon. Rather, it has a long historical past that is tied to the expansion of the U.S. nation-state. The next chapter takes a look at both the historic and current manifestations that utilize rationales emanating from the logic of policy initiatives and economic reasoning to enclose the education of Black people. Beginning in the nineteenth century and building up to the current moment, the chapter traces the genealogy of contestation of education as a central tool for Black community building and organizing.

5

By All Means Possible

The Historical Struggle over Black Education

I can remember hearing the continual inflections from family members: "Education is key." "With an education, you can do what ever you want." "Without education, you have nothing." The goal was always to improve and do better than the previous effort. Seemingly, the impetus behind the drive for education was to secure a job that meshed with my passion but also was "good"—code for a job that paid well, had health benefits, and provided some sense of long-term economic security. Just as I embarked upon maturation into young adulthood, I was made privy to a bit of family history that countered these notions of education and job security. Specifically, it detailed the journey of my mother's father. Eugene Williams had been reared just outside of Houston, Texas, in the same ethos stressing the importance of education. He received his master's degree in education from Prairie View A&M and became an instructor at a Black teaching college in Houston. However, after he and his wife moved with their children to Los Angeles in 1943, because he was Black, he could not find employment as a teacher at any local colleges or universities, nor within the secondary education system of Southern California. Determined to find employment, he settled into a job at one of the few places that was hiring Black workers: the post office. Although the position had all of the markers of a "good job," Eugene held a strong disdain for the structural processes that led him from teaching at a college to being a mail clerk.

Once I was told the story, rather than being surprised, I understood why my family had kept this seemingly benign story a secret. It flew in the face of the ideological thrust that education would ensure and, most important, the autonomy to choose your life's "passion." Rather, the lessons of my grandfather's life spoke to the centrality of race and economics within the U.S. education project.

Counter to the contemporary commonsense understanding of public education as a social good and a structural necessity within the United States, the origins of public education are situated within a jagged landscape representative of many competing interests. Although the ideology that fueled these interests varies (that is, land rights, labor, social mobility), the framing of public education beholds a dialectic contestation between forced dogma and autonomy. With respect to Black people in the United States, the notion of education was in direct opposition to the lustful greed of a predominantly white male landholding base that saw Black bodies as a source of cheap labor and vast exploitation. Contrarily, various manifestations of Black freedom movements have envisioned education as a strategic standpoint to break from the chains of dogged oppression.

Black Education, STPP, and Enclosures

Black education in the United States is rooted within a general historic tension between the libratory desires of Black communities and the attempted reinscription of Black subservience via the economic, political, and gendered demands of a racial capitalist state apparatus. A major failure of the State-to-Prison Pipeline (STPP) discourse is a structural inability to reckon with the historical reality of Black education. Schools and prisons did not spontaneously become a symbiotic phenomena in the latter half of the twentieth century; rather it was a relationship that sprung forth out of the tension marked by advances made by Black freedom struggles. In this context, the prison regime as a model of enclosure was developed from the failure and fragility of previous enclosure models' inability to thwart Black liberation. At the heart of the failure of the STPP model is an analytical framework that positions schools as separate from the political and economic realities that give structure to society as a whole. That is, it falls victim to the upward mobility logic that through reform (primarily discipline reform), education in the United States can be (and perhaps was) a utopic enterprise wherein all students can have an opportunity to learn and become productive citizens. However, a historical mapping of educational enclosures in the United States shows that not only is this impossible, state-based education has been one of the central interlocutors of structural forms of oppression. It is squarely located within the process of planned social dysfunction, so there is no way that education can be analyzed outside of its primary function.

In a departure from STPP framing model, this chapter provides a historical rendering of the political, economic, and racial intentions of Black educational enclosures. Beginning in the nineteenth century and culminating in the present moment, the chapter provides a synthesis of major enclosure models and the Black radical formations of education that they attempted to stop. The history of Black education demonstrates a key facet missing from the STPP literature: perhaps more important than visceral forms of discipline (that is, suspension and expulsions), the pedagogy, curriculum, and economics of Black education are central to the maintenance of the enclosure process. Analyzing the history recenters education within an ongoing struggle to both determine how education is developed and administered and as a key component in Black liberation struggles across the United States.

Industrial Enclosures

The primacy of education has been a focal point of Black existence in the United States. In the post-Emancipation era, the impetus of education has been continuous, and perhaps no footprint in history has loomed larger in the education of Blacks than that of Booker T. Washington. From the establishment of schools to influencing public policy, Washington's effect upon the shape of racial relations in the United States has been immense. More so than any other figure, Washington's life and pedagogical stance embodied the contested relationship between Black freedom and enslavement. In this section, I discuss not only Washington's impact but also key educational movements that his plan attempted to debunk.

Booker T. Washington's philosophy of education, although often situated within a politics of strict segregation, was built upon a complex industrial agenda. Although he (in)famously asserted, "In all things that are purely social we can be as separate as the fingers, yet one as the hand in all things essential to mutual progress," his views of segregation were not solely informed by a policy of strict racial isolation (Washington 1895/2000a, 183). Washington's motive, although assimilated into racial tropes espoused by vocal proponents of white supremacy, was not intended to further shackle Black people to the terror of white hatred. Rather, he strategically attempted to develop an economic agenda that aligned with the needs of a capitalist system in order to address issues of Black employment. The key to this system was a Black industrial school located in the South that would produce future workers.

Modeled after Hampton Normal and Agricultural Institute, Tuskegee Institute was founded in 1881 and became the hub for Black industrial training. It was within Tuskegee that the nuances of Washington's economic and education philosophy become apparent. The ideological framework that governed Tuskegee was located within progressive notions of self-reliance and sustainability. Perhaps there is no better example than the physical development of the school, which was built brick by brick by the students themselves. Additionally, the food supply that nourished the student body was farmed on the campus grounds by the Black youth who traversed across the South to attend the Alabama institution. The majority of the teaching staff was Black, and, given the opportunity, Washington gushed high praise upon their ability and knowledge capacity. Yet the radical potential of Tuskegee was dampened by Washington's immense indebtedness to northern capital.

A strident capitalist himself (as evident when he founded the National Business League in 1900), students at Tuskegee were trained in the industrial arts with the purpose of filling the coffers of northern capital investment. Although the ingenious experiments of Tuskegee's most famed professor, George Washington Carver, are discussed every February during Black History Month, what is not often analyzed is that Carver's lab work (under the direction of Washington) was underwritten and provided needed technology for a lagging white southern industrial economy. Writing about the importance of industrial education, Washington details the connection between Carver and business development:

> One of the most interesting and valuable instances of the kind that I know of is presented in the case of Mr. George W. Carver, one of our instructors in agriculture at Tuskegee Institute. . . . Some months ago a white land-holder in Montgomery County asked Mr. Carver to go through his farm with him for the purpose of inspecting it. While doing so Mr. Carver discovered traces of what he thought was a valuable mineral deposit, used in making a certain kind of paint. The interests of the land-owner and the agricultural instructor at once became mutual. Specimens of the deposits were taken to the laboratories of the Tuskegee Institute and analyzed by Mr. Carver. In due time the land-owner received a report of the analysis, together with a statement showing the commercial value and application of the mineral. I shall not go through the whole

interesting story, except to say that a stock company, composed
of some of the best white people in Alabama, has been organized,
and is now preparing to build a factory for the purpose of putting
their product on the market. I hardly need to add that Mr. Carver
has been freely consulted at every step, and his services gener-
ously recognized in the organization of the concern. (Washington
1907/2000b, 188–89)

This ethos of capitalist development enabled Washington to fund the development of Tuskegee and export the value of Black industrial development throughout the South. Although Washington's philosophy was
just what northern capital needed to extend its tentacles into the South,
Washington understood his mission as assisting the needs of free Blacks.
Importantly, Washington recognized that left to their own devices, former southern planters would reenslave the former slaves. Thus, in order
to counter the planter bloc, Washington looked to the industrial development of the South as a means to provide Black southerners with jobs and
stay out of the clutches of the planters whip. Understanding that advocating for jobs could possibly be interpreted in a threatening manner, Washington was careful to couch his ideas in extreme accommodationist terms.
Speaking before a group that included a number of northern white owners
of capital, in 1895 he stated:

The wisest among my race understand that the agitation of questions of social equality is the extremest [sic] folly, and that progress
in the enjoyment of all the privileges that will come to us must be
the result of severe and constant struggle rather than of artificial
forcing. No race that has anything to contribute to the markets
of the world is long in any degree ostracized. It is important and
right that all privileges of the law be ours, but it is vastly more
important that we be prepared for the exercise of these privileges.
(Washington 1895/2000a, 184)

However, rather than simply cowering to the demand for Black subservience, Washington was slowly setting up his real demand: Black employment. Washington extolled, "The opportunity to earn a dollar in a factory
just now is worth infinitely more than the opportunity to spend a dollar
in an opera-house" (Washington 1895/2000a, 184). It is within this context

that Washington's politics of segregation must be understood as a strategic attempt to attain Black economic security within a very harsh and terroristic white supremacist environment. As a means to achieve this goal, Washington had to navigate a thin line: stroke the ego of white capitalists and to a certain degree the southern planter class, while simultaneously pacifying the radical demands of Black southerners who wanted to form autonomous lives beyond the scope of white control.

His solution: work. In a very cunning manner, Washington attempted to frame the discussion of freedom for the Black South to mesh with the capitalist intent for the New South. He asserted, "A large element of the colored people at first interpret freedom to mean freedom from work with the hands. . . . They naturally had not learned to appreciate the fact that they had been worked, and that one of the great lessons for freemen to learn is to work. They had not learned the vast difference between working and being worked" (Washington 1907/2000b, 188).

In a sleight of hand, Washington appealed to the racist and economic sensibilities of white elites who sought to regain control of Black labor. However, more devastating for the Black south, Washington reinscripted Black sovereignty to the economic demands of white authoritarianism. Immersed within a nonthreatening position, Washington's notion of education began to gain a strong foothold throughout the South as the dominant form of training free Blacks. Yet, though Washington was a deft political tactician who was able to curry favor from powerful members of industry and U.S. House of Representatives, Senate, and Office of the President, he miscalculated the racialized underpinnings of capitalism.

Having a firm foothold within the process of Black education, industrialists turned their attention to southern white schools. White southerners, understanding the power of northern capital, realized that a direct fight against Black education meant being shut out of the new southern economy.[1] As a result, southern state legislatures reshaped white southern education to match the needs of the industrial model. Very quickly, resources that were being sent to Black schools were diverted to white schools. In 1907 Washington himself noted, "It is a fact that since the idea of industrial or technical education for white people took root within the last few years, much more money is spent annually for such education for the whites than for the colored people" (Washington 1907/2000b, 191). This is illustrated in the life of Benjamin Mays, former president of Morehouse College in Atlanta, Georgia. Writing about his educational experience in South Carolina, Mays stated:

> When I started to school at the age of six in 1900, South Carolina spent $6.51 on each white child in school; on each Negro child $1.55. Fifteen years later, in 1915, when I was a junior in high school, my state spent $23.76 on each white child in school as compared with $2.91 on each Negro child. In those years, the dollar increase for the white child was $17.25; during the same period the increase for the Negro child was $1.36. Not until Negroes began to sue in the federal courts was there any appreciable change in this situation. (Mays 1971, 44)

By 1910, industrial education was firmly entrenched within higher education in the United States. With Blacks regulated as second-class citizens within the industrial movement, Washington realized the error in advocating for a segregation-based education strategy. A firm believer in the hierarchal class separation that existed within capitalism, Washington took a tactical risk that he could create institutions within a new industrial economy which would produce a solid Black middle class. What he did not anticipate, however, was that the northern corporations that provided much of the funding for Black education would merely use Black southerners as a means to gain leverage over the southern economy. Once southern states and educational institutions fell to the pressure and genuine possibility of an employed Black laboring class, the investment into the education of the Black South had fulfilled its mission. Washington's plan of a segregated Black America was cracking at the seams. Isolated and on the periphery, Washington realized that Black industrial education would be severely marginalized because of lack of funding and resources that were placed in the hands of white students and laborers. Additionally, with the election of Woodrow Wilson as president, Washington ran into an administration that was unconcerned with the fate of Black labor or education.[2] In a complete shift of position, Washington attacked the very segregated system that he heralded twenty years prior. Washington launched a scathing critique of segregation, outlining six fundamental reasons that segregation was unjust for Black people.[3] He came to the realization that would be echoed by housing rights advocates nearly eighty years later. "The Negro objects to being segregated because it usually means that he will receive inferior accommodations in return for the taxes he pays. If the Negro is segregated, it will probably mean that the sewerage in his part of the city will be inferior; that the streets and sidewalks will be neglected, that the street lighting will be poor . . ." (Washington 1915/2000c, 196).

Although Washington came to understand the folly in his reliance upon northern capital as the major impetus that would deliver Black freedom, he still held tight to the cultural essence of bourgeois capitalism as a means for Black mobility in the United States. Washington focused a hierarchal analysis that connected morality to matters of racial superiority, class standing and economic development.[4] Born out of this logic, Black industrial schools were enclosed within a racial uplift model of success. It is within this elitist framework that the limitations of Washington's philosophy of education and critique of segregation become evident. His inability to move beyond the dangling façade that integrated capital and Black freedom rendered his industrial school movement easily co-opted and ultimately insufficient. It is from this angle that we can understand that Washington's method was subsumed within a larger industrial enclosure model financed by northern capital and importantly, was designed to counter Black communal forms of education that had posed a serious threat to expansion of a racial capitalist state. The next section will discuss these forms and the intimate connection between Black freedom and education.

Radical Black Education

In the pantheons of history, Booker T. Washington's model of education is often written as a successful entry along the trajectory of the Black freedom struggle. His autobiography, *Up from Slavery,* is part of elementary school curriculums across the country and the debate between Washington and W. E. B. Du Bois is misrepresented as a disagreement between industrial training versus a liberal arts-based education. However, an analysis of Du Bois's critique of Washington's philosophy reveals much more than a philosophical scuffle over Black education. Du Bois asserts that the timing of Washington's intervention of an industrial-based education supported by northern capital has to be understood as an effort to prevent the utilization of education as a means to radically change the social structure in the United States. Coming on the heels of Reconstruction, Du Bois argues:

Mr. Washington represents in Negro thought the old attitude of adjustment and submission; but adjustment at such a peculiar time as to make his programme unique. This is an age of unusual economic development, and Mr. Washington's programme naturally takes an economic cast, becoming a gospel of Work and Money to such an extent as apparently almost completely to overshadow the higher aims of life. (Du Bois 1935/2008, 41)

In contrast to a bourgeoisie sensibility, the higher aims of life that Du Bois references hearkens back to a radical epoch marked by the efforts of Nat Turner, Harriet Tubman, and John Brown. During a period emboldened by the organization to achieve Black freedom outside the reign of white terror and protect the sanctity of Black autonomy, Du Bois questioned the timing of Washington's assertion of a Black industrial education that was largely underwritten by northern capital.[5] Further, he positioned Washington's industrial plan outside of the historical and then-contemporary Black freedom struggle. Du Bois's critique breathed life into the trajectory of Black education that was in conversation with ongoing Black freedom movements.

Following Du Bois's lead, it is critical to trace the descendants of a Black education model that was independent of the tentacles of white control. This effort provides needed breadth through which to understand the relationship of current manifestations within public education to Blackness and the continual dialectical struggle between Black people and the various factions that have attempted to limit Black autonomy. Important within this freedom struggle was the work of David Walker, whose *Appeal,* originally written in 1829, issued a scathing critique of white supremacy in the United States. In the opening of his manifesto, Walker states, "The Blacks or Coloured People, are treated more cruel by the white Christians of America, than devils themselves ever treated a set of men, women and children on this earth" (Walker 2001, 2).

In contrast to Washington, who would follow him more than fifty years later, Walker's frank tone and broad condemnation of white terror directly attacked the racialized exploitative ideology at the heart of the capitalist enterprise. Walker connected the economic, political, and social profits gained by whites during slavery to the oblivion of Black humanity. He linked the foundation of the United States to Black labor and set forth a template to analyze the development of racism in the county. Specifically, Walker stated:

> I must observe to my brethren that at the close of the first Revolution in this country, with Great Britain, there were but thirteen States in the Union, now there are twenty-four, most of which are slave-holding States, and the whites are dragging us around in chains and in handcuffs, to their new States and Territories to work their mines and farms, to enrich them and their children—and millions of them believing firmly that we being a little darker than they, were made by our Creator to be an inheritance to them and their children for ever—the same as a parcel of brutes. (Walker 2001, 19)

Walker's work is an important antecedent in the tactical genealogy of the Black freedom struggle. Walker's *Appeal* details the interlocking structures of violence that account for white domination of Black people. As a template, his work laid out an argument tying the privileges attained by whiteness to the multifaceted oppression of Black people. In addition to processes of economic, political, and religious disenfranchisement, Walker argues that education is central to the maintenance of a white supremacist hierarchy as demanded within a capitalist system.

Walker's argument about education is a dual synthesis that details the pitfalls of a capitalist driven educative process while also asserting the importance of education within the Black freedom struggle. With respect to the former, Walker states that it is incumbent upon white slave owners to prevent Black people from learning the basic tenants of education in order that they remain enslaved.[6] Yet, even in the rare instances that Blacks are allowed within spaces of education, he argues that the education they are given is merely a sham that pacifies demands for a true education.[7]

The basis of Black education as argued by Walker is to ascertain the rudiments of grammar, history, science, and math in order to both throw off the chains of oppression and gain an accurate understanding of Africa and Africans outside of the narrow, misguided constructions ushered in with slavery. Walker writes, "When we take a retrospective view of the arts and sciences—the wise legislators—the Pyramids, and other magnificent buildings—the turning of the channel of the river Nile, by the sons of Africa or of Ham, among whom learning originated, and was carried thence into Greece . . ." (Walker 2001, 22). Further, Walker elucidates the threat inherent in the education of Blacks will have upon white control. He asserts:

> For coloured people to acquire learning in this country, makes tyrants quake and tremble on their sandy foundation. Why, what is the matter? Why, they know that their infernal deeds of cruelty will be made known to the world. Do you suppose one man of good sense and learning would submit himself, his father, mother, wife and children, to be slaves to a wretched man like himself, who, instead of compensating him for his labours, chains, hand-cuffs and beats him and family almost to death, leaving life enough in them, however, to work for, and call him master? No! no! he would cut his devilish throat from ear to ear, and well do slave-holders know it. The bare name of educating the coloured people, scares our cruel oppressors almost to death. (Walker 2001, 37)

Situated within a liberation framework, the revolutionary power of education becomes apparent. In general terms, education functions to disrupt three powerful myths that legitimate Black subjugation. First, Walker posits that with an adequate knowledge of African history, Black people in the United States will not accept the fanciful, debasing constructions of Black men and women. Largely developed out of racialized interpretations of the Bible, Walker lays the blame for this racial project at the feet of the white Christian church. Second, Walker points out that slave owners (who funded the development of the Christian church) used these mythical creations as proof for the need to subject Black families to arduous and inhumane labor conditions. Third, Walker anticipates the correlation of freedom with work that will be invoked half a century later. In a critique of the condition of supposed free Blacks, Walker states:

> Look into our freedom and happiness, and see of what kind they are composed!! They are of the very lowest kind—they are the very dregs!—they are the most servile and abject kind, that ever a people was in possession of! If any of you wish to know how FREE you are, let one of you start and go through the southern and western States of this country, and unless you travel as a slave to a white man . . . or have your free papers, (which if you are not careful they

will get from you) if they do not take you up and put you in jail,
and if you cannot give good evidence of your freedom, sell you
into eternal slavery, I am not a living man. . . . And yet some of you
have the hardihood to say that you are free and happy! May God
have mercy on your freedom and happiness!! (Walker 2001, 33–34)

Thus, the power of education becomes evident as it (1) undermines the
ideological construction of Blackness that in turn directly accounts for
the prosperity of the white planter class and simultaneously rationalizes
the enslavement of Africans and (2) asserts that Black autonomy must be
envisioned outside of the capitalist ambitions of Black freedom. Walker's
Appeal was a direct threat to the protection of white supremacy, resulting in his death in 1930, just months after the third release of the *Appeal*.[8]
The *Appeal*'s power as a key libratory antecedent to Reconstruction stands
from its being published more than fifty years prior to Washington's peak
influence. Similar to Reconstruction, it represented the possibility of a
radical democratic process infused into the fabric of the United States.
Just as Walker gave primacy to education as the key component to attain
liberation, a major focus of Reconstruction was the establishment of public education, a policy that originated from the Black freedom struggle.[9]
However, just as the policy was implemented, southern planters and legislators attacked the program with great vigor in an attempt to stop the
passage of a public education measure. In a nuanced critique that inter-
wove the capitalist greed and white male patriarchy embodied by the anti-
education bloc, Black poet, journalist, and abolitionist Francis Ellen Watkins Harper in 1894 issued the following scathing commentary,

Men may boast of the aristocracy of blood, may glory in the aristocracy of talent, and be proud of the aristocracy of wealth, but
there is one aristocracy which must outrank them all, and that is
the aristocracy of character; and it is the women of a country who
help to mold its character, and to influence if not determine its
destiny. . . . In coming into her political estate woman will find a
mass of illiteracy to be dispelled. If knowledge is power, ignorance
is also power. The power that educated wickedness may manipulate and dash against the pillars of any state when they are undermined and honeycombed by injustice. I envy neither the heart nor

the head of any legislator who has been born to an inheritance
of privileges, who has behind him ages of education, dominion,
civilization, and Christianity, if he stands opposed to the passage of
a national education bill, whose purpose is to secure education to
the children of those who were born under the shadow of institutions which made it a crime to read. (Marable and Mullings 2000,
141–42)

The question then begs, Why were the southern planter class and northern
capital so hell bent against the implementation of public education? An
analysis of the Reconstruction time period reveals the strategic attempt to
utilize education as a means to establish Black autonomy and also undo a
structure of economic apartheid levied against poor whites.

Attack of Radical Black Education: Industrial Enclosure Model

In his classic text *Black Reconstruction in America 1860–1880,* W. E. B.
Du Bois argues that the development of public education arose from the
demands of the formerly enslaved and the poor whites. Further, he posits that a state-funded public education program would drastically change
the unbalanced class structure, align the collective economic and political
interest of poor whites and Black people, and provide an entry to attain
autonomy. The white planter and northern industrial bloc fully understood the threat that public education posed to the vast coffers of accu-
mulated wealth. Primarily, it powerfully challenged their ability to extract
massive profits from a wide supply of cheap and available labor.

The trick for the white southern planter class and its collaborators in
the North was to prevent the amalgamation of class and racial interests
among poor whites and Blacks. Within a setting whereby the vast majority
of people were poor, the recreation of whiteness and Blackness was critical to the maintenance of economic exploitation. It was incumbent upon
southern planters to have poor whites adhere to the invented notions of
whiteness and Blackness because the "system was held stable and intact by
the poor white" (Du Bois 1998, 12). Du Bois notes:

Planters formed proportionally quite as small a class but they
had singularly enough at their command some five million poor

whites; that is, there were actually more white people to police slaves than there were slaves. Considering the economic rivalry of the black and white worker in the North, it would have seemed natural that the poor white would have refused to police the slaves. But two considerations led him in the opposite direction. First of all, it gave him work and some authority as overseer, slave driver, and member of the patrol system. But above and beyond this, it fed his vanity because it associated him with the masters. Slavery bred in the poor white a dislike of Negro toil of all sorts. He never regarded himself as laborer, or as part of any labor movement. If he had any ambition at all it was to become a planter and to own "niggers." To these Negroes he transferred all dislike and hatred which he had for the whole slave system. (Du Bois 1998, 12)

Du Bois's analysis brings to the fore that as a matter of ideological acceptance, poor whites, as many northern whites, were invested in the fallacy of the capitalist enterprise and the false lure of exuberant wealth afforded by a plantation lifestyle. The fact of the matter was that the southern planter class did not even recognize the existence of the masses of poor southern whites. As commented by an observer of southern social relations stated, "For twenty years, I do not recollect ever to have seen or heard these non-slaveholding whites referred to by the southern gentlemen as constituting any part of what they called the South" (Du Bois 1935/1998, 26). The majority of poor whites failed to comprehend that the largesse and conspicuous wealth of plantation owners was dependent on southern white poverty (Fogel and Engerman 1974, 171–72).[10] An account of the depths of degradation that poor southern whites faced provides clarity:

Below a dirty and ill favored house, down under the bank on the shingle near the river, sits a family of five people, all ill-clothed and unclean; a blear-eyed old woman, a younger woman with a mass of tangled red hair hanging about her shoulders, indubitably suckling a baby; a little girl with the same auburn evidence of Scotch ancestry; a boy, and a younger child all gathered about a fire made among some bricks, surrounding a couple of iron saucepans, in which is a dirty mixture looking like mud, but probably warmed-up sorghum syrup, which with a few pieces of corn pone, makes their breakfast. (Du Bois 1935/1998, 27)

Yet, the masses of southern whites elected to overlook the matter against the planter aristocracy. In allegiance to an ideological framework that ensnared their humanity, they sought to replicate that same philosophy in the stolen territory of the Western frontier. In a form of protest (and at the urging of plantation owners), poor whites migrated to the west in hopes of fulfilling their own capitalist dream. "In 1860, 399,700 Virginians were living out of their native state. From Tennessee, 344,765 emigrated; from North Carolina, 272,606, and from South Carolina, 256,868" (Du Bois 1935/1998, 28). The movement of white laborers was connected to the economic wealth of the large plantation bloc in the South and an inability to compete with the financial resources at the disposal of rich planters. Although the average wealth of a white non-slaveholding farmer in 1860 was $1,800, the average wealth for a large-scale plantation owner during the same time period was $56,000 (Fogel 1989, 82–83).[11]

However, Du Bois notes that poor whites who fled to the West "demanded not only free soil but the exclusion of Negroes from work and the franchise. They had a very vivid fear of the Negro as a competitor in labor, whether slave or free" (Du Bois, 1935/1998, 28). Not recognizing the power that they had to radically alter the shape of the United States, the further legitimization of a racial capitalism entrapped poor whites, moving out of the grasp of the planter and into the vices of northern industrial capitalists (Fogel 1989, 346–47).[12] Unwilling to fight against the tide of capitalist development, poor whites were merely pawns in a vicious struggle over wealth management.[13]

However, for those who could not or would not to take the westward plunge, life became increasingly difficult in the vicious South. With increased competition in the form of northern capital and rapid transformation of European markets, the planter bloc witnessed a decline in their overall profit margins. Because of their inability or unwillingness to stop the incoming tide of industrial-based capitalism, they sought to squeeze increasing profits out of Black laborers.[14] The logical conclusion of this strategy was the need to reduce the number of poor white laborers in order to ensure greater profit margins in tumultuous economic times. The result was that poor whites became further marginalized and built up increased hatred not toward the planter class but against their working-class counterpart, the Black laborer. Unable to realize the profits that they so desired, both the planter class and impoverished white base turned to the solution that Black workers had known all too well: war.

Although it is understandable why the southern landed class decided to engage in violence against the northern capital interests, the illogical response by poor whites with regard to a dispute between the owners of northern industrial capital and southern planter aristocracy was baffling. Du Bois beautifully provides context to the irony that was the core of the Civil War:

> Up to the time that war actually broke out, American labor simply refused, in the main, to envisage black labor as a part of its problem. Right up to the edge of the war, it was talking about the emancipation of white labor and the organization of stronger unions without saying a word, or apparently giving a thought, to four million black slaves. During the war, labor was resentful. Workers were forced to fight in a strife between capitalists in which they no had interest and they showed their resentment in the peculiarly human way of beating and murdering the innocent victims of it, the black free Negroes of New York and other Northern cities; while in the South, five million non-slaveholding poor white farmers and laborers sent their manhood by the thousands to fight and die for a system that had degraded them equally to the black slave. Could one imagine anything more paradoxical than this whole situation? (Du Bois 1935/1998, 29)

Convinced that the only way to achieve freedom was through capital accumulation and exploitation, poor whites were not able to attain the true essence of freedom. Following the defeat of the South, free Blacks attempted to use Reconstruction as a means to revolutionize social, political, and economic relations. A key component within this effort was the establishment of a free public education system. Crucial to this struggle was the removal of the veil of upward mobility within a capitalist paradigm that poor whites adopted as a social fact. Many poor whites firmly believed education was not a right, but rather a "luxury connected with wealth" (Du Bois 1935/1998, 641). The primary means to attain wealth was through the ownership of land and slaves.[15] However, this logic ran counter to the historic evidence and social reality that Black people firmly understood: the white southern planter bloc was never going to make any concessions to the working class. Rather, whether through physical violence or contractual coercion, the planter bloc's goal was to amass land and labor at

the cheapest cost possible. From the forced removal of indigenous populations, to the forced labor enacted upon Black slaves, to the displacement
of independent white farmers, the southern landowning aristocracy knew
no limits in the quest for economic power.

It was from this vantage point that Black people understood that the
only effective method to address economic exploitation was a direct attack of the landowners' wealth. During Reconstruction, the invocation of
public education enabled this fight to be fought from multiple angles. The
first was the creation of a publicly funded structure that would demand
a radical redistribution of wealth. Southern planters vigorously opposed
being taxed to support public education on the grounds that hard work
alone would allow all white men to gain social, political, and economic
mobility (Du Bois 1935/1998; Foner 2002). However, at the heart of the
ethos of individual uplift was the reality that taxation would prevent the
complete exploitation of workers. In addition to the extraction of labor,
planters wanted to ensure that laborers who toiled in southern soil would
never see substantial economic returns. It is of no surprise then, that in
1851, Virginia spent a grand total of $69,000 on education, which educated
roughly only half the white population of the state (Du Bois 1935/1998).[16]

It cannot be overstated that the southern planter bloc did everything
imaginable to prevent financial resources from being spent on public education. Among other factors, the insistent urging of the planter bloc effectively stifled the education project established by the Freedman's Bureau
during Reconstruction. Although the supposed aim of the bureau was to
prohibit "coercive labor discipline," take up the "burden of black education," "protect blacks against violence," and remove "legal barriers to black
advancement," landowners ensured that the Freedman's Bureau would
never atone for the ills of slavery (Foner 2002, 144). The reality was that
even those who were in charge of enforcing the newly constructed laws
knew the strength of the plantation economy. General William T. Sherman, speaking to the director of the Freedman's Bureau, General Oliver
Otis Howard, informed him, "It is not . . . in your power to fulfill one
tenth of the expectations of those who framed the Bureau. I fear you have
a Hercules' task" (Foner 2002, 143). Prophetic in nature, Sherman's words
rang true; only a dozen bureau agents were assigned to Mississippi, and in
the largest concentration of Black people in the state of Alabama, a mere
twenty agents were instructed to assist the former enslaved (Foner 2002).

As vicious as the planter bloc's response was toward the demands of the newly free Black population and the planters' strident attempts to reinstitute some semblance of the glorious past, they could not match the intensity and desire of northern white capital to transform the South into an industrial utopia. Although southern planters were able to limit the effect of the federal and state governments upon Black education, they could not compete with the deep pockets of their northern brethren. Northern capital realized that southern planters had blocked the traditional government route and in a bold move circumvented the governmental bureaucratic process. Owners of production such as John D. Rockefeller Sr. and George Peabody saw an opportunity to turn Black bodies into a menial labor base in order to expand their capitalist agenda and would not allow southern planters stop them (Watkins 2001). Through corporate philanthropy, Black schools were established. No longer within the realm of public education, private corporate control dictated the parameters of curriculum and instruction. Importantly, given that freedom was intimately tied to labor, Black schools were utilized as instruments to maintain racial order in a changing southern economic climate.[17] During the twentieth century, Rockefeller, Peabody, Peter Vanderbilt, and Andrew Carnegie invested huge sums of money into Black education in the South (Watkins 2001). The establishment of education for Black people ensured their subjugation within a white supremacist logic of social, political, and economic organization.[18]

The result was that this new form of education produced Black students who were caught in a perilous paradox that was untenable at best. On one hand they were being socialized to exhibit and behold particular Western moral sensibilities, cultural norms, capitalist ideologies, and gender roles in order to become citizens of the United States. They were then instructed that these traits and beliefs would uplift the Black race. Yet, the reality was that such training did nothing to assist the plight of Black sharecroppers and domestic workers who occupied the lower rungs of the working-class hierarchy. According to historian and journalist Carter G. Woodson:

> When a Negro has finished his education in our schools, he has been equipped to begin the life of an Americanized or European-ized white man, but before he steps from threshold of his alma mater he is told by his teachers that he must go back to his own people from whom he has been estranged by a vision of ideals which in his disillusionment he will realize that he cannot attain.

While serving his country he must serve within a special group.
While being a good American, he must above all things be a "good
Negro" and to perform this definite function he must learn to stay
in a "Negro's place" (Woodson 1998, 5–6)

It is within this paradox of "mis-education" that the true intent of Black
industrial education became evident. Woodson's analysis provided a bold
critique as to the limits of equating freedom with work, because such an
education agenda presented the Black freedom movement with three obstacles. First, students who matriculated from these industrial schools
were taught to be ideological managers of the masses of impoverished
Blacks who knew that waged labor was a far cry from freedom. In order
to counter the radical demands of Black freedom, it was important to in-
doctrinate a stratum of Black southerners to the strivings of a capitalist
enterprise. Similar to writer Ralph Ellison's depiction of the bifurcation
between Black collegiate students and Black rural southerners in his classic novel, *Invisible Man* (1952), a key part of the educative process was to
further demonize the Black working class as lazy and culturally lacking.

Second, the production of a class of Black people who were married to
the capitalist system created yet another obstacle to dismantle the myriad
of repressive processes that made the allowed for capitalism to be so oppressive. Thus, already faced with a dogged work schedule and the financial exploitation of a sharecropper's existence, there was now a class of
Black southerners who believed that this very system was the key to Black
freedom. For with Black industrial-trained students placed in positions of
leadership and/or power it simply meant the reification of the same oppressive system. Woodson explains:

With "mis-educated Negroes" in control themselves, however, it is
doubtful that the system would be very much different from what
it is or that it would rapidly undergo change. The Negroes thus
placed in charge would be the products of the same system and
would show no more conception of the task at hand than do the
whites who have educated them and shaped their minds as they
would have them function. (Woodson 1998, 23)

Third, the linkage of freedom with work as posited by an industrial education, coercively silenced the one group, Black southerners who, through

firsthand experience, sought to undo the capitalist nightmare. As Du Bois pointed out, impoverished rural whites connected ownership of property (in the broad sense) to advancement in society. Such ownership naturally entailed the ability to hire and exploit labor as a means to advance one's wealth. Former southern plantation owners, while upset by their loss of immense profits and invasion from the North, sought new ways of gaining control of Black labor. Northern capitalists saw the fissure between poor whites and southern Blacks as a golden opportunity to extend industrial development throughout the south. Even liberal northerners who may have been supportive of the abolitionist movement proved that freedom within a capitalist paradigm had limits. Many moved to the South in an attempt to purchase land and teach southern Blacks the "scientific methods of capitalism" that connected freedom to wage labor (Foner 2002, 138). This was evident by a northerner Henry Lee Higginson, who along with family and friends invested $65,000 into a Georgia cotton plantation only to state that uplifting free blacks would be a "long, long struggle against ignorance, prejudice and laziness. . . . It is discouraging to see how . . . much more hopeful they appear at a distance that near to" (Foner 2002, 138).[19] Thus, the only group who opposed the further development of capitalism were Blacks and with the expansion of the ideological apparatus that equated work with freedom, Black labor became increasingly superfluous. The bold irony was that as industrial education became equated with public education, Blacks were no longer needed for the jobs that they were supposedly being trained to occupy. Unlike the resistance applied to the public education model asserted by Blacks during Reconstruction, southern lawmakers were persuaded by northern capital financial power to adopt an industrial public education agenda and thus supplant Black labor with white.[20]

Whereas the southern planter bloc bitterly fought the impending takeover by northern capital, southern state legislators understood that the rules of the game had changed. Southern states slowly began implementing education reforms modeled after the northern corporate philanthropic structure and as such enforced a system of racial, class, and gender hierarchies. In addition, the influence of industrial education reached beyond the scope of collegiate education and into the wells of secondary training. Writing about the 1928 dispute between R. C. Hall, the superintendent of the Little Rock School District, and Edwin Embree, the president of the Rosenwald Fund, Anderson describes how heads of northern capital such as Embree attempted to forcefully implement industrial train-

ing upon Black southerners. When Hall rebuffed Embree's industrial program for Black high school students in Arkansas, Embree replied, "Well,
maybe they don't need a trade school in Arkansas" (Anderson 1988, 208).
However, this was not to say that Embree was going to replace a trade
school with another form of education; rather he was laying out to Hall
that either he accepted the trade school or there would be no school for
Black students in Little Rock. In an analysis of the situation in Arkansas,
Anderson writes:

> Indeed, blacks did not need the type of industrial high school the
> Rosenwald agents had in mind. It made little sense for black pupils
> to spend their time studying to become janitors, porters, chauf-
> feurs, cooks, and laundry women when such jobs did not require
> even an elementary education, not to mention a high school
> education. The Rosenwald Fund did not intend, however, to de-
> velop black industrial high schools that would produce technically
> trained young men and women for skilled jobs or for occupational
> mobility. The fund sought to develop a secondary industrial educa-
> tion that rationalized and reproduced the existing structure of
> "Negro jobs." Hence the philanthropists brushed aside Hall's con-
> cerns and insights and pushed ahead with their plans to transform
> southern black secondary education into a system of training and
> socialization primarily for prospective unskilled and semiskilled
> workers. (Anderson 1988, 208)

The development of a Black menial working-class base through the
structure of public education was solidified within the American system
of governance. Codified under *Plessey v. Ferguson,* Black schools across
the U.S. South were intentionally underfunded in order to maintain the
social reproduction of black labor. Anderson comments:

> By 1930, the ratio of black public high school enrollment to school
> population reached 10.1 percent, and it jumped to 18 percent dur-
> ing the 1933–34 academic year. Even then it was 10 percent or less
> in Alabama, Arkansas, Georgia, and Mississippi. The proportion
> of children enrolled in high school in 1934 was nearly four times as
> great for the white population as for Afro-Americans in Alabama,
> between four and five times as great in Arkansas, Florida, and

Louisiana, and slightly more than five times as great in Georgia and South Carolina. The disparity was greatest in Mississippi, where there were proportionately more than nine times as many white as black children enrolled in public high schools in 1934. Significantly, Mississippi was at that time, the only state in America in which black children constituted the majority of the total secondary school population. By the 1930's therefore, when rural whites, urban working-class, whites, and the children of European immigrants had been brought systematically into the people's "college," black children as a class were deliberately excluded. (Anderson 1988, 188)

The lack of students within the classroom reflected a continued lack of financial support for Black education. During the 1952–53 school year, the year prior to the *Brown v. Board of Education* decision, North Carolina spent an average of $133.87 on each white student in comparison to $126.80 on each Black student. In Mississippi, $98.49 was allocated to each white student and $39.12 to each Black student. Louisiana followed the same trend, with $160.21 provided for a white student and $113.67 for a Black student (Newton and West 1963). Additionally, although the Black community demanded access to a broad liberal arts education curriculum, the northern philanthropic groups who subsidized many of the Black secondary schools intentionally implemented an industrial education in order to prepare Black people for "Negro" jobs (Anderson 1988).

Anderson's point supports Woodson's analysis that the type of education northern capital had in mind for Blacks was intentionally antiquated (in terms of equipment and resources) and underfunded. Woodson commented that "the white man does not need the Negroes' professional, commercial, or industrial assistance; and as a result of the multiplication of mechanical appliances he no longer needs them in drudgery or menial service" (Woodson 1998, 25). In the face of rising inequities in financial expenditures, *Brown* attempted to remedy the situation by placing Black and white students in the same classrooms. Not that most Black people believed that somehow going to school with white people was going to somehow improve their quest for freedom; rather, it was a strategic attempt to funnel the same resources to Black and white students in an equal distribution. Yet similar to the Reconstruction period, another enclosure model countered these efforts. Based upon the logic of massive abandonment, the libratory ambitions of school integration were quickly compromised. The abandonment model was wide in scope as in addition to the removal of direct financial resources (that is, money, loans, grants), it also included the closure of government programs and ardent ideological and fiscal attacks upon the structure of education.

A Changing Enclosure: Abandonment

Although reformist efforts were successful in forcing desegregation of U.S. schools following the *Brown* decision, as I argued in previous chapters, the hegemonic response countered these efforts and incorporated a Black middle class into the larger oppressive structure.[21] The result was Blacks "brought into the fold" of desegregation while, public education as a structure still reflected the racial capitalist logic of the state apparatus that continued to marginalize Black people. This was evident in the continued disparity between Black and white school systems. Erwin Chemerinsky writes that in 1972

> the Chicago public schools spent $5,265 for each student's education, but the Niles school system, juts north of the city, spent $9,371. This disparity also corresponded to race: in Chicago, 45.4 percent of the students were white and 39.1 percent were African American; in Niles Township, the schools were 91.6 percent white and 0.4 percent African American. In New Jersey, largely black Camden spent $3,538 on each pupil, while highly white Princeton spent $7,725. (Chemerinsky 2005, 36)

Given the drastically changing nature of urban economies during this time period (1970s–1990s), public education articulated the needs of the new system of social organization; such a system was largely dictated by the confluence of finance capital and a vast enclosure model to corral Black social, cultural, and political autonomous spaces of freedom. Counter to the logic of the STPP, public education was enclosed prior to the historical explosion of prisons (Sojoyner 2014). Further, public education was a genealogical antecedent that informed the disciplinary, economic, and political processes that were key within the development of the prison regime (Rodríguez 2006).[22] Following the reformist policies during the 1950s and '60s that included government spending on school desegregation and affirmative action programs with respect to higher education, there was a massive counter response by conservative ideologies. As argued by Sidney Plotkin and William Scheuerman, in an effort to establish a new power base, there was a concerted effort to tie moral Protestant work ethic to notions of government spending (Plotkin and Scheuerman 1994). National discourse rapidly changed from addressing acts of racial and gendered discrimination through government programs to the elimination of government programs that promoted a racialized slothfulness. The main conduit by which this discourse gained credibility was through a perceived insistent need to cut taxes. This ideology, which was first adopted by the Republican Party and later utilized by the Democrats, found many suitors within the capitalist elite. Plotkin and Scheuerman detail that in order to increase profit margins, businesses actively aligned themselves with conservative politicians that would implement the reduction of government taxation and regulation. The latter facilitated the shift in labor away from union waged labor to international sites of lower wages. This had a deleterious impact upon Black workers in Los Angeles who were just beginning to enter into positions of skilled manufacturing labor but was the very first labor group to be terminated from employment (Dymski and Veitch 1996).

The combination of nongovernment regulation of the labor market and cuts on taxes virtually removed the minimal gains that Black Angelinos had made during the late 1960s and early 1970s. Plotkin and Scheuerman also describe how the conservative base utilized the Protestant work ethic as a tool to tap into white supremacist conceptualizations of undisciplined Black people taking advantage of hard-earned tax dollars generated by a white middle-class population (Plotkin and Scheuerman 1994). Within this logic, a series of laws and policies were implemented that eliminated federal government funding for social programs and simultaneously decreased wages and benefits. This reduction of federal resources placed an exceeding burden upon states to fund social programs. However, within California, the tax revolt was in full swing, and in order to protect the economic stability of racial enclaves, white Californians voted against their long-term economic interests and with their racial privilege to pass Proposition 13 in 1978 (Davis 2006). Without the assistance of federal or state-level government funding, the economic ramifications extended beyond social programs into other state structures such as education and health and human services. It was within this social, political, and economic milieu that public education in Los Angeles reflected the demands of the state.

Prior to the post-Fordist shift of manufacturing capital in urban industrial centers during the 1970s, several scholars made the point that Black students were systemically funneled into non-college based, vocational educational tracks with the intent to fill the manual labor positions within Los Angeles (Scott and Soja 1996; Wald and Losen 2003). Even students who dropped out of high school could find a well-paying job in the manufacturing industry within Los Angeles (Johnson et al. 1992). However, with the shift of the industrial capital out of Los Angeles, the closure of vocational education programs within public education corresponded with a lack of skilled labor employment. An example of this closure was the current location of the "band room" at County High School that previously housed the now-defunct wood shop class.

With the move of industrial capital signaling a shift away from vocational education projects, a huge void needed to be filled. Within this void, the timing was ripe to incorporate the education demands of the black community.[23] However, the conservative education and public policy in California removed funding from public education within Black communities (Kafka 2005; Plotkin and Scheuerman 1994). This was aided by the racially segregated nature of public education within Los Angeles that followed the 1965 Watts Rebellion. As reported by Gary Orfield, the white flight from communities in Los Angeles and Los Angeles County could be most readily seen within the halls of public schools. Specifically, "all Black-white schools moved toward segregated Black very rapidly" (Orfield 1988, 150).

Realizing the threat of a mass of formally educated Black citizens, the main priority of then-Governor Ronald Reagan was to eliminate the opportunity for Black people to utilize publicly funded education as a tool of empowerment. Roger Freeman, a key educational advisor to President Richard Nixon, was an integral member of Reagan's 1970 reelection campaign. Articulating the economic, political, and social threat that was posed by Black Angelinos, Freeman stated, "We are in danger of producing an educated proletariat. That's dynamite! We have to be selective on who we allow to go through higher education" (Franklin 2000, 6). In immediate response, Reagan completely revamped higher education in California through the implementation of a tuition-based structure for the California State University and California community college systems, which had previously been free of costs for all California residents (Franklin 2000).

The passage of Proposition 13 further weakened the structure of public education because it reduced funding that public schools received via the local property tax base (Orfield 1988). Thus, schools that formerly drew upon the property tax base to provide support now had to rely upon state and government funding for the majority of financial assistance. Given the racial disposition of home values within Los Angeles, Proposition 13 weakened an already fractured structure and placed severe limitations upon predominately Black schools in Los Angeles (Orfield 1988; Shapiro 2005).

It was also within this era that the national focus of education shifted from the educational "equity" that had been the hallmark of President Lyndon Johnson's administration to "excellence." During this shift under President Ronald Reagan, the primary shapers of educational policy had strong ties to big business and were reflected in Reagan's plan with respect to education and the use of Title I funds. Specifically, Reagan had promised during his campaign to completely dismantle the Department of Education and eliminate Title I under the mantra of "shrinking the federal government." Although his plan did not work because of strident opposition from Congress, he was able to shift federal funding away from community-based organizations in Los Angeles (McDonnell 2005; Oliver et al. 1992). These organizations had been critical to the stabilization of the Black community in Los Angeles. Education was particularly affected, given that limited local resources were available as a result of the passage of Proposition 13 and the inability of parents to provide financial resources to public education after the closure of skilled labor industry. However, under Reagan's administration, these organizations were "forced to reduce programs that benefited the most disadvantaged in the community" (Oliver et al. 1992, 364).

Crucial to Reagan's agenda was to make the abandonment model commonsense and normal in order to counter a growing tide of a progressive sentiment that saw the logic in the argument of a platform built upon Black libratory politics. Once this was achieved, the next step was to continually prove that the failure of Black communities was due to intellectual and social ineptness of Black people rather than the structural conditions that produced poverty and imprisonment. This would be achieved by the implementation of a new enclosure model within education, the testing bloc, that would supplant all other curricular modes. The testing bloc would justify Black failure and, combined with the establishment of morality arguments that were described in the previous chapter, would provide a rationale for the expansion of the prison regime.

Establishment of the Testing Bloc as Enclosure

Promoted within the crown jewel of the Reagan administration's education policy, *A Nation at Risk,* (1983) the direction of education policy dramatically changed with the introduction of specific standards required for high school graduation and the introduction of standardized testing for aspiring teachers (McDonnell 2005). The undercurrent that ran throughout these policies was a development of one particular framework that would hold schools "accountable" with respect to attainment of federal funding. Thus, if a school district did not meet particular standards, it could lose access to valuable financial resources. Given the economic recession that affected both state and federal budgets, school districts had no choice but to cower to the demands of the federal government. Anything that was deemed as unnecessary, such as art and music programs, to compete in a new "global economy" were deemed expendable (McDonnell 2005).

Rather than change the course of Reagan, Presidents George H. W. Bush and Bill Clinton intensified this process. As an example, the Clinton administration introduced standardized testing as a measure of accountability for students. His push to reading and math standards assessments continued in the trajectory of streamlining the education process to a barebones model that diminished other forms of learning. As documented by Lorraine M. McDonnell, during Clinton's administration the utilization of student testing was connected to federal funding:

> To receive Title I grants, states were required to submit plans that provided for challenging content and performance standards, state assessments and yearly reports on meeting standards, and provisions for teacher support and learning aligned with the new curriculum standards and assessments. Each section of the Title I law detailed specific requirements. For example, the assessments and reports had to be aligned with the content standards, test at three separate grade levels, be based on "multiple, up-to-date . . . measures that assess higher order thinking skills and understanding," and "provide individual student interpretive and descriptive

reports" as well as disaggregated results at the school level by race, gender, English proficiency, migrant status, disability, and economic status (P.L. No. 103–328, §1111). (McDonnell 2005, 13)

George W. Bush's administration took the testing process a step further with the establishment of No Child Left Behind (NCLB). Specifically, Bush's policies exerted greater influence and control over state and local school districts' implementation of public education. McDonnell further states, "In NCLB, more testing is required, with AYP [average yearly progress] defined more precisely and timelines for meeting state proficiency clearly delineated. NCLB also specifies the conditions under which schools needing improvement are to be remedied and the sanctions that are to be imposed" (McDonnell 2005, 33). Whereas private corporations had gained significant influence since Reagan's administration, (most notably in the development and implementation of state tests), under NCLB, private corporations were now fully incorporated into the daily operation of public education. Most notably, school districts had to meet particular AYP numbers and content standards or face possible reorganization under the direction of federally funded private corporations. As stated within the guidelines of NCLB:

If a school fails to make adequate yearly progress [AYP] for a fifth year, the school district must initiate plans for restructuring the school. This may include reopening the school as a charter school, replacing all or most of the school staff or turning over school operations either to the state or to a private company with a demonstrated record of effectiveness. (U.S. Department of Education 2003)

The explicit policy of NCLB created an educational environment at CHS in which the primary objectives were testing and standards. The collective effect upon the daily practice of learning and teaching was horrendous. Having to abide by an enclosure model that was intended to be punitive rather than instructive, the already tenuous school environment of the late 1960s and 1970s became violate and untenable. In order to provide a thick analysis of the current situation, the next section of the chapter includes ethnographic accounts that demonstrate the absurdity and cruelty of a testing bloc model that is very serious in its intentions.

These ethnographic snapshots of enrichment classes illustrate the effect that the testing bloc model ushered in by capitalists interests has had upon public education and reflects a racialized education structure wherein the absence of a formal employment economy, Black students are deemed expendable.

Enrichment Classes

During my fieldwork at CHS, I had the opportunity to teach courses that were labeled "enrichment" classes. Depending on how a student fared upon the California High School Exit Exam (CAHSEE), he or she may have been placed in either or both of the math and literature enrichment classes. Students were placed in these classes through two different means: either they performed below the proficiency level on a particular section (or sections) of the test or their test scores in middle school indicated that they might not pass a particular section of the CAHSEE.

In addition to taking the CAHSEE, students at CHS had to take part in California's Standardized Testing and Reporting (STAR) program, which was based upon a series of California State Tests (CST). During May of each school year, instruction would cease for a two-week period in order for students to take tests in various core subjects (that is, math, science, language arts). As articulated by the California Department of Education, "Test results are used for student and school accountability purposes" (California Department of Education 2009). Using test score results, each school in California was ranked based upon their AYP score. If a school performed below an assigned standard, then the state had the authority to take control (that is, daily operation, financial management, human resources) of the district.

Math Enrichment: Multiplication Tables

Enrichment classes were taught from a curriculum that focused on the memorization of basic skills. Students spent the majority of their time repeating multiplication tables and completing number sequences. While teaching a math enrichment class, I taught a twelfth-grade senior, Oscar, who told me that he had taken the CAHSEE during each of the past three years but failed to receive a passing score on the math section of the test. I questioned why he thought he was in the class for a third year in a row, and an indifferent "I don't know" was accompanied by a shrug of his shoulders. His response was a very common answer among several of the students who appeared indifferent to the CAHSEE. Although scholars have pointed out that students who receive failing marks in school very often do not attach their self-esteem and self-worth to academic performance, Oscar's reply was indicative of a structural pressure that encourages and fosters disdain for public education (Kohl 1995).

I requested that Oscar come to the whiteboard and fill in the answers to the multiplication chart that the teacher had assigned the students. A very simple task, he carefully wrote in a sequence of numbers with a red dry-erase marker. His fellow classmates, concerned only with the answers, filled in their charts based upon Oscar's responses. After he completed four series, I thanked Oscar and asked him to take a seat. Other students made their way to the board and continued the pattern. Upon reaching the upper echelons of the number pattern, I noticed that student participation declined. This was marked most notably by the fact that the talking level in the room increased while all signs of "work" came to a standstill.

A novice teacher, I searched back through the crevices of my youth and remembered one driving force that kept my attention: competition. Dividing the students into two groups consisting of roughly twelve students each, I gave them an opportunity to fill in the chart in timed conditions to see who could complete the assignment first. Initially I thought the plan worked—students pushed each other to finish in order to become the first group to complete the assignment. Yet, as the numbers reached into the higher levels, the students educated me to the rules of the game. One student was doing the work while the rest merely copied the answers and passed them along to each other. Standing there, it became all too obvious—students were rewarded for compliance, not critical thought. They received grades for turning in the correct answers; the process of reaching the answers was irrelevant and therefore not valued by the students nor the teachers (Kohn 2000). I found the same pattern within the humanities.

English Enrichment: Learning What I Already Know

The long black dials on the black-and-white clock that faced the opposite direction of the V-shaped rows of desks in Ms. Allegro's classroom indicated that it was 2:01 PM. Sixth period was scheduled to begin in seven minutes, and the lesson plan called for students to read short articles that covered various issues from opening an ice cream shop to the impact of small schools upon public education.

Two young Latina female students trickled into the room and immediately took their seats, muttering a quiet hello. As they looked shyly into their notebooks, the silence in the room seemed to elongate the time before the bell rung. Just as the second hand indicated that there were thirty seconds remaining on the clock prior to the bell was to ring, the majority of the students hurried into the room. As they threw their backpacks on their desks and shouted "hellos" and "stop bothering me's" to each other, the bell rang. As if the bell bore no impact upon the beginning of class, the students continued their conversations. I was afraid that the lesson plan was not going to work.

Gathering the students' attention, I explained the lesson plan for today. As soon as the last instruction was given, however, the students immediately returned to their prior conversations. In an attempt to get their interest in the first article on small school learning, I assigned each student a paragraph to read aloud. One student who stuck out in the class was a quick-witted, very sharp, and outright hilarious young Black male, Cedric. Having the "gift of gab," Cedric possessed a vocabulary that was astounding given that he was placed in the enrichment class. As the class progressed, I was struck by his complete mastery of all of the words. It was not just the fact that he knew the words, but he was able to assist other students to learn the words in a manner that was enticing, funny, and clever.

Each student pored through the article, and I was confounded as to why they were in the class. I asked them why they thought they were in the class. Cedric immediately responded, "I don't know, but this class is wack. We don't do anything in this class." I asked them if they had ever heard of the CAHSEE, and all responded with a despondent yes. I then questioned how many had passed the exam. Although some said that they had not taken the test as they were in the tenth grade, others said that they had passed the math section but still had to pass the English section. Rather than an original response, I soon found that students in other enrichment classes had similar attitudes as Cedric and resisted being placed in these courses. The student resistance was informed by the fact that they were both being disrespected and not being taught a skill set that reflected their lived experience. Having the opportunity to teach in Mr. Gomez's math course provided insight into the articulation of student resistance and also the manner in which these courses fostered a culture of discipline against that resistance.

Math Enrichment: Context Clues

Prior to teaching in his class, Mr. Gomez informed me that the students in his enrichment classes were a "handful" and sometimes "out of control." True to his word, the bell rang and the students had no regard for my presence as "teacher" in the room. I understood that students would often attempt to test boundaries with a substitute teacher with the intent of having to do less work in class. However, the situation in the room was organized confusion. Although the assignment called for students to focus their efforts on the multiplication section of the CAHSEE, no one opened any of the provided workbooks.

I took attendance and before I could begin to write an algebraic equation on the white board, a young Latino male roughly half my weight and 6 inches shorter than me threw a crumpled piece of paper at another young student to his left. In response, the afflicted student took the paper and threw it back. When I reprimanded the students about not throwing paper in the classroom, the same young man who threw the first piece of paper picked up a piece another piece of paper and threw it at a young woman in the class. She got out of her seat and hit the same young man. I ran quickly to defuse the situation before it escalated any further.

As I approached the young man, the school policy ran through my head. I was supposed to write a referral for this young man, send him to the principal where he would either have to serve detention or be suspended for an extended period of time. "Why are you harassing her and why are you throwing paper?," I questioned him. His response was curt and straight to the point. "Man do what you got to do. Send me to the office. I don't care. Just hurry up and do it."

Not ready for his response, I gathered my thoughts and told him, "No, that is the easy way out. You will stay in here and you will learn something today."

Realizing that I also had the attention of a young man who was later identified as his best friend, I looked at both of them and asked why they were in the class. Once again, I received the proverbial, "I don't know."

Looking at his friend's notebook I saw images of the rapper Lil Wayne in various magazine cutouts plastered on the front cover. I engaged both young men in a conversation about Lil Wayne and his keen business acuity. Realizing that I had piqued their interest, I shared with them that Wayne lived close to my family in New Orleans. Suddenly, the entire classroom was locked into our conversation. We talked for about ten more minutes about Lil Wayne and his ability to parlay his musical talents into a medium that was enjoyed by masses of people.

Lil Wayne is central to the story of students at CHS because he is one of them. He is the rebel that students pattern themselves after. Roughly the same age, Wayne is the kid that the state of Louisiana and the city of New Orleans intentionally neglected. A young man, he dropped out of school and followed his passion of making music. "Tatted up" all over his body, Wayne is the student who was too small to play sports and did not have any other sanctioned talents to allow him to fit into school. As a result, he rebelled against the system and made his own path. In essence, this represented the feelings and emotions of the vast majority of students at CHS and definitely the students in Mr. Gomez's math enrichment class.

Once the conversation ended, as a class we were able to bridge the economic principals of the hip-hop market to the multiplication tables. After we analyzed how much money was earned through album sales, we then used math to examine the financial exploitation of music artists through an interrogation of percentages, fractions, and ratios. As the students went through the exercise, it was evident that although they had the ability to engage critically with the world, they were not being provided the opportunity to further develop and enhance their skills. It was also revealed that they had a firm grasp on multiplication and that their life experiences had taught them how to apply it to real-world situations.[24] Ironically, counter to notions that the students in these classes were underachieving or low performing, they had mastered the very skills that the tests "proved" they had not.[25] Although the testing bloc adversely affected the students, they were not the only group at CHS who had to deal with the test's ugly realities. The faculty at CHS had to endure the continual questioning of their aptitude as teachers and were under the proverbial gun of a harsh bureaucratic structure.

English Enrichment: From the Teacher's Perspective

One of the teachers who had confided her frustration with the testing system to me was Ms. Allegro, a member of the Language Arts Department who taught twelfth-grade Language Arts and one period of English enrichment. Ms. Allegro's walls were adorned with a wide array of pictures, posters, and cut-out stencils. Walking into her classroom, a casual observer would be hard-pressed to find a spot that was not occupied by artwork from projects assigned during the school year, literature posters that emphasized the importance of reading Shakespeare and other English authors, motivational phrases, pictures of students from the various years that she taught at CHS, and, significantly, paraphernalia that praised student achievement. It was evident that Ms. Allegro read the local newspaper, *The Daily Observer,* for one reason: to find the achievements of her students and post them throughout her class. Primarily focusing on sports, she would change the clippings on a weekly basis to illustrate certain students' achievements.

I substitute-taught for Ms. Allegro on several occasions, and she would talk very frankly with me about her students, the direction of public education, and her family. A dedicated teacher who loved her job, she often emphasized how great her students were. Toward the latter portion of the school year, because of her father's failing health I was called on frequently to substitute-teach for her class. Having aided my grandfather while his mind slowly yet viciously became distorted by Alzheimer's disease, I had great empathy for Ms. Allegro's situation. On one occasion, although I was not scheduled to teach until the mid-morning, I came at the beginning of the school day to relieve Ms. Allegro so she could tend to her father. Surprised to see me she said, "You are not scheduled to come until 11:30 AM, but I am so glad that you are here. You are welcome to stay if you want, the kids will be so happy to see you." She then explained that she and her siblings were splitting duty taking her father to his medical treatments. "I am so glad that you are here. I have so much work to get caught up on before I leave. Do you mind covering periods two and three for me?" Responding that I would, she began to pack up papers that she had to grade for the subsequent periods. As she gathered her materials, she informed me that she had received word that her classroom was not up to standards.

She said that a school district representative had inspected her room and deemed that she did not have enough standards-based material on her walls. "Why does it matter what I have on my walls? An official came to my room and I received notice that I did not have enough of these materials on my walls. Can you believe that? After the first week of class, no one looks at that stuff. Evidently they weren't looking too hard either." She pointed right above the classroom window, and there were the very materials that the officials said were not on display. She continued in a rhetorical manner, "Now what do you think is more important to a student—the amount of standard-based stuff on a wall or to see their own work? Sometimes, these district rules just don't make any sense." Ms. Allegro was reprimanded by the official and written up in the form of a citation that was placed in a larger school report.

The Effect and Intentions of the Testing Bloc

The enrichment classrooms can be seen as a microcosm of the structural effect of testing upon Black students. Rather than encourage critical thinking skills that would provide a platform for educational growth and maturation, the testing regime demands that the teacher (as mandated by the state and school district) give primacy to the answers (McNeil 2000). Alfie Kohn points out that though the official discourse of the state is accountability and assessment, norm referenced tests (NRT), such as those within the Standardized Testing and Reporting program, "cannot tell us— indeed, were never designed to tell us—how much of a body of knowledge a student learned or a school taught. . . . Norm referenced tests are not about assessing excellence; they are about sorting students (or schools) into winners and losers." His argument is made clear with an explanation of NRTs: "No matter how many students take the NRT, no matter how well or poorly they were taught, no matter how difficult the questions are, the pattern of results is guaranteed to be the same: Exactly 10 percent of those who take the test will score in the top 10 percent, and half will always fall below the median" (Kohn 2000, 14).

Students learn very quickly that answers are the key to "success." Kohn insightfully illustrates the inherent flaw within the structure of standardized math tests that place value on the answer:

> An analysis of the most widely used standardized math tests found
> that only 3 percent of the questions required "high level conceptual
> knowledge" and only 5 percent tested "high level thinking skills
> such as problems solving and reasoning." Typically the tests aim
> to make sure that students have memorized a series of procedures,
> not that they understand what they are doing. They also end up

> measuring knowledge of arbitrary conventions (such as the ac-
> cepted way of writing a ratio or the fact that "<" means "less than")
> more than a capacity for logical thinking. (Kohn 2000, 8)

Although testing and preparatory testing material provide students with very limited ability to demonstrate knowledge, they are a product of a structure that is firmly entrenched in the removal of critical thinking that in essence denies the human existence. It is then no surprise when students such as Oscar show very little attachment to a formal education system that has attempted to render him useless and without intellectual capability. This disdain is linked to an experience whereby students such as Oscar understood that the school is a site of oppression rather than learning.

Although students resist such pressure by getting correct answers through mass replication and/or not associating their self-esteem with their academic standing, such actions reproduce their oppressed condition. Receiving failing grades and not passing the CAHSEE serve to reinforce their status as "bad students," attending a bad school, and not graduating.

Within the commonsense understanding of public education, students' worth and value is attached to the grades and scores that they receive (Kohn 2000, 6). If a student or a group of students perform well in school, it is assumed that they worked hard and earned high marks. However, this assumption cloaks processes of racial, class, gender, and sexual subjugation that lie at the root of student academic performance. Testing is the means by which understanding of student achievement or failure has become legitimated within society. As argued by McNeil, "The scores have both a highly individuated effect that ignores the social and collaborative aspects of learning. And yet in the reporting of scores, children are subsumed into depersonalized aggregates" (McNeil 2000, 262). Above all else, testing serves to individualize students as collective failures. A school such as CHS is then understood within the public psyche as a space of incompetent and inferior students. As further proof, the test results published every year in the local newspaper substantiate those beliefs.

Although there is general consensus that testing proves the (in)effectiveness of a school, what is omitted from discussion is that testing prevents Black and Brown students from learning. As an example, the enrichment classes at CHS became sites of teacher frustration and student disengagement. The combination created an environment in which students found it easier to simply ignore the work and some teachers found it less emotionally and mentally draining to force students to do things when they themselves did not see the supposed value of such activities.

On three fronts the enrichment courses were particularly disturbing: (1) students from the middle school level were being tracked into classes that offered no mastery of critical thinking skills; (2) enrichment classes took the place of electives (that is, music, art, drama) that students could take and removed a possible source of attachment and identification with the school; and (3) students in the eleventh and twelfth grades lost the opportunity to take classes that would aid them when applying to colleges and universities. This was of particular importance to students applying to the California State University and the University of California systems, which required specific classes to be completed in order to even apply to their schools. As a result, students very quickly understood that they were not on track to attend college. As argued by Linda McNeil, testing prevents students from graduating and/or entering institutions of higher education and reinforces the education process as an oppressive force with respect to their life opportunities (McNeil 2000, 247).

As standardized testing has increasingly become the sole determinant of success, it has gained top priority within the school budget. Consequently, as California has come under severe budgetary constraints, modes of learning that do not follow the testing paradigm are deemed expendable. Thus, although the school has continued to expand its tutorial programs that are designed to assist students to pass the CAHSEE, the school's music program as articulated to me by the band instructor is heavily underfunded.

The void of student electives and the closure of vocational programs were soon filled by classes focused on passing the CAHSEE. However, the question remains: What are these classes teaching the students to do? Rather intended or not, the real-life consequence of this paradigm is a warehousing effect. Students such as Oscar and Cedric are held within these classes from one year to the next, not passing the CASHEE, which in turn means not graduating from high school.

In addition to negatively affecting students, the testing regime has had profound affects upon teachers. Ms. Allegro's account with respect to the standards is not an uncommon story. The result is that teachers such as

Ms. Allegro "tire of the pressure, the skewed priorities, and the disrespect-
ful treatment as they are forced to implement a curriculum largely determined by test manufactures or state legislators" (Kohn 2000, 27).

The irony of Ms. Allegro's account is that educational researchers have
long proved that teaching standards curriculum based upon standardized
testing has dire effects upon Black students. In 2000, Linda McNeil's study
of testing in Houston, Texas, proved that "once institutionalized, standard-
ization widens educational inequalities and masks historical and persistent inequities" (McNeil 2000, 230). Although teachers worried about in-
spections from officials, students suffered the consequences of completing
mindless assignments that wore down their academic skill set and limited
their opportunities to advance beyond high school (McNeil 2000).[26] The
inequity gap is evident by the dropout rate of Black high school students
in County High School. The dropout percentage of Black high school students declined during the 1990s to a low of 18.5 percent during the 1997–98
school year (California Department of Education 2009). However, since
the implementation of NCLB during the 2000–2001 school year, the dropout rate has increased. The moment the dropout rate between Black students and white students was decreasing, the state implemented NCLB
and the high school exit exam. Consequently, the differential rate between
the two groups once again increased, widening the inequity gap.

McNeil's study also analyzed the relationship between teachers in Houston and the Texas Assessment of Academic Skills (TAAS). She assessed
that, like Ms. Allegro, teachers are severely limited in their ability to teach
critical material to students. McNeil argues:

> The limiting of the role of the teacher in shaping or negotiating
> the course content and the means of assessment causes problems
> beyond deciding what to teach. When their students' learning is
> represented by the narrow indicators of a test like the TAAS, the
> teachers lose the capacity to bring into the discussion of the school
> program, their knowledge of what children are learning. . . . The
> test scores generated by centralized, standardized tests like the
> TAAS, and by the test-prep materials which prepare them for those
> tests are no reliable indicators of learning. It is here where the ef-
> fects on low-performing students, particularly minority students,
> begin to skew the possibilities for their access to a richer education.
> (McNeil 2000, 237)

McNeil's intervention is critical with respect to the teachers at CHS and their inability to move beyond the parameters of standards and testing. Within the structure of the testing regime, this process highlights the ability of the state to control the education experiences of Black students. As McNeil points out, the focus on standards and testing is located within a system of rudimentary and repetitive tasks designed to increase test scores. However, teachers such as Ms. Allegro fully understand that the standards and test alike inhibit "rich" educative processes.

Thus school administrators who are trusted to emphasize the importance of the test are placed in a difficult position, for though they understand the limitations of the tests, their primary objectives are to ensure that students met the AYP and passed the CAHSEE. A complicated position, their role was situated within a liminal space—they were often at odds with both teachers who felt limited by the testing curriculum and students who did not see the value in testing. In addition, they were under tremendous pressure from the school district to increase test scores. While teaching at CHS, I had several conversations with the assistant principal, Ms. Shirley, who vocalized her frustration with the system of testing. Although she had several ideas about how to improve the school, if they did not align with the guidelines of state standards and testing protocol, then they were not going to be funded.

Ms. Shirley's position as a Black woman provided insight into the hegemonic response to the demands made by Black parents and students. The strategic placement of Black people in positions of perceived power served to placate protests and inserted a racialized buffer between the white power structure and the Black community. In particular, when parents at CHS brought issues of racial discrimination to the attention of the school and/or district, they would be told to address the matter with Ms. Shirley, placing her in a tenuous position. Although the school district utilized her to keep a distance between board officials and the radical demands of parents, her primary job capacity as assistant principal entailed discipline and testing. As Chris's (a young Black male at CHS) mother told me, "Ms. Shirley may be Black, but she doesn't do anything for the Black students." Many Black parents believed that Ms. Shirley was concerned only about her own personal advancement. She faced tremendous obstacles, her primary interaction with Black parents and students was interpreted as demeaning while the school district held her accountable for the test scores. Her task was unenviable; educational researchers have proven that because of systematic racial discrimination built into standardized tests, Black students are automatically at a disadvantage (Kohn 2000, 27; Neill and Medina 1989).[27]

The gross irony of Ms. Shirley's position at CHS was that the she was able to attain the title of assistant principal in part because of her extensive professional background, but also because of the historic fight that the Black community waged against white supremacist school systems during the 1970s and 1980s (Anyon 1995). However, in response to the struggle made by the Black community, the state implemented a new regime of compulsory testing that was to be administered by newly hired Black administrators. In effect, the state attempted to defuse a potentially damning blow to racial hierarchies with respect to education—an educated Black population that could not only compete in the labor market but also radically change how the process of education was delivered. As argued by Linda McNeil, testing shifted the "decisions regarding teaching and learning away from communities and educational professionals and into the hands of technical experts following a political agenda to reduce democratic governance of schooling" (McNeil 2000, 10). This agenda was directed against the demands made by the Black community, as made evident by George W. Bush's education advisor while Bush was governor of Texas:

> Now, I'm not against democracy, per se. But when it comes to
> education, it just won't work. What you need in education is
> a power board of business executives—the right people in the
> community—then your board brings in a few experts and the ex-
> perts will advise them on the plan. And then when you have your
> plan, you call the Black ministers in and tell them what you want
> them to do. (McNeil 2000, 268)

In a very shrewd manner, Black administrators such as Ms. Shirley were hired under the guise of integrating public education but were handicapped by the politics of the testing regime and thus could not make substantive changes within schools. As argued by James Anderson and William Watkins, the education of Black people has historically been linked to the needs of white capital interests (Anderson 1988; Watkins 2001). From filling manual labor roles within the Jim Crow South to being utilized as a source of cheap labor in sites of urban industry, Black education was purposefully designed to defeat the best interests of Black people. Yet, Black people have not sat by tacitly and accepted a third-tier position within U.S. society. From Du Bois's critique of the Hampton educational model to the foundation of Morris Brown College by the African Methodist Episcopal Church, Black people have consistently challenged attacks to subordinate their humanity (Du Bois 1973; Morris Brown College 2009).[28]

Given this historic dialectic, it is necessary to bring the conversation back to the shortcomings of the STPP framework. The historical realities of Black education in the United States are critical because not only have they informed education for Black people, but they have become models for maintaining power in the face of severe threats to power structures. The inability of the STPP to deal with this history and embrace the ideological premise of Black radical education as the path to oppose enclosure models has allowed the STPP framework to become severely co-opted and ineffective. In its place, we must further the scope of our debates, dialogues, and framing of the relationship between schools and prisons or we are doomed to replicate the failures endured by Booker T. Washington and educational integration strategies. Rather than seek to become inclusive within a structure intent on reproducing structures of domination, it is key that we look to models that challenge power and demand radical change.

Reading the Past and Listening to the Present

My mother, Eugenia Schnyder, worked as a special education teacher in public schools for more than thirty-five years in Southern California. Teaching predominately Black, Latino, and Pacific Islander students during that time period, she was dedicated to her craft and loved her job. Without failure she would wake up at 5:00 AM every morning, drop my sister and me off at school, and be in her classroom by 7:15 AM. Long after the last bell had rung, you could find my mom at her desk grading papers, going over a student's individualized education program, or meeting with caregivers. She would then come home and spend between one and two hours talking on the phone to parents, grandparents, uncles, aunts, and family friends who were providing for the students in her class. My mother would take the time to make sure that everybody was on the "same page" and was intent on providing the highest level of education to each of her students. In addition to the fact that she is one of the smartest, most caring, and astute individuals that I know, I tell this story about her because of the current climate with education. Across the country referendums have been issued to teachers locating them as the problem of education failure in the United States. Whether it is slick packaging such as the film *Waiting for Superman* or through superfunded legal challenges that seek to end tenure for teachers, the failure of education of primarily poor Black and Brown students had been placed squarely in the lap of teachers. From New Orleans to Chicago to Washington, D.C., to Detroit to Philadelphia to Los Angeles, the model has been to locate the locus of the problem upon one specific collective body—the teachers' union.

The logic is fairly simple: students do not receive a solid education because teachers' unions prevent administrators from excising the bad teachers from schools. Thus, schools are full of underperforming teachers who in turn produce underperforming students. However, harkening back to my mother's experience as a teacher, not only is that rationale oversimplistic, it is sinister. Starting in the middle of the 1990s, my mother

consistently stated that public education and in particular special education was changing. Three things started to happen: First, her classroom
size was slowly getting larger, and increasingly the racial and gendered
composition of her class was young Black boys. Also, the majority of the
students were placed her class for "behavioral problems." A common refrain she would utter was "This is not why I got into teaching." Though she
was glad to teach her students, she also recognized that there were serious
forces at play that were changing the dynamics of her class. Rather than
meet with caregivers, she was now having conversations with police officers and school security. She commented that as the social services that
her students desperately needed were cut, the role of counselors changed
from a focus on guidance to discipline. Additionally she was convinced
that the elimination of music, art, and extracurricular activities would do
nothing but increase student detachment from school and thus legitimate
the supposed behavior issues.

A second major shift occurred at the close of the 1990s and the start of
the 2000s. From that point forward, she would state in some form or fashion that without a serious fight, public education would cease to exist. Not
merely in the sense of public schools, but in the sense that the vast majority of people in the United States were not going to have the opportunity
to become educated. Her foresight into the demise of public education
was through her experience with the explosion of standardized testing.
Rather than an educative tool, she recognized early on that it was a device that could be used to justify the exclusion of certain students (such as
those at her school) from receiving an education. "This is not education,"
she would comment. "We are just training kids to accept failure."

Third, she was convinced that standardized testing did not prove anything other than one could take a test. Her intuition was informed by the
fact that she came from a family of educators. With more than two hundred years of collective teaching experience among her cousins, aunts,
uncles, and father, she knew that something was amiss with this new form
of education that was being thrust upon students and teachers. Her insights were confirmed nationally when the litany of research from across
the country proved the folly of No Child Left Behind and high stakes standardized testing. However, given that many of her colleagues had to spend
hours preparing students to take a test that had no bearing upon a truly
educative process, she questioned the motives behind the demand for testing. Her inquisitive nature pushed her to search for answers. She would

frequently call to inform me when she found a trail of money that connected purported education reform lobbying groups to politicians who strongly advocated for testing and charter schools.

Possessing a passion for history, she insisted that what was happening "did not just take place overnight." She was insistent on reading about the historical development of education in order to understand the current trends. It was during this search that she called me one day informing me that I had to read a book entitled *The White Architects of Black Education* by William Watkins. The title alone grabbed my attention. After reading Watkins's book, I was convinced more than ever that both a close analysis of history and policy were critical to understanding the current reality. His excavation of the motives and ideology that informed the education of Black people post-Reconstruction revealed the fallacy of education as an altruistic apparatus. When read closely alongside articles and historical texts that describe the horrors of convict lease labor, one saw that something profound was taking place. Men such as Andrew Carnegie, who had an enormous economic footprint both in the incarceration of Black people in the South and the education of Black people in the South, were not invested in the "betterment" of Black communities. Rather, through their immense economic fortune they were able to wield power in the form of policy and action in order to maintain a strict form of racial capitalism in the United States that during the time period was under threat by the actions of Black mobilization.

My mother's intuition as usual, was spot on. The path she opened for me sent me culling through the historical record to find out more about the connections among education, Black freedom movements, and formations of state repression. A child of southern migrants to California, from the lived experience of her family she learned to be highly skeptical of the ability of formal policy to bring about social change. Further, from the rigid forms of housing and education segregation in Southern California, she knew that social policy was at play in maintaining forms of racial difference. Starting my own fieldwork at County High School and getting a sliver of what she had experienced during her tenure as a teacher, I was in desperate need to understand what I was seeing. Following my mother's lead, I knew my own research had to be framed at the intersections where history and policy informed contemporary developments. Her insights and subtle nudges proved invaluable as I embarked upon a journey to understand the troubling relationship between schools and prisons.

One of the first historical texts that I turned to in my search for an explanation was W. E. B. Du Bois's classic book, *Black Reconstruction in America 1860–1880*. In *Black Reconstruction*, Du Bois implores his audience to look at two competing visions of what the future of the country could have been at the dawn of Reconstruction. The first was the radically democratic social vision of Black people in their quest to attain liberation from the brutal horrors of slavery. The second was the plan of the planter class that sought to reinscribe Black people back to the land. In a very poetic manner, Du Bois positions two chapters side by side, one entitled "Looking Backward" and the other "Looking Forward." These two chapters provide an analysis of the historical genealogies of these competing visions and what each would entail for the future. Drastically different in scope, Du Bois held education as a key component in the development of these visions. He argued that education was central to Black liberation efforts to forge a radically democratic society. Both in terms of the practical application of education, which had been largely denied to Black people during slavery, but also as a strategic move to establish a progressive taxed form of public education that would dismantle the economic stranglehold that the planter class had over the majority of southerners, both Black and white, who were greatly impoverished. The plans of the planter class ran directly counter to Black social visions of freedom. They opposed any form of taxation and given that they had been subsumed within a new industrial regime, they sought to gain control through the reestablishment of bygone laws—laws developed out of the Western Christian Church—that constricted the political, social, and economic movement of Black people in the United States. Du Bois argues that by looking back at these two competing social visions, one could tell what the future held for the country.

Following in the intellectual tradition of Du Bois, Clyde Woods, in his text *Development Arrested: The Blues and Plantation Power in the Mississippi Delta*, mapped out the social visions of both the plantation bloc and Black liberation efforts, which he coined the "Blues bloc." As a framework of analysis, Woods traced the intellectual and pragmatic roots of Black freedom efforts to the Mississippi Delta. Emanating out of the Black poor and working class, Woods argued that the Blues bloc developed a praxis of daily living and mass organizing that he referred to as "Blues Epistemology." Developed out of a rigorous analysis of history and social, political, and economic policy, Woods demonstrated how the plantation bloc attempted to thwart the efforts of the Blues bloc. As a method of understanding the dialectic relationship between the two competing social visions, Woods utilized enclosures as a model to detail the intimate and ugly connection between the blocs. Both conceptual and historic in nature, enclosures provided a way to show the effect that the plantation bloc policy agenda, as a power-making tool, had upon Black lived conditions in the Delta. Further, he argued that the specific aim of these enclosures was to counter the organizing logic of the Blues Epistemology—the shared cultural memories, practices, and history that had been forged over generations. Mapping out this relationship until the latter part of the twentieth century, Woods was adamant that the only way to understand the contemporary conditions of Black subjugation was to show how it developed and was connected to historic formations of power maintenance. In the development of his framework and argumentation, he also dismantled convenient and short-sighted theories and reactionary postulations of Black marginalization that failed to account for the longue durée of dialectical contestation that informs the current moment.

Thus, it is here, forged out of the guidance and analytic framework provided by Eugenia Schnyder, W. E. B. Du Bois, and Clyde Woods, that this book takes form. The overall goals of the text are twofold: First, through a blend of a historical rendering of enclosure processes and a contemporary ethnography of public education, my aim is to detail the complexity of the current relationship between schools and prisons in the United States in order to push the discourse beyond limited frameworks such as the School-to-Prison Pipeline (STPP). The second is to demonstrate the manner in which efforts for Black mobilization, often centered within education, have been countered by the formal and informal expressions of the state in the form of social and economic policies. Although often conveyed in altruistic language, the express intent of such a strategy has been to neutralize the radical dismantling of racial, gendered, class, and sexed hierarchies. The framework for each chapter is based upon these two goals, and, as a collective, the chapters build upon each other in order to provide a comprehensive analysis of very complex structures.

The first chapter, "The Problem of Black Genius: Black Cultural Enclosures," delves into the historical basis of one of the oldest enclosure models: Black culture. Central to the organizing and communal framework of Black life, Black culture has always posed a threat to undermine Western constructions of difference. As a result, Black culture has either been denigrated or silenced in an effort to dampen its radical potential. At the heart of these enclosures has been the Western Christian Church. The essence of the chapter traces the development of cultural enclosures at CHS back to its genealogical roots of the imposition of Western Christianity upon Black people. As a model, these forms are important, as they have been replicated again and again in an attempt to limit the impact of Black culture in the United States. In addition, the chapter points out that a serious limitation of the STPP framework is its inability to grapple with culture. While intensely focusing upon discipline, a failure to move beyond the limits of a discipline paradigm renders the analysis insufficient.

A transition from culture to its kindred spirit, ideology, is made in the second chapter. "In the Belly of the Beast: Ideological Expansion" explores the logic that undergirds the prison regime, the ideological enclosure apparatus that is present in all facets of the U.S. nation-state. Building upon the work of Dylan Rodríguez and Ruth Wilson Gilmore, the chapter analyzes the totality of the prison regime as a method of U.S. domination both domestically and on the international front. Arguing for a paradigm shift against the linear pathway of the STPP, education is positioned as a historical and ideological antecedent to the rampant explosion of prisons in the United States. This forces us to rethink of the intent of education in terms of the work that is done to legitimize the prison regime as a necessary entity of the nation-state and also the portrayal of education as a sight of supposed enlightenment.

The third chapter of the book, "Land of Smoke and Mirrors: The Meaning of Punishment and Control," resituates the framing of increased modalities of discipline within public education. Counter to a top-down model that positions Black communities as passive subjects, we must recenter the intent of discipline within schools. One of the goals of the chapter is to situate the manner in which policy was utilized as a tool to delegitimize Black organizing efforts through the development of a massive physical enclosure apparatus within public education under the guise of public safety. The reframing of punishment in this manner forces us to reconsider a problematic assertion made by advocates of the STPP position. Based upon the policy initiatives that deemed Black organizing a threat, the STPP model similarly blames student discipline issues upon student behavior. As a solution, the model claims that students need behavior intervention programs rather than address the root causes of the establishment of a massive punishment apparatus. The ethnography details the oppressive weight of this enclosure model and the extent to which is seeks to control the movement of students.

Building upon the policy analysis within chapter 3, the fourth chapter, "Troubled Man: Limitations of the Masculinity Solution," calls into question the formulation of a state based Black masculine subject. Indebted to the work of Beth Richie, the chapter looks into the problematic centering of Black boys and men as the key to the development of Black communities. Utilizing Richie's framework and needed theoretical interventions, the chapter demonstrates that a state-based masculine policy model reproduces oppression upon Black communities through a silencing of violence enacted upon Black women. The chapter details the manner in which education has been a central facet in the production of a particular type of heteronormative masculine subject. Through a close read of recent history, I argue that such a construction was done with the explicit intent to counter Black organizing.

The fifth and final chapter, "By All Means Possible: The Historical Struggle over Black Education," culls through the historical record of Black education in the United States to demonstrate the manner in which education has played a critical role in the development of Black communal enclosures. Starting at the nineteenth century and working to the current moment, the chapter demonstrates how processes of enclosure within education had profound impacts upon both Black life and also the shape of the nation. From industrialization to the prison regime, education enclosure models provided the impetus to counter Black freedom movements and establish new regimes of power to replace broken models (such as industrialization). An important discussion in the chapter points to a major fault within the STPP discourse: the omission of significance of education to enclosure models and an analysis of the core function of Black education within a racial capitalist framework.

As I was writing this book, I was often left with more questions that answers. Questions such as, What are the connections between neoliberal models of education (that is, charter schools) and the persistence of the prison regime? How do we account for the diminishment of and lack of sophistication with regard to race, and in particular Blackness, within analysis of education and prisons during some of the most racially charged times? Within the ever cutthroat world of the nonprofit industrial complex, how does one offer critique and solutions that directly counter reform program agendas that provide much needed short-term financial capital?

Whether it has been searching through policy briefs, talking with students and parents, or reading through historical records, I have been often left to ponder about possible solutions. However, the more I read and communicated with people, the more I realized that the solutions were right in front of me. Whether in the form of knowledge that students bring with them to school or historic strategies employed by Black mobilization efforts, the solutions to current problems are at our disposal. Rather than rely upon state-sponsored ideological or policy-driven models that do nothing more than maintain structures of hierarchal domination, I hope that this book will allow us to resituate our epistemological framework and begin looking for solutions in spaces that are readily available and are immersed in radically democratic social visions of the future.

Acknowledgments

The writing of *First Strike* has taken me on a fruitful journey that has been both parts agonizing and euphoric. Yet through it all, I have had the pleasure to work with some of the most brilliant and energetic young people who were simply amazing in the face of what can only be described as very arduous circumstances. As a whole, I thank the many teachers, staff, and students at County High School who talked with me about my project. The needed pedagogical techniques that were imparted to me were vital to my success in the classroom. The honesty and spirit of the students and their family members made my time there enjoyable and rewarding.

I am especially grateful for the opportunity afforded me by the University of California President's Postdoctoral Fellowship. Through the postdoc, I was most fortunate to spend time with a collection of the most thoughtful and considerate people at the University of California, Santa Barbara. I am extremely grateful to Debra Nash, Toni Moore, Vanessa Moore, and Ashley Davis for helping to make the impossible possible. The faculty in the Black Studies Department at UCSB—including Gaye Theresa Johnson, Jeffrey Stewart, Stephanie Batiste, Earl Stewart, Chris McAuley, Otis Madison, Mirelle Miller-Young, Jude Akudinobi, Ingrid Banks, Roberto Strongman, and Douglas Daniels—were simply tremendous in helping me craft my ideas and providing feedback in the direction of the work. I am especially thankful to Julie Carlson, Elizabeth Robinson, and George Lipsitz, who read over chapter drafts and provided great suggestions and much-needed and appreciated guidance. The wonderful comments from participants in the Prisons and Public Education class, including Angelica Camacho, Amber Bailey, and Morgan Twiggs, pushed me to further my intellectual project.

During my time at UCSB I had the great fortune to work under the guidance of two mentors who greatly affected the framing and analysis of the book. While serving in the capacity of mentor professor as a part of the UC President's Postdoctoral Fellowship, Cedric Robinson was much more than a formal mentor. His dedication to going over every word of every chapter and spending the time to discuss the project as a whole was more than I could ever ask for. In addition to being on call via e-mail or phone, Cedric imparted a seemingly endless fountain of knowledge that I could never repay in a million lifetimes. Simply the most brilliant scholar that I have had the pleasure to meet, Cedric's selflessness and dedication to the creation of both my book and the work of all of his students is a model that I hope to be able to live up to as I proceed through this journey within academia.

The second person who functioned in an informal but nevertheless very important mentor capacity at UCSB was the late Clyde Woods. Clyde, who passed away far too soon, brought needed levity and an intellectual breadth that pushed me beyond what I thought were my limits. From informal conversations in the middle of a hallway to panel presentations at major academic conferences, Clyde was seemingly always thinking about how to make my project better. His insistence on centering my analysis on the lives of Black people was very influential in the development of the text, and I can only hope that I did right by him as this book goes out into the world.

A very warm thanks to the editorial staff at the University of Minnesota Press. The editor for the project, Pieter Martin, put forth a great amount of energy and time to make sure that the book was reviewed and provided copious notes and instructions in order to enhance the manuscript. I am also very appreciative of the assistance of Kristian Tvedten, whose work was crucial to the completion of the book. Many, many thanks to the readers of the book and editorial board who gave their time to provide much-needed feedback and critique in order to develop the main arguments of the text.

To my many friends and colleagues who read chapter drafts and mulled over ideas with me, I am truly appreciative. While at the University at Texas at Austin I had the pleasure of engaging with the smartest and kindest people. I am especially thankful for the generosity put forth by Raja Swamy, Raquel DeSouza, Sonia dos Santos, Mohan Ambikaipaker, Arin Hill, Keisha-Khan Perry, Octavio Barajas, Tiriza Saziru, Naomi Reed, Alysia Childs, Nedra Lee, Jaime Alves, Marcia Lopes, Alix Chapman, Lynn Selby, Jodi Skipper, Courtney Morris, Peggy Brunache, Jamahn Lee, Tifani Blakes, Bavu Blakes, Jafari Allen, Alex Chavez, Santiago Guerra, Amy Brown, Kenneth MacLeish, Lidia Marte, Martín Perna, Linda Prieto, Sharon Bridgforth, Teresa Velasquez, Vivian Newdick, Takkara Brunson,

Spencer Platt, Keila Murray, Jacqueline Smith, Madlene Hamilton, Pablo Gonzalez, Celeste Henery, Heather Teague, Stephanie Lang, Jemima Pierre, Silvia Castro, Natasha Jarvis, Kyle Clark, and Angel Wilson. From the University of California, Santa Barbara, I thank Jordan Camp, Nadege Clitandre, Che Rodríguez, Daniel Olmos, Jonathan Gomez, Steven Osuna, and all of the good people from the SOUL collective who reviewed several iterations of this book. I extend a special thank you to my colleague, officemate while on the Black Studies Dissertation Writing Fellowship at UCSB, writing partner, African Diasporic dance aficionado, and good friend, Erica Williams, who put up with my eccentric behavior, continual inquiries, and moments of insanity during some pretty perilous times.

I am truly appreciative to the Center for African and African American Studies at the University of Texas at Austin. I cannot overstate my gratitude for the generous financial and spatial support offered by the center under the directorship of Edmund T. Gordon and Omi Oshun Olomo. In particular, the high level of scholarship that was offered through lectures, speaker series, conferences, symposiums, and community events was an educational and social experience that developed both critical thinking and academic skills.

The intellectual support from the Department of Anthropology at the University of Texas at Austin paved my way as a scholar. The guidance and mentorship of Kevin Foster was an invaluable learning experience. His belief in developing young academics enabled me to be apart of a great group of graduate students and professors, including Doug Foley, Angela Valenzuela, Linda Prieto, and Joel Dorwin, who were on the editorial board of *Anthropology and Education Quarterly*. In addition, the support of Gregory Vincent enabled me to continue my research in Los Angeles during the summers in Austin.

I am indebted to the hard work of my dissertation committee who guided me through the critical thinking and writing process. Edmund T. Gordon, Doug Foley, João Costa Vargas, Christen Smith, and Ruth Wilson Gilmore provided brilliant insight and poignant critique of my work. I have been shaped and molded by the caring, intellectual proclivity and multidimensional nature of João Costa Vargas. His dedication to my development as a scholar has sharpened my critical thinking skills, pushed me to deepen my theoretical analysis, and always maintain a close connection to the Black community.

I am extremely grateful for the support that I have received from

Scripps College and the Claremont Colleges as a collective. Having the opportunity to work with Seanna Cade Leath, André Larry, Ayanna Harris, Richard Roderick, Romarilyn Ralston, and Kristie Hernandez was especially fruitful to the development of crucial ideas. The guidance and support of Sid Lemelle, Salima Lemelle, Matt Delmont, Eric Hurley, Alicia Bonaparte, Lara Deeb, Susan Rankaitis, and Sheila Walker was invaluable in making sure that I had time to complete the project.

I give special thanks to my Southern California–based crew who have been instrumental in making this project come to fruition. From the Southern California Library, Yusef Omowale, Michele Welsing, and Raquel Chavez have been bedrocks in providing an abundance of resources. Much of this project would not have been made possible without the efforts of Mrs. Johnnie Savoy, whose mentorship and leadership were a steady bridge over tumultuous waters. Kirk Kirkwood, Antoinette Andrews, Shawnie Dockery, Jia Wang, Carla Appling, Yessenia Henriquez, Danielle Brown, Lee Modster, Lettie Totah, LouEllen Guidry, Sharon Goff, and Jonathon Harper all provided valuable insight and positive reinforcement throughout the duration of the work. The staff at the San Pedro Regional Library was especially gracious during the completion of the project. A most sincere thanks to librarians Ednita Kelly and Emma Roublow for allowing me to stay just a little bit after closing and being sounding boards for the book. Longtime friend and colleague Juli Grigsby has been vital in providing needed feedback and helped to provide needed nuance to the project. Shana Redmond has been a continual rock in making sure that the work gets done and ensure that I maintain sanity throughout the process. Connie Wun was instrumental in providing some of the most clear and coherent advice for shaping my ideas throughout the book. I am extremely thankful to Sarah Haley, Craig Gilmore, Deborah Vargas, Erica R. Meiners, Erica Edwards, Dylan Rodríguez, Robin D. G. Kelley, Tiffany Willoughby-Herard, and Kris Peterson, who provided me with opportunities to push my research and made me rethink my approach. There are many people who have helped in the development of this book, and I have sincerely tried to include them all—however, I may have forgotten key people in the process, and for that I offer my most sincere apology.

This book would not have been possible without the continual support of my loving and caring family and close friends. Through the formative years of my graduate training, the hospitality provided by Janet and

Ron Jones and their children, Rashida Butler and Ron Jones, provided me a home away from home. I am thankful for the beautiful and consistent generosity of David and Denise McLeod and their daughter Hope, who have provided a wonderful model of a warm family. The intellectual and emotional support of Alicia Kester and Laura Kester has been tremendous to my development as a scholar and overall person. The words of wisdom from longtime friends Brian Rikuda, Amika Rikuda, John Norwood, Tula Orum, Leslie Poston, Asmahan Thompson, Sofia Martos, Reggie Fears, Jerrin West, Chris Harris, Hyman Scott, Nesanet Abegaze, Anthony Johnson, Johanna Almiron, Pamela Davis, Byron Davis, Jamila Webb, and Dermar Moses have been invaluable and much needed.

The encouragement that was extended to me by Elouise McLemore, Alison McLemore, Darrizet and Jimmy Moore, Aunt Sweet, Silena Morris, Richard James and Janie Morris, Brenda Morris, Constance Lynn Morris, Lolita and Anthony Johnson, Tracy and Ron Prince, Mr. and Mrs. Addison, and Mr. and Mrs. Cook provided me with the warmth and love of family while I was in Texas. The perseverance of a strong Southern California family network, including Esther, Earl, Lela, and Cheryl Bohannon; Ann, Tony, Jasmine Hardy, and Tanner Livingston; Renee Sherman; Bobby, Carolyn, Sheldon, and Austen Lawrence; Richard Lawrence; Curtis, Diana, Carter, and Christian McIntyre; Aunt Imani, Jamila, and Kamilah Williams; Aunt Jesse; Aunt Joe; and Jo-Carolyn Dent-Clark have inspired me to continue to want to do better and place the needs of the Black community within all of my actions. Shelia and Wilson Crawford and their children Nikia and Wilson provided me with continual support and laughter. Michael Johnson's funny wit and understanding demeanor provided me with relief during the most stressful of times. Herbertean and Keith Morris and their wonderful family, Keiana Morris and Rodney, Whitneigh, and Taran Braxton, and Andreas Beasley have made my stay in Los Angeles always warm and inviting.

My sister, Leslie Schnyder, has been a wonderful, supportive sibling whose passion for life is matched only by her energy. Godfrey and Elaine Schnyder have been kind, caring, and most of all, loving parents who have had the patience to support me through all of my good and bad decisions. Their ability to make life fun and enjoyable enabled me to get through some of the most difficult times of completing this project.

Finally, this book is a reflection of both Shana and Naima Sojoyner.

Shana has supported me through countless revisions, copyedits, proofs, late-night study sessions, and chapter drafts. Her willingness to place her interests on hold to assist me cannot be quantified nor ever adequately repaid. I could have not finished this work without her, and I thank her for taking each step with me along the way. Naima has brought a sense of calm to the final stages of the process. She has given me an unnerving sense of focus, and I hope that the unconditional love that I have for her is felt throughout the pages of this book.

Notes

Introduction

1. This was the case at Charles Lindbergh Middle School in Long Beach, California, where the school district erected a ten-foot wall to separate the school from the Carmelitos Housing Project directly adjacent to the school in the name of student safety (Kopetman 1989).

2. To provide context for the demographics of Ranchos Palos Verdes for the time period I am writing about, according to figures from the 1990 census, the population of Ranchos Palos Verdes was 76 percent white. The numbers slightly changed over a ten-year period whereby the 2000 census found that 67 percent of the population was white (*Los Angeles Almanac* 2015).

3. It is important to point out that the phrasing of the School-to-Prison Pipeline has been used in different contexts. On one hand, it has been employed by community activists since the early part of the 1990s in an attempt to describe the relationship between a burgeoning prison system and failing education system. On the other, the mantra took hold within public policy, academics, and the private foundation discourse at the turn of the twenty-first century. The differences between the two are very distinct: the former often operated (and continues to operate) within a paradigm that centered the discussion on the abolition or a severe scaling back of prisons in the United States. The latter has focused the discussion primarily upon a reformist vision of education that has omitted prisons from the conversation. Although the two understandings of the phrase are very different, a central critique that holds true for both meanings rings the same: there is a need to resituate the understanding of schools and prisons within a historic framework that accounts for the economic, political, and planning realities that have led to the current moment.

4. Commenting on the rift that developed in the antiviolence movement, Richie states, "The challenges that emerge for the anti-violence movement because of the broader political changes became key sources of tension between distinct groups of anti-violence activists during this era. One group remain committed to a broader analysis of the systemic causes of violence against women, arguing as strongly as ever for the need for radical social change work based on an understanding of the role that systems efficacy and coalition politics could play in

that. For this group, the problem of persistent gender inequality, as a structural problem, remained at the center of the analytical paradigm that activists remained committed to. Another group coalesced around a different formation. Compelled to respond to conservative state tendencies regarding families, gender, and sexuality, they pursued a safer, less antagonistic strategy that they expected would be more acceptable to the new conservative national, legislative, and local leadership. This group distanced itself from the former activist-oriented agenda aimed at social change and developed a more professional identity as 'specialists' who worked with women who experienced male violence. Believing that politically they would be better position to compete for public support, the feminist activists in this later group became counselors, community organizers became project administrators, and advocates became apologists for the system" (Richie 2012, 75).

5. Writing about the importance of myths to the nation-state process, Cedric Robinson argues, "It is by now generally understood that the formation of nation-states and political reigns precipitate the development of founding myths—myths of origin, in the language of anthropologists." He further argues that myths are vital to the amalgamation of ideology that gives meaning to the nation-state stating, "Founding myths were substituted for history, providing the appearance of historical narrative to what was in actuality part fact and part class-serving rationales. Endlessly elaborated, these myths were produced by ideologues who identified with the dominant creed and depended upon those classes in the society that possessed power and the capacities to extend social privilege" (Robinson 2000, 186).

6. Erica Meiners discusses the often-unseen impact of soft discipline policies in her text, *Right to Be Hostile: Schools, Prisons, and the Making of Public Enemies* (Meiners 2007). Drawing comparisons between soft discipline policies and constructions of helping, Meiners states, "Similar to the 'soft' practices of school discipline, with disrespect and insubordination moving select youth into the juvenile justice system, the 'helping' discourses can also function to produce a highly individuated subject that is prepared for surveillance, and a self that is trained to separate the individual from his or her sociocultural contexts" (Meiners 2007, 144). Borrowing from Meiners's intervention, I argue that the current models of testing and standards-based curriculum are key to soft-side disciplining techniques that have functioned to counter Black demands for education.

1. The Problem of Black Genius

1. Specifically, I am referring to Black cultural constructions that are independent from Western, white supremacist interpolations of Blackness. In particular, these spaces are dual sites of Black resistance to racial hierarchal modes of oppression and a continuity of Blackness that is authentically distinct from Western epistemologies of thought. Based upon Cedric Robinson's Black Marxism, sites

of African Diasporic radical Black contestation to white supremacy were lodged within epistemological frameworks that were distinct and located within West African cosmologies.

2. The removal of the wood, metal, and auto shop classes was in line with the massive shift in capital in Southern California from the 1970s through the 1980s. As major corporations within the automotive and defense industry moved out to sites of lower wages, schools followed their cue and began removing vocational programs from the curriculum.

3. "On the quest for green" is a colloquial term in reference to earning money.

4. In comparison, Black marching bands, though very precise and organized, incorporate cultural elements of dancing and freedom of movement that is counter to the limited range of expression allowed in traditional white marching bands.

5. Rabateau argues that "one of the principal reasons for the refusal of English planters to allow their slaves to receive instructions was the fear that baptism would emancipate their slaves. The notion that if slaves were baptized, 'they should, according to the laws of the *British* nation, and the canons of its church' be freed was legally vague but widely believed" (Rabateau 1980, 99).

6. Noting the importance of African spiritual practices to Black freedom, Robinson comments, "After all, voodoo, which James termed 'the medium of the conspiracy' (of 1791), had also inspired earlier maroon revolts, the most important of which had occurred barely thirty years before under the guide of Mackandel . . ." (Robinson 2000, 147).

7. Genovese writes, "Before the insurrectory plot of 1822 the planters generally opposed religious instruction of the slaves. In part this hostility derived from a suspicion that many ministers and preachers held antislavery views. William W. Freeling, our best authority, has even suggested that the ministry did not become safely proslavery until about 1840. After the Denmark Vesey plot, however, despite the momentary hysteria over the alleged role of the church in encouraging slave insubordination, South Carolina's great planter aristocracy began going to church, or rather began making sure the slaves were going. As was to happen in Virginia a decade later, once faced with an insurrection of slaves who displayed religious inclinations, the slaveholders sobered up. If the slaves were going to get religion, then religion had to be made safe for the slaveholders" (Genovese 1976, 186).

8. Southern preachers such as Reverend C. C. Jones interpreting the work of Paul, stated, "Servants, obey in all things your masters according to the flesh; not with eye service, as menpleasers; but in singleness of heart, fearing God. . . ." Additionally he claimed, "Servants, be subject to your masters with all fear; not only to the good and gentle, but also to the forward" (Genovese 1976, 208).

9. These actions should be read and understood as part of the fight waged by plantation owners against the liberation schemes enacted by Black people. Genovese argues, "As apart of the white attempt to control black religion, the slave-holder's

regime tried to supervise slave funerals and feared their providing the occasion for insurrectionary plots. . . . These fears betrayed caution, not paranoia. The famous insurrectory plot associated with Gabriel Prosser in Virginia in 1800 had, as its organization occasion, the gathering of slaves for a child's funeral, and the circumstances surrounding the Nat Turner revolt of 1831 chilled the white South" (Genovese 1976, 194).

10. Coming out of the same political and cultural trajectory as Turner, Tubman used the song "Go Down, Moses" as a means to gather the slaves she was preparing to liberate through the myriad of points that formed the Underground Railroad (Cruz 2001, 109).

11. This sentiment of the Catholic Church was made most popular by the Spanish priest Juan Ginés de Sepúlveda, who between 1550 and 1551 took part in a series of debates in Valladolid, Spain, against fellow clergyman Bartolomé de Las Casas regarding the position of slavery within the Spanish war of aggression against indigenous populations of North America.

12. Davis notes that during the period of 1700 to 1763, former Black plantation workers founded a free Black community, Palenque, and its accompanying fort, just east of St. Augustine and the famous Spanish fort, Castillo de San Marcos.

13. With regards to Hughes, Sharrow cites the many conflicts that Hughes had with preachers such as Theodore Parker and abolitionist William Lloyd Garrison. Sharrow writes, "Hughes compared the abolitionist plan for removing slavery to a physician's prescription for burning a city as the surest means to cure cholera. Such a remedy, he concluded, might be worse than the disease. Hughes criticized the abolitionist solution as too simple because it failed to make careful provisions for the welfare of the nearly four million slaves who were to be freed. Hughes assumed that it would be most difficult, if not impossible, for the recent bondsman to function in free society. To the Archbishop, who placed a high premium on property rights, the abolitionist failure to compensate the master for his loss of property bordered on national larceny. Finally, Hughes asserted, that the abolitionists, in their simplicity, had neglected to make adjustments for the regional and national economic disruption which would be caused by the death of the South's peculiar institution (Sharrow 1972, 262).

14. Writing of Brownson, Davis states, "Brownson, on the other hand, insisted that slaves were private property. One could not divest someone of his or her property without recompense. It is for this reason that he both opposed the abolitionist and defended the Fugitive Slave Act of 1850" (Davis 1990, 60).

15. Rabateau argues that African-based religion has been critical to revolts launched across the African Diaspora and Haiti in particular. He states, "The revolt led by Boukman in 1791 was inaugurated by an awesome religious ceremony concluded by a blood pact" (Raboteau 1980, 26).

16. In regards to the limitations of the Catholic Church, Ochs writes of the

Sherriff in Natchez, Mississippi, who during Reconstruction had severe issues with the church. He states, "The black Catholic sheriff of Natchez during Reconstruction, for example, though sending his children to what was designated as the 'colored Catholic School,' refused to attend mass at the local Catholic church because of the church's rules requiring blacks to sit in the aisle. Neither did Catholic worship allow for the range of emotional expression that many freedmen found attractive in the Protestant churches" (Ochs 1990, 36).

17. This pattern was first established by the Portuguese government and then later adopted by the French and Spanish in their proclamations regarding slavery. Raboteau states, "It was the settled policy of Portugal that all slaves brought into her New World colony of Brazil had to be baptized before the slave ships set sail from Africa. Similarly, the slave codes of the French and Spanish colonies legislated that slave owners baptize and instruct their slaves in the Catholic faith" (Raboteau 1996, 118).

18. Raboteau, commenting on the work of Catholic historian Roger Baudier, stated, "The situation of Catholicism among Louisiana's black population at the end of the Civil War was summarized by Roger Baudier, a historian of Catholicism in Louisiana: '. . . Many attempts were made to give instructions on the plantations, but this was extremely difficult. All of this, however, was spasmodic and unorganized. There was always present the prejudices of slave owners. . . . Negroes were freely admitted to Catholic Church and to the Sacraments; but even in this there was some opposition, though the clergy resisted any interference with the practice of their religion by the slaves. . . . Baptism of slave children was very generally practiced . . . in some parishes the practice being generally followed of baptizing many in a group on Holy Saturday and the Vigil of Pentecost. As a whole, however, the work of the evangelization was certainly far from what it should have been" (Raboteau 1980, 271).

2. In the Belly of the Beast

1. The naturalization of work as an ideological human endeavor was key to Gramsci's theorization of the school in the formation of the state. He stated, "Human work cannot be realized in all its power of expansion and productivity without an exact and realistic knowledge of natural laws and without a legal order which organically regulates men's [sic] life in common. Men [sic] must respect this legal order through spontaneous assent, and not merely as an external imposition—it must be a necessity recognized and proposed to themselves as freedom, and not simply coercion. The idea and the fact of work (of theoretical and practical activity) was the educational principle latent in the primary school, since it is by means of work that the social and state order (rights and duties) is introduced and identified within natural order. . . . It provides the basis for the

subsequent development of a historical, dialectical conception of the world, which understands movements and change, which appreciates the sum of effort and sacrifice, and which conceives the contemporary world as synthesis of the past, of all past generations, which projects itself into the future. This is the real basis of the primary school" (Gramsci and Hobsbawm 1988/2000, 312).

2. Gilmore identifies these points of transition as crises. She states, "Crisis is not objectively bad or good; rather it signals systemic change whose outcome is determined through struggle. Struggle, which is a politically neutral word, occurs at all levels of a society as people try to figure out, through trial and error, what to make of idled capacities. . . . What are the possible outcomes of crises? Households can reorganize internal relations of authority and dependence according to who can find work or receive income assistance, creating both tensions and opportunities that significantly alter 'traditional' household hierarchies. Community institutions, such as churches, unions, or street gangs, can gain or lose adherents and experience new pressures because of excessive or vanished reliance on the services and security they provide" (Gilmore 2007, 54). Gilmore makes note that rather than a conspiratorial act, agents of the state make cognitive decisions during such crises that have major implications upon communities. She highlights the late twentieth-century gubernatorial reign of Jerry Brown during the wake of prison reform in California to address prisoners' writs of habeas corpus with regard to prison conditions, specifically overcrowding. Gilmore states that "Brown could have used his power as the state's chief executive to relieve overcrowding by ordering parole for indeterminate-sentence prisoners who had served time equal to the new sentencing requirements and by commuting sentences for others who had been in the system a long time. Instead, he began to investigate the best way to improve plans and modestly expand capacity, intending—or so he claimed—to use state-of-the-art prisons for the benefit of prisoners and society" (Gilmore 2007, 92).

3. Ruth Wilson Gilmore argues that during this shift to a "post-Keynesian militarism, the owners of capital were invested in not only maintaining their capital, but ensuring that the masses of workers become increasingly economically subjugated to their needs." Gilmore states in reference to late twentieth century globalization, "The nation was being 'prepped' for global developments by operators firmly ensconced in state institutions, such as the Federal Reserve Bank governors, who as Edwin Dickens argues, powerfully insisted that the state's capacity to discipline labour was politically and economically more important than the state's capacity to guarantee labor a decent share of surplus value" (Gilmore 2007, 179).

4. Rodríguez points out throughout his text that the vast irony within this configuration is that the very existence of Blackness is negated within the construction of American life, thus the only option for Black people is to resist against assertions that demand subservience and allegiance (Rodríguez 2006).

5. Minimum wage in California as of January 1, 2008, and had not increased as of May 2009.

6. The *California Progressive Message* notes that in order to understand the scope of rapid rate of expansion of prisons, is that in between 1852 and 1964 only twelve prisons were built in California. The development of prisons has been aided by the growth of the prison guard union, the California Correctional Peace Officers Association (CCPOA), which has been a major player in draconian policy formation such as Proposition 184 (Three Strikes Law). Since then, "the CCPOA, its subsidized crime victims groups, lobbyists and its members have contributed nearly $38 million to the California legislative and election process . . ." (CPM 2011).

7. As explained by Dylan Rodríguez, "The current era of mass imprisonment, white-supremacist unfreedom—specifically, carceral technologies of human immobilization and bodily disintegration—provides the institutional form, cultural discourse, and ethical basis of social coherence, safety, and civic peace" (Rodríguez 2006, 14). In an ironic twist, such logic implies that prisons provide for the very freedom that in practice they negate. The realty is that the expansion of the prison regime has served to make Black communities more economically, politically, and socially unstable (Clear 2007).

8. Rodríguez borrows the term *capillary* from Foucault's theoretical intervention of "capillary power." Rodríguez builds upon this claim to describe the conduit-like effect that prison has upon state structures. He states, "Capillaries, in the medical definition, are 'the tiny blood vessels that connect the arterioles (the smallest division of the arteries) and the venules (the smallest divisions of the veins).' These blood vessels, like the prison, from crucial sites of passage for the transfer of the (social) body's life-sustaining nutrients as well as for the spread of (alleged social) disease, infections, and impurity. They are evidence of a functioning order, a living organism. . . . Apropos of this medical definition, an essential (warfare) technology of the prison regime is its circulation of violence through its legitimated parishioners—the bodies of designated agents (guards, doctors, wardens, prison educators) and guardians of the dominion—and simultaneous performance and materialization on the bodies of an immobilized captive population. This is to extrapolate Foucault's conception of capillary power beyond its metaphorical deployment, and to suggest its relevance a literal designation for the materiality of the prison regime's modalities of violence on the imprisoned subject's bodily capillaries, that is, her or his flesh and blood (Rodríguez 2006, 46).

9. Hardt and Negri explain the confluence of power being dispersed and internalized through the dismantling of that which is considered "inside" and "outside" as key in the shift from the modern mode of economic and social relations to the postmodern. They state, "In the passage from modern to postmodern . . . there is progressively less distinction between inside and outside. This transformation is

particularly evident when viewed in terms of the notion of sovereignty. Modern sovereignty has generally been conceived in terms of a (real or imagined) territory and the relation of that territory of its outside." Explaining the intricacies of the shift they comment, "In the imperial world, this dialectic of sovereignty between the civil order and the natural order has come to an end. This is one precise sense in which the contemporary world is post-modern. . . . The modern dialectic of inside and outside has been replaced by a play of degrees and intensities, of hybridity and artificiality" (Hardt and Negri 2001, 187–88). They further describe the effect of the dispersal upon the internal politics of nation states as breaking down previous jurisdictions of control. They state, "There is no outside in a military sense. When Francis Fukuyama claims that the contemporary historical passage is defined by the end of history, he means that the era of major conflicts has come to an end: sovereign power will no longer confront its Other and no longer face its outside, but rather will progressively expand its boundaries to envelop the entire globe as its proper domain. The history of imperialist, interimperialist, and anti-imperialist wars is over. Or really, we have entered the era of minor and internal conflicts. Every imperial war is a civil war, a police action—from Los Angeles to Granada to Mogadishu and Sarajevo. In fact, the separation of tasks between the external and internal arms of power (between the army and the police, the CIA and the FBI) is increasingly vague and indeterminate (Hardt and Negri 2001, 189).

10. Hardt and Negri state, "The process of formation, and the subjects that act in it, are attracted in advance toward the positively defined vortex of the center, and this attraction becomes irresistible, not only in the name of the capacity of the center to exercise force, but also in the name of the formal power, which resides in the center, to frame and systematize the totality" (Hardt and Negri 2001, 15).

11. Gordon posits that the politics of "Respectability" have a "long trajectory" rooted within "African patriarchy and segmentary lineage socio-political organization. It emerged during slavery as the practice of male slaves who, despite the destructive pressures of slavery, were pillars of slave communities and their institutions." He further argues, "Despite the barbarities and hardships of 'Jim Crow' apartheid, many Black males played pivotal roles in such institutions as patriarchal extended families, Black religious and educational institutions, lodges, social clubs, 'civic' organizations, the Black media, and Black-owned and operated small businesses and farms. In this context values and practices that complemented positions of responsibility within these institutions and enhanced community survival, such as hard work, economic frugality and independence . . . and conservative styles of self-presentation were basic to the achievement of 'respectable' male status" (Gordon 1997, 42).

12. Within contemporary civic society the distinction between respectable and reputation performances of masculinity has been heightened by a body of literature that negatively stigmatizes the "urban underclass" for their improvised state.

Gordon states, "'Respectable' males are family heads who are preeminently successful economic providers as well as responsible husbands and fathers. Many are also successful in comparison with other males in their public sphere activities: assertive, ambitious, self-reliant, principled, successful at their work and economically viable" (Gordon 1997, 42).

13. One of the key elements of respectable behavior is validation by whites of Blackness. Gordon argues, "Respectability is clearly infused with hegemonic patriarchy. . . . Many, though not all, of the core values of 'Respectability' are shared with Anglo middle-class male culture. . . . Further, as practice, 'Respectability' is informed by accommodationist, Black male concern with White perceptions of African American individuals and community. Validation by White society is often an important component of 'Respectability' . . . [and] is understood by Whites to be similar to their own valued practice and therefore non-threatening. Perhaps a legacy of a more coercive past, 'Respectability' also involves a level of deference to dominant authority" (Gordon 1997, 42).

14. Kelley insightfully argues that social relations based upon individual notions of achievement and success do little more that stigmatize the failings of the Black poor onto their "moral deficiencies such as the lack of a work ethic, frugality, and thrift." The result is that although the Black poor are denigrated for abuses of the welfare system and lack of desire to work, the greatest beneficiaries of government subsidized programs, white males increase power. He provides the example of Ross Perot, who was a strong advocate for the removal of direct government spending on social programs. A strong proponent of privatization of social services, Perot's company, Electronic Data Systems, according to Kelley made "millions providing computer management services for welfare administrations in thirty states" (Kelley 1997, 97).

15. Alexander's study of the neocolonial Black masculine Bahamian governance ideology points out the many limitations of the adoption of a respectable politics that reifies heteronormativity. She states, "Nationalism may have contradicted the imperial discourse that used the fictions of science to explain 'native' incapacity to govern in terms of biology, but the psychic residue of colonization continued to operate to convert double consciousness into a double bind. Acting through this psychic residue, neocolonial state managers continued the policing of sexualized bodies (as a way of denying it), as if the colonial masters were still looking on, as if it to convey legitimate claims to being civilized. . . . Not having dismantled the underlying presuppositions of British law, however, black nationalist men, now with some modicum of control over the state apparatus, continue to administer and preside over these same fictions. Moreover, no nationalism could survive without heterosexuality—nationalism needs it no matter how criminal, incestuous, or abusive it might be. Heterosexuality still appears more conducive to nation-building than does same-sex desire, which appears hostile to it—for

women presumably cannot love themselves, love other women, and love the nation simultaneously" (Alexander 2005, 45–46).

16. Davis, in linking the INS and the production of racialized subjects within the prison regime, states, "Penal infrastructures must be created to accommodate this rapidly swelling population of caged people. Goods and people must be provided to keep imprisoned populations alive. Sometimes these populations must be kept busy and at other times—particularly in repressive super-maximum prisons and in Immigration and Naturalization Service (INS) detention centres—they must be deprived of virtually all meaningful activity" (Gordon 1999, 146).

17. Seale in critique of the antiwar movement during the Vietnam War stated, "To the Peace Forces, the progressive forces in America, the protestors, those who know the war in Vietnam is unjust, those who are going to the streets and demonstrating, those who think they're really doing something—what they're doing in trying to end the war in Vietnam, is not meaningful at all, yet. It's not meaningful at all and will not become meaningful at all if you really want to stop the war in Vietnam, until you take some action here in America against the fascist brutal forces against Black people here in America. . . . Because the Black Panther Party itself has moved in this direction from its very inception to get rid of those fascist forces that corral us. This is the kind of action that has to be taken on the part of the Peace Forces in America and the progressive forces in America. And until they begin to do that they will not begin at all to stop imperialism; they will not begin at all to stop domestic imperialism right here at home. YOU MUST MOVE AGAINST DOMESTIC IMPERIALISM, GROWING RAMPANT FACISM—RIGHT HERE IN AMERICA BEFORE YOU CAN END THE WAR IN VIETNAM OR ALL FORMS OF AGGRESSIVE WARS LIKE THAT AGAINST OTHER PEOPLES ABROAD. The very fact that Black, Brown, Red, and other peoples in America and poor people, even poor White people, are corralled in wretched ghettos, especially those in the fashion they are and murdered. No, we can't continue to allow ourselves to be duped with the notion that we're doing something good until we learn to smash imperialism right here at home. Because to smash imperialism right here at home is to smash imperialism abroad. Smashing imperialism means taking action, demanding that those prisoners of war be allowed to come home. When you say 'Bring the GI's home,' bring the GI's home. And we can bring the prisoners of war home by demanding that the U.S. government release political prisoners here in America. . . . People move. Black brothers and sisters, American people, it's time that we moved against fascism at home because to smash fascism at home is to smash fascism forever abroad" (Seale 2002, 96).

18. Hardt and Negri provide a concise conceptualization of the function of both the military and the police within the current epoch of war. They claim, "War thus seems to be heading at once in two opposite directions: it is, on one hand, reduced to police action and, on the other, raised up to an absolute, ontological

level by technologies of global destruction. These two movements, however, are not contradictory: the reduction of war to police action does not take away but actually confirms its ontological dimension. The thinning of the war function and thickening of the police function maintain the ontological stigmata of absolute annihilation: the war police maintain the threat of genocide and nuclear destruction as their ultimate foundation" (Hardt and Negri 2005, 19).

19. Kaplan's study of single Black mothers in Oakland provides the terrain to understand the limits of ideological adherence. She posited that the mothers in her study abided by the myth of the U.S. nation-building project. They were "trying to achieve the American Dream. . . . Having a baby was an act of individualism and achievement." However, they castigated as sexually immoral for not abiding by social conventions of getting married and having a baby in the "proper order." "According to mainstream ideology," Kaplan states, "men who through hard work have moved up the career ladder and provide their families with decent food on the dinner table, clothes on their backs, and occasional family vacation have achieved the American Dream. Women's achievements are measured by their marriage and child rearing. . . . Teenage girls are expected to replicate these values by refraining from sexual relations before adulthood and marriage" (Kaplan 1997, xx). However, she points out that these conventions are designed along racialized gender lines: "The young Black women in this study are like most Black women today. They want the traditional American Dream. They do not reject the idea of marrying before having a baby, as many of today's White women do. I thought about the facetiousness of the morally superior 'good girl' when a White teenager told me that she became sexually active at thirteen. She liked boys, she said, but she did not plan on being with anyone at this time of her life. . . . The irony here is that while White women might flaunt their autonomy and the independence of traditional values and are accepted and even admired by some people for doing so, Black women who do not act according to traditional values, even though they desire to, are blamed" (Kaplan 1997, 186–87).

20. Fanon writes, "What? While I was forgetting, forgiving, and wanting only to love, my message was flung back in my face like a slap. The white world, the only honorable one, barred me from all participation. A man was expected to behave like a man. I was expected to behave like a black man—or at least like a nigger. I shouted a greeting to the world and the world slashed away my joy. I was told to stay within bounds, to go back where I belonged. They would see, then! I had warned them, anyway. Slavery? It was no longer even mentioned, that unpleasant memory. My supposed inferiority? A hoax that it was better to laugh at. I forgot it all, but only on condition that the world not protect itself against me any longer. I had incisors to test. I was sure they were strong. And besides . . . What! When it was I who had every reason to hate, to despise, I was rejected? When I should have been begged, implored, I was denied the slightest recognition? I resolved, since it

was impossible for me to get away from an *inborn complex,* to assert myself as a BLACK MAN. Since the other hesitated to recognize me, there remained only one solution: to make myself known" (Fanon 1967, 114–15).

21. In reference to schools and the elimination of culture, Gramsci states, "The scientific ideas the children learned conflicted with the magical conception of the world and nature which they absorbed from an environment steeped in folklore. . . . The school combated folklore, indeed every residue of traditional conceptions of the world. It taught a more modern outlook based essentially on an awareness of the simple and fundamental fact that there exist objective, intractable natural laws to which man must adapt himself if he is to master them in his turn— and that there exist social and state laws which are the product of human activity, which are established by men and can be altered by men in the interests of their collective development" (Gramsci and Hobsbawm 1988/2000, 311).

22. Such action is perhaps best exemplified by the FBI's surveillance of the rap group N.W.A. following the release of their album *Straight Outta Compton* that contained the popular song "Fuck the Police" (Hochman 1989). The FBI issued a letter to the record label, Priority Records, in which the FBI accused the group of supporting "violence and disrespect" against law enforcement (Hochman 1989). This surveillance of hip-hop artists was later developed into a full-fledged program within police departments. The *Miami Herald*'s 2004 investigative report, "Police Secretly Watching Hip-Hop Artists," was eye-opening in that it detailed the degree to which the panopticon was upon young Black artists (White and McDonnell 2004). Yet, perhaps even more astounding was that the Miami police officers were in fact trained by the New York Police Department, which had started the program during the 1990s and had an entire unit dedicated to surveilling hip-hop artists (Allah 2004).

23. Negri and Hardt argue, "Empire is not based upon force itself but on the basis of the capacity to present force as being in the service of right and peace. All interventions of the imperial armies are solicited by one or more of the parties involved in an already existing conflict. Empire is not born of its own will but rather it is called into being and constituted on the basis of its capacity to resolve conflicts" (Hardt and Negri 2001, 15).

24. Writing about Genovese's bold claims about the lack of Black agency in the abolishment of slavery, Robinson writes, "In 1966, Eugene Genovese, the radical historian, neatly asserted all three propositions in an attack on the idea of a Black radical tradition in America: 'American radicals have long been imprisoned by the pernicious notion that the masses are necessarily both good and revolutionary. . . . This viewpoint now dominates the black liberation movement, which has been fed for decades by white radical historians who in this one respect have set the ideological pace for their liberal colleagues. It has become virtually sacrilege—or at least white chauvinism—to suggest that slavery was a social system within which

whites and blacks lived in harmony as well as antagonism, that there is little evidence of massive, organized opposition to the regime, that the blacks did not establish a revolutionary tradition of much significance, and that our main problem is to discover the reasons for the widespread accommodation and, perhaps more important, the long-term effects both of the accommodation and of that resistance which did occur.' Thus opposition to slavery was minimal; in 'absence or extreme weakness of such tradition,' Black nationalism as a movement was a twentieth-century phenomenon; and the regard accorded to the revolutionary politics of the Black masses has its source in 'white' radicalism" (Robinson 2000, 176).

25. The power that foundations and philanthropic groups wielded cannot be overstated. Watkins borrowing from Edward H. Berman's 1984 work, *The Influence of the Carnegie, Ford and Rockefeller Foundations on American Foreign Policy: The Ideology of Philanthropy* recounts Berman's analysis: "The major American foundations were established to accomplish certain ends in the heyday of capitalist accumulation. These included the stabilization of the rapidly evolving corporate and political order and its legislation and acceptance by the majority of the American population; the institutionalization of certain reforms, which would serve to preclude the call for more radical structural change and the creation through educational institutions of a worldwide network of elites whose approach to governance and change would be efficient, professional, moderate, incremental and nonthreatening to the class interests of those like Messrs. Carnegie, Ford, and Rockefeller had established the foundations. The subsequent support by the foundations for various educational configurations both at home and abroad cannot be separated from their attempts to evolve a stable domestic polity and a world order amenable to their interests and the strengthening of international capitalism" (Watkins 2001, 19).

26. The corporate industrial class held a level of disdain and hatred toward Black people that rivaled that of southern plantation owners and slave traders. Newton Baker, who was on the board of the Carnegie Corporation, wrote to the president of the company, F. P. Keppel, in 1935 concerning the Carnegie's role in the fufure direction of Black people in the county. Keppel's influence was enormous given that the Carnegie Corporation would later commission the infamous 1944 study, *An American Dilemma*. Baker wrote, "I think anybody who has read Anthony Adverse, will share my feeling of unlimited amazement at the courage of the white people in this country who received the slaves from slave ships and undertook to make useful laborers of them. How many white civilizations could have dared to receive so many wild savages who were practically un-caged animals and spread them over their farms in contact with their own families passes human comprehension? What has been done for the negro in one hundred years is an unparalleled achievement and nothing but a theoretical, democratic impatience can make us critical of it, though of course much more remains to be done" (Jackson 1994, 21).

27. The significance of attempted capitalist manipulation cannot be overstated within the affairs of Black freedom movements. South Carolina's being an early site over the contestation of Black cultural practices was one of the primary examples of the intervention of the Black freedom struggle. Perry L. Kyles notes that the plantation government of South Carolina implemented many measures in an effort to counter Black autonomy. He states, "It was a common practice for planters and colonial authorities to reward slaves who collaborated with those in power and the Afro-Carolinian population was certainly mindful of this practice. There are several recorded instances of the Commons House of Assembly rewarding Afro-Carolinians who acted in the interest of their masters, especially in the wake of the 1739 Stono Rebellion. For example, 'a Negro Man named July belonging to Mr. Thomas' was 'chiefly instrumental in saving his Master and his Family [the master's family] from being destroyed by the rebellious Negroes.' July 'had at several Times bravely fought against the Rebels, and killed one of them.' July received 'his Freedom, and a Present of a Suit of Clothes, Shirt, Hat, a Pair of Stockings, and a Pair of Shoes.' This reward was for 'his faithful Services, and for an Encouragement to other Slaves to follow his Example in Cases of the like Nature.' Thus July's emancipation served as an example of how acting in defense of the status quo could yield distinct advantages. Other women and men often received lesser rewards for their collaborationist activities. Sixteen Afro-Carolinian men and one woman were acknowledged as having 'behaved themselves very well and been of great Service in opposing the rebellious Negroes.' As a reward for their loyalty, the males received 'a Suit of Clothes, Hat, Shirt, a Pair of Shoes and a Pair of Stockings.' The woman received 'a Jacket and Petticoat, a Shirt, a Pair of Stockings and a Pair of Shoes.' In addition, both the men and the woman each received twenty pounds Carolina money. Three other Afro-Carolinians received the same allotment of clothing, but only ten pounds in cash. The committee also rewarded Afro-Carolinians who assisted 'in the taking and apprehending some of the rebellious Negroes,' for which they received clothing and five pounds. Another Afro-Carolinian, Quash, 'did endeavour to take one of the rebellious Negroes' and received ten pounds as reward" (Kyles 2008, 503–4). Such a point was of vital importance because South Carolina planters were acutely aware (especially after the Stono Rebellion) that the targets of revolt were the landed gentry class. Kyles points out, "The Stono rebel's actions reflected their extreme contempt for the plantation elites, and their decision to kill certain planters, but to spare the lives of whites they considered hospitable toward enslaved black workers, revealed their acute awareness of the racial dynamics in the South Carolina colony" (Kyles 2008, 505).

In regards to the appropriation of state funds as a strategy for Black freedom, Du Bois notes that during the state convention during Reconstruction, Blacks in South Carolina forged political alliances with poor whites in order to gain control of the state budget and the form of a new constitution. This resulted in funding for a major restructuring of the state, including the redistribution of land, free public education, and the building of infrastructure within Black communities (Du Bois 1935/1998, 381–430).

28. Rather than attack just one modality of capitalism (i.e., business exploitation of Black communities), the Panthers sought to undo the entire apparatus. Calling for Black control over material and cultural resources, they envisioned that the only solution was to disavow the system as one unworthy of reform.

29. Evidence of this concern was stated by Roger Freeman, then-California Governor Ronald Reagan's Educational Advisor, who in the face of Black radicalism that demanded control of public education stated, "We are in danger of producing an educated proletariat. That's dynamite! We have to be selective on who we allow to go through higher education" (Franklin 2000, 6).

30. In writing about the power of the Panthers in Los Angeles, the threat that they posed, and the repression levied against them, Widener writes, "As Ward Churchill observed, more than half of all Black Panther Party members killed in the United States died in Los Angeles at the hands of the police" (Widener 2010, 12).

3. Land of Smoke and Mirrors

1. Most notably this has been done by well-meaning advocates of reformation within state structures (i.e., public education and the criminal justice system).

2. The formation of a system of public education in the United States during Reconstruction was a contestation of capital against the demands of Blacks for a truly democratic institution that countered the plutocracy that was marked by the white landed class's exploitation of labor from Blacks and working-class whites throughout the South. Though not necessarily a "friend" of Black folks, the federal administration, through the urging of Black activists and white abolitionists, played a crucial role in the development of the Freedman's Bureau, which ushered in for the first time a taxed system to pay for a general public education system. In an attempt to undermine this system, the corporate class (i.e., John D. Rockefeller, Andrew Carnegie, George Peabody) circumvented the government in the establishment of Black institutions that sought to reinscribe Black subservience to the needs of the capitalist agenda (Watkins 2001). In the decades that followed, Black activists continually pushed against industrial forms of education as the sole pedagogical method of instruction. Thus, as an example, public school integration as a strategy had nothing to do with conceptualizations that white schools were inherently better because they were white; rather there was an understanding that integration could possibly lead to a redistribution of resources in much more equitable manner. Yet, it wasn't until after the recognition that integration not only did not work, but exacerbated white control of Black education, did radical organizations begin to employ the structure of public education as a model to

both raise consciousness and also utilize the energy of youth as a tool to undo the fundamental tenets of capitalism that were key to Black oppression.

3. The enclosures worked in a multifaceted manner (i.e., political, social, cultural, economic, sexual, health, and educational) in an attempt to stifle Black libratory practices. From the sixteenth century to the present, enclosure strategies, in a broad sense, have changed from plantations, to sharecropping, to corporate farms in the South and industrial centers in the North to urban blight (brought on by abandonment through economic disinvestment) to the current form of prisons. Perhaps there has been no better scholar to detail and analyze the relationship between enclosures and Black freedom than Clyde Woods. Analyzing the effect of the planter bloc upon the Mississippi Delta, Woods argues, "The Delta enclosure movement decimated the region's democratic constituency just as the African American return to electoral activity was on the horizon. It also guaranteed the derailment of movements for land and resource redistribution while preserving the White supremacy alliance. As with the Choctaw removal, efforts were made to limit the historical vision of African Americans; the rights obtained earlier were now deemed revolutionary, while the violence of mass eviction and the total monopolization of resources were depicted as the inevitable march of progress" (Woods 1998, 121). Similarly, writing about the struggle between Black folks in Louisiana and the long-standing Bourbon regime, Woods notes, "When confronted by the growing alliance among African Americans, national unions, and progressive movements, the Bourbons pushed for the expulsion of these groups from the rural areas and then from the economic and political life of the urban areas between 1945–1954. The rural population in Louisiana declined by 286,000 persons during the 1940s and by another 334,000 persons during the 1950s. Numerous African-American rural communities collapsed during this period while starvation and flight to the cities became central narratives of Black Louisiana life. Enclosure and expulsion also defined urban life in the areas of employment and housing. Due to pressure from the Bourbon bloc and its allies on the House Un-American Activities Committee and the Senate Internal Security Committee, the Louisiana Civil Rights Congress, the Louisiana Committee on Human Rights, and the Southern Conference for Human Welfare were forced to disband and the Congress of Industrial Organizations and the National Association for the Advancement of Colored People (NAACP) purged its ranks of progressives and radicals. In Louisiana, the Dixiecrat movement against the civil rights agenda in the Democratic Party received strong support as did right to work legislation designed to cripple the union movement" (Woods 2009, 440–41).

4. Writing about the conflict between STEP and penal code limits, Sigal wrote about a case of a young man who at the age of nineteen was charged with the robbery of two men at gunpoint. The prosecution proved through the vagueness of the law that the young man had loose affiliations with gangs, and, with the en-

hancements initiated through STEP, faced more than one hundred years in prison for an offense in which no one was injured and all property was returned to the owner. Sigal also brings this to the fore because even though this was the young man's first offense, the utilization of STEP "effectively destroyed the young man's life" (Sigal 2007, 2).

5. A key aspect of the amendment of Penal Code 272 was that its legality was brought into question when in 1989 a Black woman, Gloria Williams of Los Angeles County, was brought under charges for the actions of her seventeen-year-old son accused of sexual assault. Ms. Williams was arrested when the police searched her house and according to the report found a "gang museum" consisting of family members and friends posing with weapons and hand signs. Ms. Williams was subsequently taken to jail, but the case was dismissed after she took parenting classes. As a result of Ms. Williams's case, the American Civil Liberties Union (ACLU) and Gary Williams, a law professor at Loyola University Law School in Los Angeles, brought forth a suit on behalf of the Los Angeles County taxpayers against the office of the Los Angeles County District Attorney (Office of Juvenile Justice, U.S. Department of Justice). The ACLU charged that the amended version of Penal Code 272 was a violation of the Fourteenth Amendment with regards to privacy and was too vague in application. The ACLU originally lost the case but won the appeal. This victory was short-lived, however, because in 1993, the California Supreme Court overturned the appeal, and Penal Code 272 stood in its amended form (Clements 1995).

6. The Abolish Chronic Truancy legislation states the following: "ACT places prosecutors in elementary schools to work with administrators, teachers, parents and students to intervene at the very beginning of the truancy cycle. Prosecutors inform parents that it is their legal responsibility to ensure their children attend school and that education is as essential as food, clothing, and shelter in a child's life. If there are problems interfering with the ability of the child to go to school, prosecutors attempt to find community resources to help overcome those problems. If the child continues to be truant, the prosecutor can take legal action, prosecuting the student, the parent, or both."

The District Attorney's Office lists the following reasons for the policy:

"1.) Truant behavior is not as ingrained at this age as it will later become. 2.) The parent of the elementary school-aged child still has control over the child and can, therefore, be held accountable. 3.) If intervention occurs later in the child's life, he will have fallen so far behind academically as a result of truancy that getting the pupil back in school will be a matter of winning the battle having already lost the war. While prosecution can result from A.C.T. intervention, the focus of the program is not to punish parents and students, but to get truants off the streets and back in the *classrooms*" (Los Angeles District Attorney's Office, 2007).

7. In 1995, the *Los Angeles Times* reported that Los Angeles County Office

of Education issued a report that "concluded that school absences are 'the most powerful predictor' of delinquent behavior" (Shuster 1995a). In 1996, the *Los Angeles Times* issued a quote from then–Deputy District Attorney Kim Menninger, who stated, "I've never seen a gang member in Santa Ana who wasn't a truant first" (Kass 1996). In 1998, the *Los Angeles Times* commenting on the district attorney's effort to "Head Off Truancy Early" noted that Higgins approach was "schizophrenic" (Higgins's own words) in that it "weav[ed] together a pep talk and a threat" (Mozingo 1998).

8. Higgins was an open advocate of changing the funding procedure of public education. Within California, schools were paid based upon the number of students in attendance on a given day. If a student was absent and brought in a note from a parent or doctor, then the absence was legitimated as excused (i.e., appointment, funeral, sick, etc.) and the school could then count the student as present and collect revenue. Whether the absence from school was proven through a note from a parent or a doctor, Higgins argued that the school should not be able to count the student as present and subsequently receive funding. Higgins stated, "I think you'd see a substantial impact on truancy, dropout rates and ultimately crime rates" (Shuster 1995a). Although Higgins's commentary seems well intentioned, as a strategy, Higgins was attempting to get rid of the laws of excusable absence in order that officers could issue more truancy tickets to Black and Latino youth.

9. This sentiment perhaps is best encapsulated by David Halberstam, who in reference to the *LA Times* ownership stated, "Journalism, as an expression of restraint and judgment on a community, journalists as the spiritual monitors of a community, those were the things Harry Chandler never heard of. His was advocacy journalism of a primitive kind of brutal economic advocacy" (Halberstam 2000, 138).

10. Writing about the origins of the *Los Angeles Times,* the extent to which the paper was used to change the landscape of Los Angeles to a capitalist utopia cannot be overstated. Halberstam argues, "The event (economic bust of 1888) was to produce, overnight, a permanent scar on Los Angeles, making it in the two decades to come one of the bloodiest battlegrounds between labor and capital in the nation, and making the *Times* one of America's most reactionary papers. For the next sixty years, the *Times* was not just a voice of anti-unionism, but an outspoken, relentless instrument for all conservative policies and candidates, wedded to the Republican Party but wary of the party lest it become too soft. *Time* magazine, quite conservative itself in the thirties, could say of General Otis he "lived to make the *Times* the most rabid Labor-baiting, Red-hating paper in the United States" (Halberstam 2000, 154).

11. Davis cites coalescence of Police Chief William Parker with the leadership of the *Times* to prevent the development of public housing as a key model to dis-

seminate law and order propaganda in the name of public safety. Davis asserts, "Chief Parker also did his bit to support the *Times*'s crusade against 'socialist' public housing by using phony crime statistics to paint lurid images of 'jungle life' in the projects a political manipulation of police data which some critics feel has continued through the present" (Davis 2006, 295).

12. Mike Davis, commenting on the role of the *Times* ownership in the destruction of public housing, writes, "Aided by local McCarthyism, the Old Guard was more successful in 1953 in restoring a pliant, *Times*-dominated regime in City Hall. The pretext of their municipal counter-revolution was the 'creeping socialism' (their turn to make the accusation) of Mayor Fletcher Bowren's low-rent public housing program, especially where it cut across elite plans for Downtown—as in Chavez Ravine, or potentially, Bunker Hill. What Bowren would latter denounce, as 'a small, immensely wealthy, incredibly powerful group'—i.e., Chandler, Cal Petree and Beebe—drafted right-wing Congressman Norris Poulson as the torchbearer of their crusade against 'socialism.' According to Gottlieb and Wolt, Poulson accepted the nomination only after being assured by Chandler that the mayor was 'entitled to strut around in a Cadillac and chauffer supplied by the city.' With Norman Chandler's editorial pages pounding away at Bolshevism and public housing, Poulson got his ride in the Cadillac. Within a few years, the *Times*-made mayor, in return gave the Downtown interests what they really wanted: the removal of 12,000 low-income residents to pave the way for Bunker Hill redevelopment and Dodger Stadium in Chavez Ravine" (Davis 2006, 122–23).

13. The basic planning of Los Angeles as antipedestrian urban space built around a series of freeways and cars is directly attributed to the Chandlers' desire and ability to kill off a public transportation system in order to best suit their investments within the property, oil, and the automobile industries (Halberstam 2000, 164). Thus, the mythical organization of Los Angeles as an urban sprawl has to be understood within the context that such a system promotes the necessity of automobile ownership, opens up large swaths of land to sell as feasible options (through the connection of freeways), provides an opportunity to control racial regimes through property ownership, and dictate labor in relation to the spatial proximity to work (i.e., length of time to get to work, utilizing the police to keep Black people out of certain locations to secure an all white labor base, ensuring that certain locations will be pools of surplus labor).

14. The struggle over school bussing was intense throughout the San Fernando Valley and the board meetings alike. The *New York Times*, which picked up an Associated Press report on the bussing issue in Los Angeles, noted, "A school bus was blocked briefly and some students picketed today as eight more schools were added to a court-ordered desegregation plan. Meanwhile, there was angry shouting at a Board of Education meeting. Black civic leaders demanded the resignation of Roberta Weintraub, president of the board, and her supporters, demanding that

Mrs. Weintraub apologize for calling Rita Walters, the board's only black member, an insulting name in a radio interview last week" (National Desk 1980).

15. Given the enormity of the Los Angeles metro area and the various political and cultural leanings of these areas, the *Times* created distinct editions that were sold and catered to those specific locals. The Valley (the San Fernando Valley), Orange County, Inland Empire (the San Bernardino Valley), San Diego, and Ventura received different editions that focused on issues pertaining to those areas. In this case it is of note that the *Times* editorial staff depicted a vastly different type of truancy program for the white residents of the San Fernando Valley (via the Valley edition) that was absent of police, economic sanctions, and the LA County District Attorney's Office.

16. Henry Chu of the *Times,* reporting from a planning meeting of the new truancy ticket initiative, stated, "Opponents of the toughened policy fear that minority students in poorer areas and youths with valid reasons for being out of school will be unfairly targeted by police. To answer those concerns, city officials sought assurance Monday from police that officers would not enforce the law in a discriminatory way or employ 'new techniques' for corralling youngsters that would infringe on their civil liberties, said Marvin Braude, chairman of the council's public safety committee" (Chu 1995). As a matter of appeasement, the city council moved back the implementation date to October 1995 to ensure that the tickets would not be deployed in a discriminatory manner (Chu 1995).

17. Ironically, Shuster mentions the Southgate program, which was buried near the first part of the series. Giving it only a few lines worthy of attention, she comments, "Although school board members applauded the methods used at South Gate, they have not ordered them to be used at any other school. Critics of the district say that is evidence the massive bureaucracy is too big to respond even when solutions are found to the problem" (Shuster 1995a).

18. Browne, Losen, and Wald argue, "Like mandatory sentencing schemes in the criminal law system, zero-tolerance policies were supposed to remove (or at least minimize discretion and therefore ensure objectivity and the unbiased application of discipline. This is not how these practices were in fact adopted or are implemented. School officials continue to retain discretion in interpretation and application of zero-tolerance policies. Students of color disproportionately receive harsh punishments under zero-tolerance policies, due in large part to the expansion of these policies to cover a range of nonviolent behaviors that are not objectively defined (Browne, Losen, and Wald 2002, 73–74).

19. Browne et al. cite the work of Brenda Townsend, professor of special education at the University of South Florida. They state, "[Townsend] argues that when the majority of school suspensions and expulsions are meted out to a minority of the school population, these students are likely to interpret the disparity as rejection and as a result develop a collective self-fulfilling belief that they are inca-

pable of abiding by schools' social and behavioral codes. Susan Black . . . notes that 'these kids often interpret suspension as a one way ticket out of school—a message of rejection that alienates them from ever returning to school.' This may explain recurring suspensions of students and the correlation between dropout rates and suspensions and expulsions" (Browne et al. 2002, 76–77).

20. Kelley notes during the 1980s that in addition to South Central Los Angeles, "Black communities like Southgate, Carson, Northwest Pasadena, Paramount, and North Long Beach . . . became the battlefield of the so called 'war on drugs' . . ." (Kelley 1994, 202).

21. More than a decade after the introduction of DARE into Los Angeles public schools, several studies had been conducted to test the effectiveness of DARE. A five-year longitudinal study implemented by Richard Clayton, Anne Cattarello, and Bryan Johnstone revealed that in fact DARE had "limited effects" upon "drug abuse" (Clayton et al. 1996, 1). In addition, the study noted a "general tendency for curriculum effects to decay over time." In a similar study conducted in 1994 by Susan Ennett, Nancy Tobler, Christopher Ringwalt, and Robert Flewelling found that DARE's "short term effectiveness for reducing or preventing drug use behavior is small and is less than for interactive prevention programs" (Ennett et al. 1994).

22. Ennett et al. stated that "DARE is the only drug use prevention program specifically named in the 1986 Drug-Free Schools and Communities Act. Some 10% of the Drug-Free Schools and Communities Act governors' funds, which are 30% of the funds available each fiscal year for state and local programs, are set aside for programs such as Project Drug Abuse Resistance Education, amounting to much of the program's public funding" (Ennett et al. 1994, 1). Gorman notes that "the [drug] prevention budget increased by close to $400 million as a result of the first Anti-Drug Abuse Act rising from $195 million in 1986 to $577 million in 1987. Following the Anti-Drug Abuse Act of 1988, the budget rose to $870 million, and by 1992 the federal government was spending almost $1.7 billion on drug abuse prevention efforts" (Gorman 1998, 121). Further, "the Department of Education drug prevention budget underwent a massive increase between 1986 and 1987 rising from just $3.9 million to $263.9 million. By 1992, the budget was more than $660 million" (Gorman 1998, 121).

23. Writing about the origins of the Gang Truce, Joao Vargas comments, "Most O.G.'s (Original Gangsters) underline that the current cease fire between gangs established in March 1992 was preceded by several years of difficult meetings and negotiations. Since at least 1988, a truce had been the object of discussion between the gangs that were based in each of the four main housing projects in Watts: Nickerson Gardens, Jordan Downs, Imperial Courts, and Hacienda Village. . . . In this atmosphere, the idea of the ceasefire emerged, first within the Crips of Jordan Downs, and then between the various gangs in Watts. In order to 'stop the killings and the drive-bys and all of the negative things that affect our community daily,'

Crips from the Grape Street Watts gang, mostly residents of Jordan Downs, began holding meetings with the Crips of Imperial Courts. These groups had a long bloody history of vendettas. . . . Once the beginnings of an accord were set, both Crip groups sought to start a dialogue with the Bloods of the Nickerson Gardens housing projects. The next step was to go over to Hacienda Village, dominated by Piru Bloods, where a similar agreement was approved" (Vargas 2007, 185–86).

24. Writing about the influence that CAPA had upon the Gang Truce, Zinzun stated, "We found out that the vast majority of complaints about police brutality come from youth. Youth tend to be more attentive, to listen more, when they're in this type of situation. As a result, we began to develop a plan that showed them how important it is to come together rather than fight each other. When they're in trouble with the law, or have been abused, they find out that the police tend to be more of a threat than the person on the next block or from a different set. We participated in the formation of The Gang Truce before the Los Angeles uprising [in response to the Rodney King verdict]. The L.A. uprising galvanized the gang truce . . ." (Zinzun 1997, 259).

25. The analysis of capital as a major obstacle to Black freedom was central to the Truce. In light of the Redevelop Los Angeles (RLA) plan that was issued in response to the 1992 rebellion, the architects of the Truce understood that proposed corporate sponsorship of any development within South Central Los Angeles would only lead to further exploitation. Writing about the tension between RLA and the Truce, Vargas noted, "The main problem stemming from RLA and other similar corporate centered initiatives is that, even though these initiatives promote and indeed speak for large corporations, the rhetoric that accompanies such initiatives tends to exalt small business as the main, if not the only, salvation for dilapidated neighborhoods. . . . According to the members of CAPA and CSGT, this rhetoric not only fuels divisions and competition within the inner city, but also diverts attention from the necessity of investments in other areas besides small businesses. Because small businesspersons are usually well organized, they tend to attract large proportions of public funds destined for the inner city. . . . One activist complained: These business groups in the community are driving me crazy. Every time we try to pressure elected officials to talk about money for schools, hospitals, public health centers, and transportation they talk about loans for themselves. Every time we talk about curbing police brutality they talk about more police and making the community safer for business. And every time we talk about cleaning up toxins and the environment, they talk about how all the rules are killing them. I want to work with these people, but not for the business class, black or white" (Vargas 2007, 192–93).

26. Vargas comments that the Truce "demands better and more recreational facilities—more parks, arts and sports programs, a 'midnight basketball league' for teens supervised by community residents, and more theaters staffed by local

residents. It demands better health care, especially for senior citizens, family plan-ning clinics to provide birth control and sex education, free pre and postnatal care, and abortions. As well, it calls for an end to forced sterilizations. Furthermore, CSGT makes claims for tenant's rights, demanding enforcement of health and safety codes in all residents and public housing, more senior citizen housing, low-income housing, and to 'cease eviction of entire families because of a problem of relatives or a single family member'" (Vargas 2007, 191).

27. Foot Action and Footlocker are chains of stores, primarily located within malls, that sell brand-name athletic wear (shoes, shorts, hats, and shirts).

28. The reference to Home Depot is in regards to day laborers who congregate near sites of manual labor (i.e., construction zones, hardware stores) with the in-tention of finding work from contractors. The majority of these laborers tend to be immigrants from Mexico and other Central American countries.

29. During the course of my fieldwork, the normalized antagonistic relation-ship between the students and the state was quite stark. Students often engaged with teachers expecting hostility and confrontation. Rather than being afraid of disciplinary procedures (as the fact that Los Padrinos was expected strike fear in the students), students such those in the Enrichment Classes and Rashad from Mr. Davies's classroom had so become accustomed to the severity that these policies no longer caused fear; rather they brought out a particular type of anger and frus-tration that was utilized by the school as a rationale for further disciplinary action.

4. Troubled Man

1. In her 2012 text, *Arrested Justice*, Beth Richie's utilization of the prison na-tion is analogous to my framing of the prison regime. Writing about the many conceptualizations that describe the development of prisons in the United States, Richie comments, "In this framing of Black women's experience of male violence, I am using the notion of the prison nation metaphorically. I borrow the notion from scholars who use the term more literally to signal the situation in which a neoliberal, law-and-order-oriented social agenda has supplanted the state's will-ingness to provide basic material resources and opportunity for self-sufficiency for low-income groups. This trend has been called mass incarceration or imprison-ment, lockdown, the prison industrial complex, carceral archipelago, the celling of America, the American gulag and the New Jim Crow" (Richie 2012, 103).

2. A major contribution that Beth Richie makes is to re-center the conversa-tion pertaining to prisons and gender. Although current popular rhetoric is fo-cused upon masculinity, Richie argues that at the core of the development of the prison nation are multiple forms of violence enacted upon Black women that have been hidden and exacerbated by the co-optation of the anti-violence movement by the state bureaucratic structure. Richie states, "Indeed, there is evidence that

some women are safer in 2012 than they were 25 years ago because of the success of the anti-violence movement in changing policy and because of America's growing prison nation and the concurrent focus on punishment in the United States. At the same time, there is growing concern about women with less power who are in as much danger as ever, precisely because of the ideological and strategic direction the anti-violence movement has taken during the buildup of America's prison nation. . . . . Still, after 25 years, racism persists in the mainstream anti-violence movement, and some leadership in communities of color refuse to pay sufficient attention to gender inequality" (Richie 2012, 3–4).

3. Black incarceration rates in the United States have reached points of absurdity beyond explanation. Black men's rates of incarceration are important because one in six Black men are in prison, and it is predicted that if the expansion of the prisons continues at the current rate, that statistic will increase to one in three (NAACP 2013). The expansion of the prison system has been a totalizing force within the United States. Pam Oliver states, "Even the majority White population has a very high incarceration rate by international standards: the 2005 rate of incarceration for U.S. Non-Hispanic Whites—414 per 100,000 (Harrison and Beck 2006)—is higher than the total incarceration rate for all but 15 of the 216 countries listed in the World Prison Population List (Walmsley 2007) and is two to four times the rate of Western European nations" (Oliver 2008, 1).

4. Agnew's harsh and condemning feelings and actions toward Black forms of resistance are well documented. Commenting upon Agnew's stance toward Black education, Franklin writes, "Vice President Agnew (not yet indicted for his own criminal activities) was even more explicit. In early 1970, Agnew argued that there was too high a percentage of Black students in college and condemned 'the violence emanating from Black student militancy.' Declaring that 'College, at one time considered a privilege, is considered to be a right today,' he singled out open admissions as one of the main ways "by which unqualified students are being swept into college on the wave of the new socialism" (Franklin 2000).

5. In writing about the invocation of Aristotelian forms of democracy, Robinson writes, "Aristotle saw slavery as necessary for the self-sufficiency of the *polis,* and in only rare instances were slaves expected to achieve a virtuous life. Given their marginal intelligence and development, Aristotle found no compelling reason for inquiry into the ethics, consciousness, or desires of slaves, content to state that 'the slave is in a sense apart of his master, a living but separate part of his body'" (Robinson 2000, xxix).

6. According to Danifu, the constitution of the CRIPS charter was based upon the charter of the Black Panther Party. Discussing the development of the constitution, Danifu stated, "By the time of '72, we knew that it was so many of us, we were shooting each other. So we knew that we had to put more order into it because of the criticism and self-criticism of what we were doing to ourselves . . .

Raymond [Raymond Washington] said you the one to do that kind of the stuff . . . Automatically, I'm going to come from the Panther Party and say this is how it goes right here [speaking about the Panther Constitution]" (Sloan 2005).

7. Amde Muhammad's description of the role of the city in relation to gangs was second by Mike Davis's description of the relationship between gangs and the city. Davis stated, "I don't think there is anything that the police really fear more than an end to gang warfare. For them, it's the perfect situation, a war that they can't really ever stop, but they constantly profit from" (Sloan 2005).

8. As told by Chili, a former member of the Gladiators, "The police didn't want people to work with gangs. Not people like me. What they want, they wanted to do it their way. They told me, you'll go back to the penitentiary if you don't stop" (Sloan 2005).

9. It is important to note that the student action was also informed by and informed the politics of some of the small cadre of Black faculty at Stanford during this time period. Anthropologist St. Clair Drake, who was a mentor to many of the Black students at Stanford, issued a clear direction for Black Studies both at Stanford and across the nation. In 1969 he stated, "The very use of the term Black Studies is by implication an indictment of American and Western European scholarship. It makes bold assertion that what we have heretofore called 'Objective' intellectual activities were actually white studies in perspective and content; and that a corrective bias, a shift in emphasis, is needed, even if something called 'truth' is set as the goal. To use a technical sociological term, the present body of knowledge has an ideological element in it, and a counterideology is needed. Black Studies supply that counterideology" (Marable 2000, 21). Drake's assertion of a particular type of Black Studies caused tremendous waves at Stanford both within the student body and within the faculty base led by Nobel Prize physicist professor, William Shockley, who was an adamant supporter of eugenics and philosophies pertaining to the degeneration of the Black population within the United States.

10. According to Geronimo Ji Jaga (Pratt) former Minister of Defense of the LA chapter of the Black Panther Party, "The day before that meeting Bunchy and I, went to the US headquarters and met with Ron Karenga and Jomo. Jomo was in charge of their military. We had an agreement that however the students voted, if they voted for cultural nationalism, the Panthers would support that. If they voted for revolutionary nationalism, US would support that . . . [The incident at UCLA was manifested] by the FBI. But at the time we were naïve and thought that it was just another move by the US organization. For all of these years, the US organization has been getting a bum wrap behind that killing. I'm sure Bunchy above all would be turning over in his grave if we were not to straighten this out." This was furthered by Panther member Ericka Huggins who stated, "Some kind of memorandum was uncovered from the FBI which declared that though we did not pull

the trigger on that day January 1969, we did cause the unrest that preceded it" (Sloan 2005).

11. The dates are in question, as investigators are still unsure of how many murders Lonnie Franklin Jr. committed. While the total was originally thought to be ten, after searching Franklin Jr.'s home, the investigation quickly broadened as it appeared that Franklin Jr. could have been involved with the deaths of more than forty women.

12. In June 2013, the Supreme Court ruled that DNA swabbing of those arrested but not convicted of any crime was legal. In a five-to-four decision, the Court overturned the State of Maryland's highest court which had ruled that such swabbing was illegal. The case was widely followed, and the Court's ruling further complicated notions of privacy pertaining to "individual rights" versus "rights of the State" ("Supreme Court Rules" 2013).

13. Trouble in this sense refers to things such as burglaries, selling of drugs, and bringing unwanted attention to the neighborhood. Yet, because of the historic and current forms of disrespect, harassment, and abuse that many residents face at the hands of the police, there is no trust that the police have the best intentions of the community in mind. Thus, when police conduct investigations there is an intense unwillingness to implicate fellow neighbors in criminal activity.

14. Williams's claim about Franklin Jr. can also be read as an extension of Richie's postulation of the "trap of loyalty." Although Richie's analysis focused on intimate relationships, there is a natural pathway to neighbors and close friends. She states, "The notion of a trap of loyalty includes (1) the obligation that Black women feel to buffer their families from the impact of racism in the public sphere; (2) the pressure to live up to the expectations that they, as Black women, will be able to withstand abuse and mistreatment more than other members of their households; and (3) an acceptance of the community rhetoric that argues that Black women are in a more privileged position than are African American men (including those who abuse them)" (Richie 2012, 37).

15. Several of the family members who lost loved ones during Franklin Jr.'s alleged killing spree articulated that he was able to kill freely in large part because of who was being killed and where they were being killed. Diana Ware, stepmother of Barbara Ware who was killed in 1987, questioned, "I just have to wonder if it'd been a different part of town, would these things have been done?" (Coolican 2010). Further, the blog site *Crunk Feminist Collective* argued, "You would think the separate news stories about the systematic killing of Black women and girls in different regions would launch a national conversation about gender violence in Black communities. In the same week that a major network news station reported the LA murders, it also celebrated the No. 1 YouTube video called 'Bed Intruder.' The video has been watched more than 54 million times. It uses actual news footage of Antonio Dodson, a concerned brother who reports on the attempted rape

of his sister, Kelly. I remain dumbfounded by the complete thematic disconnect and the utter disregard for the actual loss of Black girls and women. It is as if media makers and the consuming public are unable to see Black women unless we are repackaged as entertainment" ("Do We Need a Body Count" 2010).

16. In a similar fashion, Leah Donella writes about her experience in Brazil while conducting ethnographic research. Donella, a Black women, writes that she was approached on several occasions by white male tourists who assumed that because she was Black, she was a sex worker (Donella 2013).

17. The wait time for basic and emergency services became the butt of many jokes, such as the classic refrain "Killa-King," insinuating that King–Drew was the hospital that you went to not to be saved but to die.

18. Kelley notes, "The loss of manufacturing jobs was accompanied by expansion of low wage 'service' jobs—retail clerks, janitors, maids, data processors, security guards, waitresses, and cooks, which tend to be part-time and offer limited health or retirement benefits" (Kelley 1997, 46).

19. Radatz (2009), in going through the literature pertaining to sex work, writes, "Additionally, policing prostitution is highly focused on female offenders while it leaves the male 'johns' (the customers) out of the legal ramifications. Raymond (2004) discusses the legislation and explains that the penalization of 'the male customer whose right to buy women and children for prostitution activities remains unquestioned' (1156). As female prostitutes carry the brunt of the offense, they are also subjected to police officers' personal beliefs and values that may affect their experiences with the legal system" (Radatz 2009, 1–2). Further, in citing from "Police-Prostitute Interactions: Sometimes Discretion, Sometimes Misconduct" by Williamson et al. (2007) she states, "Prostitutes have found that their cases involving complaints of sexual assault are not typically prosecuted and are generally dismissed" (Radatz 2009, 2).

20. Narratives of Black women's sexual deviancy as being the key to the Black community were especially salient during a rash of Black films during the 1990s such as *New Jack City, Jungle Fever,* and *Malcolm X,* which situated the failure of Black community squarely upon Black sex work and drug usage.

21. William (Willie) Horton was the target of racial propaganda during the 1988 presidential race between George H. W. Bush and Michael Dukakis. Horton was a prisoner serving a life sentence for murder in Massachusetts where Dukakis was presiding as governor. Horton was released on a furlough plan on June 6, 1986, but did not return back to the prison as outlined in the furlough agreement. In April 1987 Horton, then residing in Maryland, raped a woman and upon his arrest was sentenced to two life sentences. The Bush campaign used Horton as fodder to link Dukakis to black criminality during the campaign. Horton's picture was plastered side-by-side with Dukakis and the two become synonymous. The effect of this ad campaign bolstered Bush to the White House and had a

tremendous effect upon prison policy. Shortly after the campaign, Massachusetts did away with its furlough program and Bush's administration ushered in tough prison legislation aimed at poor Black people.

22. The reliance upon policing as the solution as purported by the state has had devastating effects on Black women. Beth Ritchie's commentary following her analysis of numerous cases of law enforcement violence against women of color is very poignant. Ritchie states, "Society's reliance on law enforcement-based responses to violence against women has had a number of unintended consequences, not the least of which is increased vulnerability of survivors to violence—at the hands of both their abusers and law enforcement officers. Often, police brutality against women of color and their families occurs when they seek assistance in the context of domestic violence or sexual assault. As a result, 'law and order' agendas and 'tough on crime' policies have not necessarily increased women of color's safety from violence—instead, fear of police violence or of inappropriate responses to interpersonal violence by law enforcement agents, combined with the lack of alternative responses, often leaves women of color with nowhere to turn when we face violence in our homes and communities" (Ritchie 2006, 150–51).

23. This is done masterfully in Beth Richie's development of a violence matrix to understand the impact of gendered violence upon Black women. Richie states, "Specifically, the male violence matrix I am advancing here does two things. First, using a Black feminist standpoint, the matrix makes it possible to comprehend the tenacious grip that male violence has on Black women and the ways that the various kinds of abuse in multiple contexts line up to leave Black women uniquely vulnerable. Equally important, the male violence matrix highlights the intersectional relationship between male violence and ideology around race, gender, sexuality, and class. In particular, it allows us to consider the consequences when ideology shifts in more conservative directions, when resources are constrained, and communities of color are disadvantaged by the buildup of a prison nation" (Richie 2012, 132).

5. By All Means Possible

1. Writing about industrial education, Washington remarked, "A careful investigation of the subject will show that it was not until after industrial education was started among the colored people, and its value proved, that it was taken up by the southern white people. Manual training or industrial and technical schools for the whites have, for the most part, been established under state auspices, and are at this time chiefly maintained by the states. An investigation would also show that in securing money from the state legislatures for the purpose of introducing hand work, one of the main arguments was the existence and success of industrial training among the Negroes. It was often argued that the white boys and girls would be

left behind unless they had the opportunities for securing the same kind of training that was being given the colored people" (Washington 1907/2000c, 191).

2. Though Teddy Roosevelt and to a certain extent William Taft are characterized as "friends of the Negro," because of their support of specific measures that were underwritten by northern capital, Woodrow Wilson was notorious for his blatant disregard for Black people. Perhaps most notable and emblematic of his disdain for Black folks during his presidential tenure was his view upon D. W. Griffith's 1915 film *Birth of a Nation*. Although organizations such as the NAACP protested the movie, Wilson screened the film at the White House and praised the white supremacist mythical tale, stating that it was "history writ with lightning." Further, Cedric Robinson posits, "Like Woodrow Wilson, Griffith repositioned his moral fulcrum from a support for justice to the preoccupation with race. Both men impersonated history, transferring the crimes of the slave order onto their fantastic myth of Reconstruction" (Robinson 2007, 102–3). In response to the open hatred that Wilson issued to Black people, Washington openly took Wilson to task over his position on the segregation of Blacks. He stated, "I have never viewed except with amusement the sentiment that white people who live next to Negro populations suffer physically, mentally and morally because of their proximity to colored people. Southern white people who have been brought up in this proximity are not inferior to other white people. The President of the United Stats was born and reared in the South in close contact with black people. Five members of the present Cabinet were born in the South; and many of them, I am sure, had black 'mammies' " (Robinson 2007, 195).

3. Arguing against segregation, Washington stated, "Summarizing the matter in the large, segregation is ill advised because

1. It is unjust.
2. It invites other unjust measures.
3. It will not be productive of good, because practically every thoughtful Negro resents its injustice and doubts its sincerity. Any race adjustment based on injustice finally defeats itself. The Civil War is the best illustration of what results when it is attempted to make wrong right or seem to be right.
4. It is unnecessary.
5. It is inconsistent. The Negro is segregated from his white neighbor, but white business men are not prevented from doing business in Negro neighborhoods.
6. There has been no case of segregation of Negroes in the United States that has not widened the breach between the two races. Wherever a form of segregation exists it will be found that it has been administered in such a way as to embitter the Negro and harm more or less

the moral fiber of a white man. That the Negro does not express this constant sense of wrong is no proof that he does not feel it. (Washington 1915/2000c, 197).

4. Although Washington became critical of segregation, his position was situated within a framework that placed Black people in the clutches of white subjectivity with respect to morality and cultural development. In doing this, he was cowing to white supremacist sensibilities that demanded Black degradation even while pleading for justice. As an example, Washington stated, "White people who argue for the segregation of the masses of black people forget the tremendous power of objective teaching. To hedge any set of people off in a corner and sally among them now and then with a lecture or a sermon is merely to add misery to degradation. But put the black man where day by day he sees how the white man keeps his lawns, his windows; how he treats his wife and children, and you will do more real helpful teaching than a whole library of lectures and sermons. Moreover, this will help the white man. If he knows that his life is to be taken as a model, that his hours, dress, manners, are all to be patterns for someone less fortunate, he will deport himself better than he would otherwise. Practically all the real moral uplift the black people have gotten from the whites—and this been great indeed—has come from this observation of the white man's conduct. The South today is still full of the type of Negro with gentle manners. Where did he get them? From some master or mistress of the same type" (Washington 1915/2000c, 197).

5. Du Bois realized that although Washington's intent may not have been to further the oppression of Black southerners, his alliance with capitalist and southern heads of state proved to be disastrous for Black folk. He argued, "Mr. Washington distinctly asks that black people give up, at least for the present, three things,—First, political power, Second, insistence on civil rights, Third, higher education of Negro youth,—and concentrate all their energies on industrial education, the accumulation of wealth, and the conciliation of the South. This policy has been courageously and insistently advocated for over 15 years, and has been triumphant for perhaps 10 years. As a result of this tender of the palm-branch, what has been the return? In these years there have occurred:

The disfranchisement of the Negro.
The legal creation of a distinct status of civil inferiority for the Negro.
The steady withdrawal of aid from institutions for the higher training of the Negro.

These movements are not, to be sure, direct results of Mr. Washington's teachings; but his propaganda has, without a shadow of doubt, helped their speedier accomplishment" (Du Bois 1903/2008, 41–42).

6. Walker provides an account of a student in Massachusetts as an example

of the intent of the education system. He writes, "Here is a fact, which I this very minute take from the mouth of a young coloured man, who has been to school in this state (Massachusetts) nearly nine years, and who knows grammar this day, nearly as well as he did the day he first entered the school-house, under a white master. This young man says: 'My master would never allow me to study grammar.' I asked him, 'why?' 'The school committee,' said he 'forbid the coloured children learning grammar'—they would not allow any but the white children 'to study grammar.' It is a notorious fact, that the major part of the white Americans, have, ever since we have been among them, tried to keep us ignorant, and make us believe that God made us and our children to be slaves to them and theirs" (Walker 2001, 39).

7. In discussing the pretential veil that is pulled down upon the face of Black people to hide a false education system, Walker writes, "Most of the coloured people, when they speak of the education of one among us who can write a neat hand, and who perhaps knows nothing but to scribble and puff pretty fair on a small scrap of paper, immaterial whether his words are grammatical, or spelt correctly, or not; if it only looks beautiful, they say he has as good an education as any white man—he can write as well as any white man. The poor, ignorant creature, hearing, this, he is ashamed, forever after, to let any person see him humbling himself to another for knowledge but going about trying to deceive those who are more ignorant than himself, he at last falls an ignorant victim to death in wretchedness. I pray that the Lord may undeceive my ignorant brethren, and permit them to throw away pretensions, and seek after the substance of learning" (Walker 2001, 36–37).

8. Neither substantiated nor refuted, it is believed that Walker was poisoned and succumbed to the deadly toxins within his home (Marable and Mullings 2000, 23).

9. Even Booker T. Washington, while lambasting Reconstruction, recognized the connection between education and Reconstruction. Washington stated, "I want to call attention here to a phase of Reconstruction policy which is often overlooked. All now agree that there was much in Reconstruction that was unwise and unfortunate. However, we may regard that policy, and much as we may regret mistakes, the fact is too often overlooked that it was during the Reconstruction Period that a public school system for the education of all the people of the South was first established in most states. Much that was done by those in charge of Reconstruction legislation has been overturned, but the public school system still remains. True, it has been modified and improved, but the system remains and is everyday growing in popularity and strength" (Washington 1907/2000b, 186).

10. Citing the work of Fredrick Law Olmsted, Fogel and Engerman point out that "he [Olmsted] concluded that the peculiar institution kept not just slaves but virtually the entire free population in deep poverty. The deeply impoverished included not just landless free farmers but even those owning substantial land and

as many as five slaves. In Olmsted's words, the 'majority of those who sell the cotton crop,' were 'poorer than the majority of our day-laborers at the North.' Planters with as many as thirty-five slaves still could barely eke out a living, earning an average 'hardly more than that of a private of the New York Metropolitan Police Force.' To live 'in a moderately comfortable way,' a planter had to own at least fifty slaves. Thus slavery was a boon only for those at the very top of the southern economic pyramid-for just the top 2 percent of the slaveholders" (Fogel and Engerman 1974, 171).

11. Writing about the economic wealth of the large southern planter class, Fogel states, "When the yeoman class of the South is defined to include both non-slaveholding farmers and farmers with seven or fewer slaves, their average wealth is nearly identical with that of northern farmers, although the distribution of wealth is somewhat more concentrated among southern yeoman. On the other hand, the average wealth of gang-systems farms exceeded $56,000, which is more than 15 times the average either for southern yeoman or for northern farmers. Thus, the distribution of wealth among northern farmers had "an upper limit which did not exist in the South." It was not the pauperization of the small farmer but the existence of huge agribusiness—the gang-system plantations—that made the rural wealth distribution of the South so much more unequal than that of the North (Fogel 1989, 83).

12. The failure of this recognition was enormous. Du Bois writes, "It was thus the presence of the poor white southerner in the West that complicated the whole Free Soil movement in its relation to the labor movement. While the Western pioneer was an advocate of extreme democracy and equalitarianism in his political and economic philosophy, his vote and influence did not go to strengthen the abolition-democracy, before, during, or even after the war. On the contrary, it was stopped and inhibited by the doctrine of race, and the West, therefore, long stood against that democracy in industry which might have emancipated labor in the United States, because it did not admit to that democracy the American citizen of Negro decent" (Du Bois 1998, 28).

13. Fogel points out that the thrust of the Free Soil Party was to protect the interests of northern capital in the fight against the plantation bloc. Fogel writes, "More secular in its orientation, and led by more sophisticated politicians than the party it supplanted [Liberty Party], the emphasis of the Free Soil party was more on the political than on the economic threat slaveholders to northern interests. The principal plank of the new party was the barring of slavery from all territories. Unlike the Liberty party, the principal rationale for the plank was not concern for the blacks but defense of northern political interests against the political aggrandizement of the Slave Power" (Fogel 1989, 346). It is important to note that the propagation of "free labor" as a viable option for white labor was within a social and economic context that was seriously debating the viability of enslaving

all labor. Fogel writes, "By the mid-1850s southern writers, newspapers, and politicians were widely proclaiming the superiority of slave labor and commending it to the elite of the North. They announced that slavery was the natural and normal condition of the laboring man, white or black'; that free society was a disastrous 'little experiment,' originally designed 'in a corner of Western Europe,' which had 'failed dismally' both there and in the North; that the free society of the North was a 'self destroying' and unstable form of social organization which alternated between famine and insurrection; that the North was an insufferable 'conglomeration of greasy mechanics, filthy operatives, and small-listed farmers'; that is the 'laboring man' of the North became 'the slave of one man instead of the slave' of the economic system, 'he would be far better off' . . . The struggle against the Slave Power conspiracy was thus nothing less than the struggle to prevent the free workers of the North from becoming white slaves" (Fogel 1989, 343–44). It is within this social milieu that poor white laborers' decision to betray their commonalities with Black laborers resulted in their ensnarement by northern industrialists who equated "freedom" with "labor."

14. The planter class was done in by sheer greed and arrogance. In a powerful critique of the class position, Du Bois argues, "Since it was beneath the dignity of a 'gentleman' to encumber himself with the details of his finances, this lordly excuse enabled the planter to place between himself and the black slave a series of intermediaries through whom bitter pressure and exploitation could be exercised and large crops raised. For the very reason that the planters did not give attention to details, there was wide tendency to commercialize their growing business of supplying raw materials for an expanding modern industry. They were the last to comprehend the revolution through which that industry was passing and their efforts to increase income succeeded only at the cost of raping the land and degrading the laborers" (Du Bois 1935/1998, 36).

15. Du Bois insightfully points out that "White laborers did not demand education, and saw no need of it, save in exceptional cases. They accepted without murmur their subordination to the slaveholders, and looked for escape from their condition only to the possibility of becoming slaveholders themselves" (Du Bois 1935/1998, 641).

16. The same situation held true for other southern states such as Alabama. In 1851, the comptroller of the state treasury, Joel Riggs, stated, "Perhaps of all trust-funds, none has been so greatly mismanaged as the school fund of Alabama" (Du Bois 1935/1998, 641).

17. Watkins makes a strong connection between Black education and philanthropic interests. He states, "Race philanthropy emerged by the 1880s as a major approach to policy making. It was quick, avoided the slow deliberative processes of law making, and could be expeditiously and unilaterally started and/or halted at will. Race philanthropy was ideally suited to educating Blacks as well as other

minorities. The building and support of schools, the training of teachers, and very important, the construction of curriculum could be accomplished handily by corporate philanthropies" (Watkins 2001, 19).

18. Watkins insightfully analyzes the development of Black education during the post–Civil War era as a process by which "Blacks . . . [had] to learn their 'place' in the new industrial order." Specifically he links the political economy of the United States during this time period to the subjugation of Black people. "Politics was the noteworthy feature of educating Blacks after the Civil War. While Blacks had the desire to uplift themselves, join the social mainstream of American life, and break forever with the bondage of the past, they lacked the resources to achieve either education or their larger freedom. . . . The new corporate hegemonists needed to work toward their political and policy objectives. Among those objectives was a stable and orderly South where subservient wage labor and debt farming or share-cropping would provide the livelihood for Black Americans" (Watkins 2001, 23).

19. Illustrating the true intentions of northerners and the limits of the capitalist enterprise to be humanitarian, Foner comments that "as time passed, the Northern planters sounded and acted more and more like Southerners. Some sought to restore corporal punishment, on to find that freedman would not stand it" (Foner 2002, 138).

20. With the South adopting the new industrial model of education, Black education became obsolete and easily expendable. Woodson writes, "Negroes attended industrial schools, took such training as was prescribed, and received their diplomas; but few of them developed adequate efficiency to be able to do what they were supposedly trained to do. The schools in which they were educated could not provide for all the experience with machinery which white apprentices trained in factories had. Such industrial education as these Negroes received, then, was merely to master a technique already discarded in progressive centres; and even in less complicated operations of industry these schools had no such facilities as to parallel the numerous processes of factories conducted on the plan of the division of labor. Except what value such training might have in the development of the mind by making practical applications of mathematics and science, then, it was a failure" (Woodson 1933/1998, 13).

21. W. E. B. Du Bois issued a critique of Black education that cautioned of reformist efforts that simply chose to become incorporated within the system. In a speech to the Howard University graduating class of 1930 he issued the following analysis, "There is no doubt but that college and university training among us has had largely the exact effect that was predicted; it has turned an increasing number of our people not simply away from manual labor and industry, not simply away from business and economic reform, into a few well-paid professions, but it has turned our attention from any disposition to study or solve our economic

problem. A disproportionate number of our college-trained students are crowding into teaching and medicine and beginning to swarm into other professions and to form at the threshold of these better-paid jobs, a white-collared proletariat . . ." (Du Bois 1973, 67).

22. Dylan Rodríguez states, "The contemporary prison regime is . . . simultaneously the materialization of U.S. civil society's presumptive white corporate identity (inclusive of its post-civil rights 'multicultural' articulations) and the production of a social logic essential to the current social order—a fabrication and criminalization of disorder for the sake of extracting and dramatizing order, compliance, authority. . . . Thus, I am arguing that in the current era of mass imprisonment, white supremacist unfreedom—specifically, carceral technologies of human immobilization and bodily disintegration—provides the institutional form, cultural discourse, and ethical basis of social coherence, safety, and civic peace" (Rodríguez 2006, 14).

23. As shown in the documentary *The Fire This Time*, the Black community in Los Angeles had stressed that their education was irrelevant within the political economy of the city (Holland 1995). Additionally, all social services that prevented Black students from participating in extracurricular activities (music, art, dance, film, etc.) had been stripped from the schools. There was a demand to institute a curriculum that would flow into the labor market and college while providing students with viable outlets during school.

24. Kohn analyzes the effect of standardized testing of mislabeling students who actually understand the process of math rather than memorizing steps. "On the other hand, standardized tests underestimate what others can do because, as any teacher can tell you, very talented students often get low scores. . . . Consider a fifth grade boy who, researchers found, could flawlessly march through the steps of subtracting 2⅚ from 3⅓, ending up quite correctly with ¾ and then reducing that to ½. Unfortunately, successful performance of this final reduction does not imply understanding that the two fractions are equivalent. In fact, this student remarked in an interview that ½ was larger than ¾ because 'the denominator is smaller so the pieces are larger.' Meanwhile, one of his classmates, whose answer had been marked wrong because it had not been expressed in the correct terms, clearly had a better grasp of the underlying concepts. Intrigued, these researchers proceeded to interview a number of fifth graders about another topic (division) and discovered that 41 percent had memorized the process without really understanding the idea, while 11 percent understood the concept but made minor errors that resulted in getting the wrong answer. A standardized test therefore would have misclassified more than half of these students" (Kohn 2000, 11).

25. Similarly, McNeil makes reference to a case of an eighth grade student, Elaine. "In the previous grade, she won the citywide short story writing award conferred by

the local chapter of the National Council of Teachers of English. [During the eighth grade] she failed to pass the eighth grade writing section of the TAAS because she *failed to provide sufficient supporting detail*" (McNeil 2000, 240).

26. McNeil points out, "Students who practice these reading exercises day after day for months show a decreased ability to read longer works. A sixth-grade teacher who had selected a fourth-grade Newbery Award book for her class, thinking all the students could read and understand it, found that after reading for a few minutes the students stopped. They were accustomed to reading very brief, disjointed passages; they had difficulty carrying over information from the first chapter to a later one" (McNeil 2000, 238).

27. Indeed Ms. Shirley faced tremendous odds given how standardized test are designed. As argued by Kohn, "The people who produce non-referenced tests not only want questions that are answered correctly by only some students; they also want questions that are answered by those who do well on the test overall. . . . They want a nice, clean correspondence between the whole and the parts." Regarding Black students at CHS, Neill and Medina explain that "a test item on which African-Americans do particularly well but whites do not is likely to be discarded because of the interaction of two factors: African Americans are a minority, and African Americans tend to score low" (Neill and Medina 1989, 692).

28. Morris Brown College was the first Historically Black College in the Atlanta University Complex founded by Black people (African Methodist Episcopal Church). As stated within the founding resolution, the mission of the college was to foster "the moral, spiritual, and intellectual growth of Negro boys and girls" (Morris Brown College 2009).

Bibliography

Adler, Lisa. 2009. "Ticketing towards Prisons: LAUSD's Truancy Tickets and the Pre-Prisoning of Our Youth." *Community Rights Campaign.* March 19. http://www.thestrategycenter.org/blog/2009/03/19/ticketing-towards-prisons -lausd%E2%80%99s-truancy-tickets-and-pre-prisoning-our-youth.

Alexander, M. Jacqui. 2005. *Pedagogies of Crossing: Meditations on Feminism, Sexual Politics, Memory, and the Sacred.* Durham, N.C.: Duke University Press.

Alexander, Michelle. 2010. *The New Jim Crow: Mass Incarceration in the Age of Colorblindness.* New York: New Press.

Allah, Sasun. 2004. "NYPD Admits to Rap Intelligence Unit." *Village Voice*, March 16. http://www.villagevoice.com/news/nypd-admits-to-rap-intelligence-unit -6407962.

Anderson, James D. 1988. *The Education of Blacks in the South, 1860–1935.* Chapel Hill: University of North Carolina Press.

Anyon, Jean. 1995. "Race, Class and Social Reform in an Inner-City School." *Teachers College Record* 97, no. 1: 69–94.

Awkward, Michael. 1995. *Negotiating Difference: Race, Gender, and the Politics of Positionality.* 1st ed. Chicago: University of Chicago Press.

Becerra, Hector, and Scott Gold. 2010. "'Everybody Knew Lonnie.'" *Los Angeles Times,* July 9. http://articles.latimes.com/2010/jul/09/local/la-me-grim-sleeper -profile-20100709.

Brown, Brian, and Greg Jolivette. 2005. "A Primer: Three Strikes: The Impact after More Than a Decade." Sacramento, Calif.: Legislative Analyst's Office. http:// www.lao.ca.gov/2005/3_strikes/3_strikes_102005.htm.

Browne, Judith, Daniel Losen, and Johanna Wald. 2002. "Zero Tolerance: Unfair, with Little Recourse." In *Zero Tolerance: Can Suspension and Expulsion Keep Schools Safe?* New Directions for Youth Development, no. 92, ed. Russell J. Skiba and Gil G. Noam, 73–101. San Francisco, Calif: Jossey-Bass.

Burton, Paul. 1995. "Black Panthers Push Gang Truce." *Valley Advocate,* April 22. http://la.indymedia.org/news/2006/07/168587.html.

California Department of Corrections. 2008. "Peace Officer Careers." http://www .cdcr.ca.gov/Career_Opportunities/POR/Pay.html.

California Department of Education. 2009. "Data and Statistics." http://Dq.Cde .Ca.Gov/Dataquest/.

California Progressive Message. 2011. "The California Prison Guards Union: Still Profiting from Incarceration-Mania." *A Publication of Jim Gonzalez & Associates.* https://caprogressivemessage.wordpress.com/2011/03/04/the-california -prison-guards-union-still-profiting-from-incarceration-mania/.

Chemerinsky, Erwin. 2005. "The Segregation and Resegregation of American Public Education." In *School Resegregation: Must the South Turn Back,* ed. John Charles Boger and Gary Orfield, 29–50. Chapel Hill: University of North Carolina Press.

Chu, Henry. 1995. "Enforcement of Truancy Law Delayed: Schools: New L.A. City Ordinance Will Be Implemented Oct. 1. Police Say the Move Gives Them Time to Educate the Public and Work out Details." *Los Angeles Times,* June 20. http:// articles.latimes.com/1995-06-20/local/me-15186_1_city-schools.

Churchill, Ward, and Jim Vander Wall. 2002. *Agents of Repression: The FBI's Secret Wars against the Black Panther Party and the American Indian Movement.* Boston: South End Press.

Clayton, R. R., A. M. Cattarello, and B. M. Johnstone. 1996. "The Effectiveness of Drug Abuse Resistance Education (Project DARE): Five-Year Follow-Up Results." *Preventive Medicine* 25, no. 3: 307–18. doi:10.1006/pmed.1996.0061.

Clear, Todd R. 2007. *Imprisoning Communities: How Mass Incarceration Makes Disadvantaged Neighborhoods Worse.* Studies in Crime and Public Policy. Oxford: Oxford University Press.

Clements, Catherine. 1995. "*Williams v. Garcetti:* The Constitutionality of Holding Parents Criminally Liable for the Acts of Their Children." *Golden Gate University Law Review* 25: 417.

Community Coalition. 2009a. "City Upholds Conditions on South LA Nuisance Business." http://www.cocosouthla.org/node/530.

———. 2009b. "We Closed 150 Liquor Stores to Make South LA Safer and Healthier." http://www.cocosouthla.org/bethechange/bruce-patton.

———. 2013. "About Us." http://www.cocosouthla.org/about/ourmission.

Cooley, Steve. 2004. "Authorize District Attorney to Accept Grant Funds." Los Angeles, Calif.: Los Angeles County District Attorney. http://file.lacounty.gov/ bos/supdocs/11028.pdf.

Coolican, Patrick. 2010. "Family of Barbara Ware, Victim of Grim Sleeper, Reflect on an Eventful Week." *Informer.* http://blogs.laweekly.com/informer/2010/07/ family_of_barbara_ware_victim.php.

Coutin, Susan Bibler. 2007. *Nations of Emigrants: Shifting Boundaries of Citizenship in El Salvador and the United States.* Ithaca, N.Y.: Cornell University Press.

Crunk Feminist Collective. 2010. "Do We Need a Body Count to Count? Notes on the Serial Murders of Black Women." December 23. http://www

.crunkfeministcollective.com/2010/12/23/do-we-need-a-body-count-to-count
-notes-on-the-serial-murders-of-black-women/.

Cruz, Jon D. 2001. "Historicizing the American Cultural Turn: The Slave Narrative." *European Journal of Cultural Studies* 4, no. 3: 305–23. doi:10.1177/
136754940100400304.

Cube, Ice. 1993. "Ghetto Bird." Priority.

Davis, Cyprian. 1990. *The History of Black Catholics in the United States*. New York:
Crossroad.

———. 1998. "God of Our Weary Years." In *Taking Down Our Harps: Black Catholics in the United States*, ed. Diana L. Hayes and Cyprian Davis, 17–48. Mary-
knoll, N.Y.: Orbis.

Davis, Mike. 2006. *City of Quartz: Excavating the Future in Los Angeles*. New ed.
London: Verso.

Dolan, Maura, Joel Rubin, and Mitchell Landsburg. 2010. "DNA Leads to Arrest
in Grim Sleeper Killings." *Los Angeles Times*, July 8. http://articles.latimes
.com/2010/jul/08/local/la-me-grim-sleeper-20100708.

Donella, Leah. 2013. "Commoditized Pleasure: Neocolonial Sexual Landscapes in
Salvador Da Bahia." Claremont, Calif.: Pomona College.

Du Bois, W. E. B. 1903/2008. *The Souls of Black Folk*. Rockville, Md.: Arc Manor.

———. 1935/1998. *Black Reconstruction in America, 1860–1880*. New York: Free
Press.

———. 1973. *The Education of Black People; Ten Critiques, 1906–1960*. Amherst:
University of Massachusetts Press.

Dymski, Gary, and John Veitch. 1996. "Financial Transformation and the Metropo-
lis: Booms, Busts, and Banking in Los Angeles." *Environment and Planning* 28,
no. 7: 1233–60.

Eckholm, Erik. 2013. "With Police in Schools, More Children in Court." *New York
Times*, April 12, Education sec. http://www.nytimes.com/2013/04/12/education/
with-police-in-schools-more-children-in-court.html.

Ellison, Ralph. 1952. *Invisible Man*. New York: Random House.

Ennett, S. T., D. P. Rosenbaum, R. L. Flewelling, G. S. Bieler, C. L. Ringwalt, and
S. L. Bailey. 1994. "Long-Term Evaluation of Drug Abuse Resistance Education." *Addictive Behaviors* 19, no. 2: 113–25.

Epstein, Dena J. 1977. *Sinful Tunes and Spirituals: Black Folk Music to the Civil
War*. Urbana: University of Illinois Press.

Fanon, Frantz. 1967. *Black Skin, White Masks*. New York: Grove Press.

Ferguson, Ann Arnett. 2001. *Bad Boys: Public Schools in the Making of Black Masculinity*. Rpt. ed. Ann Arbor: University of Michigan Press.

Fogel, Robert William. 1989. *Without Consent or Contract: The Rise and Fall of
American Slavery*. New York: Norton.

Fogel, Robert William, and Stanley Engerman. 1974. *Time on the Cross: The Economics of American Negro Slavery*. Boston: Little, Brown.

Foley, Douglas E. 1990. *Learning Capitalist Culture: Deep in the Heart of Tejas*. Philadelphia: University of Pennsylvania Press.

Foner, Eric. 2002. *Reconstruction: America's Unfinished Revolution, 1863–1877*. New American Nation Series. New York: Harpers Perennial Modern Classics.

Foucault, Michel. 1979. *Discipline and Punish: The Birth of the Prison*. New York: Vintage.

———. 1990. *The History of Sexuality: An Introduction*. New York: Vintage.

Franklin, Bruce H. 2000. "The American Prison in the Culture Wars." Modern Language Association. http://andromeda.rutgers.edu/~hbf/priscult.html.

Franklin, Vincent. 1974. "Education for Colonization: Attempts to Educate Free Blacks in the United States for Emigration to Africa, 1823–1833." *Journal of Negro Education* 43, no. 1: 91–103.

Freidrichs, Chad. 2012. *The Pruitt-Igoe Myth*. Documentary, Drama, History, News. Unicorn Stencil. Video Recording.

Fuentes, Annette. 2003. "Discipline and Punish." *The Nation*, November 26. http://www.thenation.com/article/discipline-and-punish.

Genovese, Eugene D. 1976. *Roll, Jordan, Roll: The World the Slaves Made*. New York: Vintage.

Gilmore, Ruth Wilson. 1999. "Globalisation and US Prison Growth: From Military Keynesianism to Post-Keynesian Militarism." *Race and Class* 40, nos. 2–3: 171–88. doi:10.1177/030639689904000212.

———. 2002. "Race and Globalization." In *Geographies of Global Change: Remapping the World*, 2nd ed., ed. R. J. Johnston, Peter J. Taylor, and Michael Watts, 261–74. Malden, Mass.: Wiley-Blackwell.

———. 2007. *Golden Gulag: Prisons, Surplus, Crisis, and Opposition in Globalizing California*. Berkeley: University of California Press.

Gordon, Avery F. 1999. "Globalism and the Prison Industrial Complex: An Interview with Angela Davis." *Race and Class* 40, nos. 2–3: 145–57. doi:10.1177/030639689904000210.

Gordon, Edmund T. 1997. "Cultural Politics of Black Masculinity." *Transforming Anthropology* 6, nos. 1–2: 36–53. doi:10.1525/tran.1997.6.1–2.36.

Gorman, D. M. 1998. "The Irrelevance of Evidence in the Development of School-Based Drug Prevention Policy, 1986–1996." *Evaluation Review* 22 (February): 118–46.

Gramsci, Antonio, and Eric J. Hobsbawm. 1988/2000. *The Antonio Gramsci Reader: Selected Writings 1916–1935*. Ed. David Forgacs. New York: New York University Press.

Grigsby, Juli. 2014. "Grim Sleeper: Gender, Violence, and Reproductive Justice in Los Angeles." PhD diss. Austin: University of Texas.

Halberstam, David. 2000. *The Powers That Be.* Urbana: University of Illinois Press.

Hall, Stuart. 1990. "Cultural Identity and Diaspora." In *Identity: Community, Culture, Difference,* ed. Jonathan Rutherford, 222–37. London: Lawrence & Wishart.

Hardt, Michael, and Antonio Negri. 2001. *Empire.* Cambridge, Mass.: Harvard University Press.

———. 2005. *Multitude: War and Democracy in the Age of Empire.* New York: Penguin.

Hawkins, Augustus. 1989. *Drug-Free Schools and Communities Act Amendments of 1989.* Washington, D.C.: 101st Congress of the United States of America. https://www.congress.gov/bill/101st-congress/house-bill/3614.

Hochman, Steve. 1989. "Compton Rappers versus the Letter of the Law: FBI Claims Song by N.W.A. Advocates Violence on Police." *Los Angeles Times,* October 5. http://articles.latimes.com/1989-10-05/entertainment/ca-1046_1_law-enforcement.

Holland, Randy. 1995. *The Fire This Time: Why Los Angeles Burned.* Rhino/Wea. VHS.

Hull, Gloria, Patricia Scott, and Barbara Smith. 1982. *All the Women Are White, All the Blacks Are Men, but Some of Us Are Brave: Black Women's Studies.* Old Westbury, N.Y.: Feminist Press.

Hyman, James. 2006. "Men and Communities: African American Males and the Well-Being of Children, Families, and Neighborhoods." Washington, D.C.: Joint Center Health Policy.

Incite! Women of Color against Violence. 2006. *Color of Violence: The Incite! Anthology.* Boston: South End Press.

James, C. L. R. 1989. *The Black Jacobins: Toussaint L'Ouverture and the San Domingo Revolution.* 2nd ed. New York: Vintage.

Jackson, O'Shea. 1993. *Ghetto Bird.* Priority. Audio CD.

Jackson, Walter. 1994. *Gunnar Myrdal and America's Conscience: Social Engineering and Racial Liberalism, 1938-1987.* Chapel Hill: University of North Carolina Press.

Jeong, Helen. 2011. "Making a Difference in South Los Angeles, One Block at a Time | Watt Way Blog." *Watt Way.* February 3. http://wattway.org/2011/02/making-a-difference-one-block-at-a-time/.

Johnson, Gaye Theresa. 2013. *Spaces of Conflict, Sounds of Solidarity: Music, Race, and Spatial Entitlement in Los Angeles.* Berkeley: University of California Press.

Johnson, James, Jr., Cloyzelle Jones, Walter Farrell Jr., and Melvin Oliver. 1992. "The Los Angeles Rebellion: A Retrospective View." *Economic Development Quarterly* 6, no. 4: 356–72.

Kafka, Judith Rachel. 2005. *From Discipline to Punishment: Race, Bureaucracy, and School Discipline Policy in Los Angeles, 1954–1975.* Berkeley: University of California Press.

Kaplan, Elaine Bell. 1997. *Not Our Kind of Girl: Unravelling the Myths of Black Teenage Motherhood*. Berkeley: University of California Press.

Kass, Jeff. 1996. "Curfew Mulled as Way to Stem Truancy, Crime." *Los Angeles Times*, March 31. http://articles.latimes.com/1996–03–31/local/me-53388_1_ orange-county.

Kelley, Robin. 1996. *Race Rebels: Culture, Politics, and the Black Working Class*. New York: Simon and Schuster.

Kelley, Robin D. G. 1997. *Yo' Mama's Disfunktional!: Fighting the Culture Wars in Urban American*. Boston: Beacon Press.

Klein, Patricia. 1985. "Police Ram Opens Door to Debate." *Los Angeles Times*, June 4. http://articles.latimes.com/1985-06-04/news/mn-6473_1_military-vehicle.

Kohl, Herbert R. 1995. *"I Won't Learn from You": And Other Thoughts on Creative Maladjustment*. 2nd ed. New York: New Press.

Kohn, Alfie. 2000. *The Case against Standardized Testing: Raising the Scores, Ruining the Schools*. Portsmouth, N.H.: Heinemann.

Kopetman, Roxana. 1989. "School Erecting 10-Foot-High Wall to Deflect Bullets." *Los Angeles Times*, April 16. http://articles.latimes.com/1989–04–16/news/mn-2498_1_carmelitos-housing-project-school-erecting-10-foot-high-wall-physical-education.

Kuti, Fela. 2006. *Stalemate / Fear Not for Man*. Polygram Int'l. Audio CD.

Kyles, Perry. 2008. "Resistance and Collaboration: Political Strategies within the Afro-Carolinian Slave Community, 1700–1750." *Journal of African American History* 93, no. 4: 497–508.

Ladson-Billings, Gloria, and William Tate. 1995. "Toward a Critical Race Theory of Education." *Teachers College Record* 97, no. 1: 47–68.

Lark, Melody. 1995. "The Drug-Free Schools and Communities Act of 1986: Policy, Formation, Causation, and Program Implementation." San Francisco, Calif.: American Education Research Association. http://files.eric.ed.gov/fulltext/ED389994.pdf.

Levine, Lawrence W. 2007. *Black Culture and Black Consciousness: Afro-American Folk Thought from Slavery to Freedom*. 30th anniv. ed. Oxford: Oxford University Press.

Lipsitz, George. 2011. *How Racism Takes Place*. Philadelphia: Temple University Press.

Lomawaima, K. Tsianina. 2009. "Domesticity in the Federal Indian Schools: The Power of Authority over Mind and Body." *American Ethnologist* 20, no. 2: 227–40.

Los Angeles Almanac. 2015. "City of Palos Verdes Estates-Los Angeles Almanac." www.laalmanac.com/.

Los Angeles District Attorney's Office. 2007. "Abolish Chronic Truancy." http://da.lacounty.gov/cr/act.htm#act.

Manes, Hugh R. 1963. *A Report on Law Enforcement and the Negro Citizen in Los Angeles.* Los Angeles, Calif.: Author.

Marable, Manning. 2000. "Black Studies and the Racial Mountain." *Souls: A Critical Journal of Black Politics, Culture, and Society* 2, no. 3: 17–36.

Marable, Manning, and Leith Mullings, eds. 2000. *Let Nobody Turn Us Around: Voices of Resistance, Reform, and Renewal: An African American Anthology.* Lanham, Md.: Rowman & Littlefield.

Massey, Douglas S., and Nancy A. Denton. 1993. *American Apartheid: Segregation and the Making of the Underclass.* Cambridge, Mass.: Harvard University Press.

Mauer, Marc, and Tracy Huling. 1995. "Young Black Americans and the Criminal Justice System: Five Years Later." Washington, D.C.: Sentencing Project.

Mays, Benjamin Elijah. 1971. *Born to Rebel: An Autobiography.* New York: Scribner.

McDonnell, Lorraine. 2005. "No Child Left Behind and the Federal Role in Education: Evolution or Revolution." *Peabody Journal of Education* 80, no. 2: 19–38.

McGreevy, Patrick, and Steve Hymon. 2007. "L.A. to Seek a Tax to Fight Gangs." *Los Angeles Times,* January 24. http://articles.latimes.com/2007/jan/24/local/me-gangs24.

McNeil, Linda M. 2000. *Contradictions of School Reform Educational Costs of Standardized Testing.* New York: Routledge. http://search.ebscohost.com/login.aspx?direct=true&scope=site&db=nlebk&db=nlabk&AN=71499.

Meiners, Erica R. 2007. *Right to Be Hostile: Schools, Prisons, and the Making of Public Enemies.* New York: Routledge.

Melody. 2013. "Yet Another Harrowing Tale of White Collar Addiction | Cargo Cult Contrarian, Scientific American Blog Network." February 4. http://blogs.scientificamerican.com/cargo-cult-contrarian/2013/02/04/adderall/.

Miller, Jerome G. 1996. *Search and Destroy: African-American Males in the Criminal Justice System.* Cambridge: Cambridge University Press.

Morris Brown College. 2009. "College History." http://morrisbrown.edu/history-morris-brown/.

Mozingo, Joe. 1998. "D.A.'s Program Tries to Head Off Truancy Early." *Los Angeles Times,* August 30. http://articles.latimes.com/1998/aug/30/local/me-17972.

Myers, Dowell. 2002. "Demographic and Housing Transitions in South Central Los Angeles, 1990 to 2000." Los Angeles: University of Southern California. www.usc.edu/schools/price/research/census2000/pdf/SoCentral_DM.pdf.

NAACP. 2011. "Misplaced Priorities: Over Incarcerate, Under Educate." Baltimore, Md.: Author.

———. 2013. "Criminal Justice Fact Sheet." http://www.naacp.org/pages/criminal-justice-fact-sheet.

Na, Chongmin, and Denise C. Gottfredson. 2013. "Police Officers in Schools: Effects on School Crime and the Processing of Offending Behaviors." *Justice Quarterly* 30, no. 4: 619–50. doi:10.1080/07418825.2011.615754.

National Center for Education Statistics. 2003. "Status and Trends in the Education of Blacks." NCES 2003–034. Washington, D.C.: U.S. Department of Education. http://nces.ed.gov/pubs2003/2003034.pdf.

National Desk. 1980. "Some Protests Mark Los Angeles Busing Effort." *New York Times*, September 24, Late City final edition, sec. A, p. 16, col. 6.

Neill, D. Monty, and Noe J. Medina. 1989. "Standardized Testing: Harmful to Educational Health." *Phi Delta Kappan* (May): 688–97.

Newton, Eunice S., and Earle H. West. 1963. "The Progress of the Negro in Elementary and Secondary Education." *Journal of Negro Education* 32, no. 4: 466–84.

New York Civil Liberties Union. 2007. "Criminalizing the Classroom: The Over-Policing of New York City Schools." New York: Author.

Nolan, Kathleen. 2011. *Police in the Hallways: Discipline in an Urban High School*. Minneapolis: University of Minnesota Press.

Ochs, Stephen J. 1990. *Desegregating the Altar: The Josephites and the Struggle for Black Priests, 1871–1960*. Baton Rouge: Louisiana State University Press.

Office of Juvenile Justice and Delinquency Prevention. 2009. "Recovery Act Local Youth Mentoring Initiative." Washington, D.C.: U.S. Department of Justice.

Oliver, Pamela. 2008. "Repression and Crime Control: Why Social Movement Scholars Should Pay Attention to Mass Incarceration as a Form of Repression." *Mobilization: The International Quarterly* 13, no. 1: 1–24.

Orfield, Gary. 1988. "Exclusion of the Majority: Shrinking College Access and Public Policy in Metropolitan Los Angeles." *Urban Review* 20, no. 3: 147–63.

Pelisek, Christine. 2008. "Grim Sleeper Returns: He's Murdering Angelenos, as Cops Hunt his DNA." *LA Weekly*, August 27. http://www.laweekly.com/news/grim-sleeper-returns-hes-murdering-angelenos-as-cops-hunt-his-dna-2155416.

———. 2009. "Grim Sleeper's Sole Survivor." *LA Weekly*, March 11. http://www.laweekly.com/2009-03-12/news/grim-sleeper-39-s-sole-survivor/full/.

———. 2013. "The Grim Sleeper's Trial Is Moving at Snail's Pace, and Victims' Families Are Furious." *Daily Beast*, March 21. http://www.thedailybeast.com/articles/2013/03/21/the-grim-sleeper-s-trial-is-moving-at-snail-s-pace-and-victims-families-are-furious.html.

Phillips, Steven C. 1990. *Justice and Hope: Past Reflections and Future Visions of the Stanford Black Student Union, 1967–1989*. Stanford, Calif.: Stanford Black Student Union.

Plotkin, Sidney, and William E. Scheuerman. 1994. *Private Interest, Public Spending: Balanced-Budget Conservatism and the Fiscal Crisis*. Boston: South End Press.

Raboteau, Albert J. 1980. *Slave Religion: The "Invisible Institution" in the Antebellum South*. Oxford [Oxfordshire]: Oxford University Press.

———. 1995. *A Fire in the Bones: Reflections on African-American Religious History*. Boston: Beacon Press.

Radatz, Dana. 2009. "Systematic Approach to Prostitution Laws: A Literature Review and Further Suggestions." Master's thesis, Eastern Michigan University. http://commons.emich.edu/cgi/viewcontent.cgi?article=1230&context=theses.

Richie, Beth E. 2012. *Arrested Justice: Black Women, Violence, and America's Prison Nation*. New York: NYU Press.

Ritchie, Andrea. 2006. "Law Enforcement Violence against Women of Color." In *The Color of Violence: The Incite! Anthology*, 138–56. Cambridge, Mass.: South End Press.

Robinson, Cedric J. 2000. *Black Marxism: The Making of the Black Radical Tradition*. Chapel Hill: University of North Carolina Press.

———. 2007. *Forgeries of Memory and Meaning: Blacks and the Regimes of Race in American Theater and Film before World War II*. Chapel Hill: University of North Carolina Press.

Rodríguez, Dylan. 2006. *Forced Passages: Imprisoned Radical Intellectuals and the U.S. Prison Regime*. Minneapolis: University of Minnesota Press.

Roper, L. H. 2007. "The 1701 'Act for the Better Ordering of Slaves': Reconsidering the History of Slavery in Proprietary South Carolina." *William and Mary Quarterly* 64, no. 2: 395–418.

Rose, Tricia. 1994. *Black Noise: Rap Music and Black Culture in Contemporary America*. Middletown, Conn: Wesleyan University Press.

Rose, Willie Lee, ed. 1999. *A Documentary History of Slavery in North America*. Athens: University of Georgia Press.

Schnyder, Damien. 2010. "Enclosures Abound: Black Cultural Autonomy, Prison Regime and Public Education." *Race, Ethnicity and Education* 13, no. 3: 349–65.

Schnyder, Damien M. 2012. "Masculinity Lockdown: The Formation of Black Masculinity in a California Public High School." *Transforming Anthropology* 20, no. 1: 5–16. doi:10.1111/j.1548-7466.2011.01142.x.

Schwarz, Alan. 2013. "Concerns about A.D.H.D. Practices and Amphetamine Addiction." *New York Times*, February 2, U.S. sec. http://www.nytimes.com/2013/02/03/us/concerns-about-adhd-practices-and-amphetamine-addiction.html.

Scott, Allen, and Edward Soja. 1996. *The City: Los Angeles and Urban Theory at the End of the Twentieth Century*. Berkeley: University of California Press.

Seale, Bobby. 2002. "Bring It Home." In *The Black Panthers Speak*, ed. Philip S. Foner, 2nd ed. New York: Da Capo Press.

Shapiro, Thomas M. 2005. *The Hidden Cost of Being African American: How Wealth Perpetuates Inequality*. Oxford: Oxford University Press.

Sharrow, Walter G. 1972. "John Hughes and a Catholic Response to Slavery in

Antebellum America." *Journal of Negro History* 57, no. 3: 254–69. doi:10.2307/2717338.

Shuster, Beth. 1995a. "L.A. School Truancy Exacts a Growing Social Price: Education: Diminishing Resources Curb Efforts to Prevent It. Crime and Financial Losses Are among Results." *Los Angeles Times,* June 28, p. 1.

———. 1995b. "New York Gets Tough on Truancy Prevention: City Police Round Up Students Playing Hooky and Cart Them Back to School." *Los Angeles Times* [Valley ed.], June 28, p. 12.

———. 1995c. "Taft Student Tries to Ditch a Bad Habit Series: L.A. School Truancy Exacts a Growing Social Price." *Los Angeles Times* [Valley ed.], June 28, p. 13.

Sigal, J. Franklin. 2010. "Out of Step: When the California Street Terrorism Enforcement and Prevention Act Stumbles into Penal Code Limits." *Golden Gate University Law Review* 38, no. 1. http://digitalcommons.law.ggu.edu/ggulrev/vol38/iss1/1.

Simon, Mallory. 2010. "Grim Sleeper Serial Killer Suspect Known as Nice, Funny 'Fix-It' Man." *CNN.com.* July 8. http://www.cnn.com/2010/CRIME/07/08/grim.sleeper.profile/index.html.

Sloan, Cle Shaheed. 2005. *Bastards of the Party.* Home Box Office. Video Documentary.

Smith, Dante. 2002. *Black on Both Sides.* Rawkus. Audio CD.

Sojoyner, Damien M. 2013. "Black Radicals Make for Bad Citizens: Undoing the Myth of the School to Prison Pipeline." *Berkeley Review of Education* 4, no. 2. http://escholarship.org/uc/item/35c207gv.

———. 2014. "Changing the Lens: Moving Away from the School to Prison Pipeline." In *From Education to Incarceration: Dismantling the School-to-Prison Pipeline,* ed. Anthony Nocella II, Priya Parmar, and David Stovall, 54–66. New York: Peter Lang.

"Supreme Court Rules Police Can Swab for DNA upon Arrest." 2013. June 3. http://www.pbs.org/newshour/rundown/2013/06/supreme-court-rules-police-can-swab-for-dna-upon-arrest.html.

Tee, Toddy. 1985. *Batterram.* Epic. Audio Recording.

Toldson, Ivory. 2008. "Breaking Barriers: Plotting the Path to Academic Success for School-Age African-American Males." Washington, D.C.: Congressional Black Caucus Foundation.

Urizar, Cesar. 2009. "Three Strikes Law of California. Proposition 184 of March 1994: A Policy Analysis." PhD diss. Long Beach: California State University.

U.S. Department of Education. 2003. "No Child Left Behind: A Parents Guide." Washington, D.C.: Author.

Vargas, João Helion Costa. 2006. *Catching Hell in the City of Angels: Life and Meanings of Blackness in South Central Los Angeles.* Minneapolis: University of Minnesota Press.

Wald, J., and D. Losen. 2003. *Deconstructing the School-to-Prison Pipeline.* New Directions for Youth Development. San Francisco, Calif.: Jossey-Bass.

Walker, David. 2001. *Walker's Appeal, in Four Articles; Together with a Preamble, to the Coloured Citizens of the World, but in Particular, and Very Expressly, to Those of the United States of America.* Chapel Hill, N.C.: University of North Carolina Academic Affairs Library. http://docsouth.unc.edu/nc/walker/walker .html.

Warnick, Mark. 1985. "Long Ram of the Law LAPD New Weapon." *Los Angeles Herald Examiner,* February 8.

Washington, Booker T. 1895/2000a. "Atlanta Exposition Address." In *Let Nobody Turn Us Around: Voices of Resistance, Reform, and Renewal: An African American Anthology,* ed. Manning Marable and Leith Mullings, 182–85. Lanham, Md.: Rowman & Littlefield.

———. 1907/2000b. "The Fruits of Industrial Education." In *Let Nobody Turn Us Around: Voices of Resistance, Reform, and Renewal: An African American Anthology,* ed. Manning Marable and Leith Mullings, 185–95. Lanham, Md.: Rowman & Littlefield.

———. 1915/2000c. "My Views of Segregation Laws." In *Let Nobody Turn Us Around: Voices of Resistance, Reform, and Renewal: An African American Anthology,* ed. Manning Marable and Mullings, 195–97. Lanham, Md.: Rowman & Littlefield.

Watkins, Thomas. 2010. "California Serial Killer 'Grim Sleeper' Dropped Hints, Friends Say." *Memphis Commercial Appeal.* July. http://www.commercialappeal .com/news/2010/jul/15/california-serial-killer-grim-sleeper-dropped-hint/.

Watkins, William H. 2001. *The White Architects of Black Education: Ideology and Power in America, 1865–1954.* New York: Teachers College Press.

Welfare Planning Council. 1961. "Youth Problems and Needs in the South Central Area." Part 1. Los Angeles: Author.

White, Nicole, and Evelyn McDonnell. 2004. "Police Secretly Watching Hip-Hop Artists." *Miami Herald,* March 9, p. 1A.

Widener, Daniel. 2010. *Black Arts West: Culture and Struggle in Postwar Los Angeles.* Durham, N.C.: Duke University Press.

Williams, Erica. 2013. *Sex Tourism in Bahia: Ambiguous Entanglements.* Urbana: University of Illinois Press.

Williamson, Celia Baker, Morris Jenkins, and Terry Cluse-Tolar. 2007. "Police–Prostitute Interactions: Sometimes Discretion, Sometimes Misconduct." *Journal of Progressive Human Services* 18, no. 2.

Willis, Paul E. 1977. *Learning to Labor: How Working Class Kids Get Working Class Jobs.* New York: Columbia University Press.

Winton, Richard, and Patrick McGreevy. 2007. "Will the Strategy to Battle Gangs Work?" *Los Angeles Times,* February 11. http://articles.latimes.com/2007/feb/11/ local/me-gangs11.

Woods, Clyde. 1998. *Development Arrested: The Blues and Plantation Power in the Mississippi Delta*. London: Verso.

———. 2009. "Katrina's World: Blues, Bourbon, and the Return to the Source." *American Quarterly* 61, no. 3: 427–53.

Woodson, Carter G. 1919. *The Education of the Negro Prior to 1861: A History of the Education of the Colored People of the United States from the Beginning of Slavery to the Civil War*. New Brunswick, N.J.: Association for the Study of Negro Life and History. http://andromeda.rutgers.edu/~natalieb/The_Education_Of_The_Negro_P.pdf.

———. 1933/1998. *The Miseducation of the Negro*. 10th ed. Trenton, N.J.: Africa World Press.

Zinzun, Michael. 1997. "The Gang Truce: A Movement for Social Justice." *Social Justice* 24, no. 4: 258–66.

Index

abandonment model, 169–73

Abolish Chronic Truancy (ACT), 75, 76, 77, 84, 115, 219n6

abolition, 25, 26, 30, 166

achievement gap, xiv, 68, 180

Act of 1701, 15–16

African Diaspora, xviii, 14, 16, 205n1, 206n15

African Methodist Episcopal Church, Morris Brown College and, 187

Afro-Carolinians, 216n27

Agnew, Spiro, 126, 226n4

Alabama Baptist Association, 19

Alexander, M. Jacqui, 52–53, 211n15

Alexander, Michelle: Black men/prison regime and, 72

American Civil Liberties Union (ACLU), 219n5

American Dilemma, An, 215n26

American Social Science Association, 18

Anderson, James D., 166, 167, 168, 186

Anglican Church, baptism/freedom and, 15

Anti-Drug Abuse Act (1988), 223n22

apartheid, 132, 159, 210n11

Appeal (Walker), 155, 156, 158

Aristotle, slavery and, 226n5

Arrested Justice (Richie), 225n1

Assembly of the Presbyterian Church, 19

attendance policy/rates, 74, 83, 107, 178, 220n8

average yearly progress (AYP), 174, 175, 185

Azurara, Gomes Eannes de, 23, 24

Baker, Newton, 215n26

baptism, emancipation and, 15, 205n5, 207n18

Basic Correctional Juvenile Academy, 39

Bass, Karen, 142

Baudier, Roger, 207n18

behavior, xix, 37, 114; Black, 122, 126; civic, 52; delinquent, 81, 219–20n7; drug use, 223n21; heteronormative, 125, 137; nonviolent, 222n18; problems with, 60, 61, 190; respectability, 211n13

Berman, Edward H., 215n25

biopower, xix, 64

Birth of a Nation (film), 231n2

Black, Susan, 223n19

Black arts movement, 2

Black autonomy, 1, 216n27; education and, 159; limiting, 155

Black clergy, 23, 29, 30

Black Codes, 67–68

Black community, xv, xix, 36, 74, 83, 87, 136; attacks on, 87, 145; decline of, 34–35, 144, 146; demands of, 71; desegregation and, 82; development of, 91, 191, 195; dissention within, 72–73; education and, xxi, 115, 119, 146, 171, 172; ideological remapping of, 35; militarizing, 127–28; NAO and, 143; organization of, 20, 64, 130; as passive subject, 194; problems within, 115, 124; punitive enclosure in, 84; racial terror and, 36; resources of, 66; riots/social disorder and, 72; support

Danifu, 129, 226n6
Darwin, Charles, 7
Davis, Angela Y., 54, 133
Davis, Ashley, 94
Davis, Cyprian, 25
Davis, Mike, 220–21n11; Black community and, 206n12; on Brownson,
206n14; gangs and, 227n7; on *Los
Angeles Times,* 221n12; on prison
infrastructure, 212n16
Davis, Miles, 9
democracy, xiii, 127, 234n12; Aristotelian forms of, 226n5; education
and, 186
Department of Education, 172, 223n22
desegregation, 82, 169
development: collective, 214n21;
cultural, 232n4; economic, 91, 132,
155; historical, 191; industrial, 151;
intellectual, xi
*Development Arrested: The Blues and
Plantation Power in the Mississippi
Delta* (Woods), xiii, 192
Dickens, Edwin, 208n3
Dickinson, Emily, 102
discipline, 62, 63, 79, 90, 128, 130, 133,
148, 169, 185, 190, 222n18, 225n19,
225n29; analysis of, 71; behavior
and, 194–95; culture of, 177–78;
effective, 19; harsh, xviii, 53, 61, 114,
122, 126, 127, 149; labor, 163, 208n3;
lack of, 14; policies, xix, xx, 36, 68,
204n6; racialized, 35, 60, 61; technology of, 37, 65, 67
discrimination: employment, 131; gendered, 170; racial, 170, 185–86
disinvestment, 6, 34, 59, 123, 132, 218n3
dissent, 31, 35, 73, 91, 133
District Attorney Hearing Officers
(HOs), 75, 76
Dodson, Antonio, 228n15
Dodson, Kelly, 229n15
Donella, Leah, 229n16
Drake, St. Clair, 131, 132, 227n9

dropout rate, 184, 220n8, 223n19
drug abuse, 86, 87, 141, 223n21, 229n20
Drug Abuse Resistance Education
(DARE), 86, 87, 115, 223n21, 223n22
Drug Enforcement Agency, 85
Drug-Free Schools and Communities
Act (1986), 86, 223n22; amendment
(1989), 87
Du Bois, W. E. B., 162, 193, 235n14;
analysis by, 159–60, 187; Black education and, 236n21; Black freedom
and, 216n27; education and, 154–55,
192; first strike and, x–xi; poor
whites and, 161, 166, 234n12; Washington and, 154, 232n5; white labor
and, 235n15
Dukakis, Michael: Horton and, 229n21
Dunkin, John, 80

economic issues, xiii, xiv, 33, 34, 39, 79,
130, 144, 159, 160, 161, 163
economic relations, 162, 203n3, 209n9
economics, 97, 98, 101, 102, 132
education, xviii, xix, 107, 121, 130,
158–59, 170; as altruistic apparatus,
191; attachment to, 182; attacks on,
169; Black community and, xxi, 115,
146, 159, 171, 172; criminal justice
and, 105; democracy and, 186;
enclosure and, xviii, xxi, 69, 172;
freedom and, 168, 191; higher, 153,
170, 171; industrial, xx, 152, 153, 155,
165–66, 168, 230n1, 230n5, 236n20;
integrational strategies for, 187; job
security and, 147; liberal arts–based,
154, 168; nation-building and, 31;
neoliberal models of, 195; physical,
96, 112; process, 41, 173, 183, 186, 189,
190; racialized, 175; secondary, 167;
structure of, 123, 217–18n2; system,
203n3, 233n6, 233n7; technical, 152;
vocational, 171, 183, 205n2; white
labor and, 235n15. *See also* Black
education; public education

DAMIEN M. SOJOYNER is assistant professor of anthropology at the University of California, Irvine.